IMAGES
of America

FANEUIL HALL AND QUINCY MARKET

ON THE COVER: Faneuil Hall and Quincy Market were all decked out on June 17, 1875, to celebrate the 100th anniversary of the Battle of Bunker Hill. (Photograph by James Wallace Black, Boston Public Library.)

IMAGES
of America

FANEUIL HALL AND QUINCY MARKET

Susan Mara Bregman

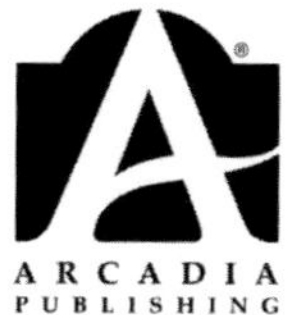

ISBN 978-1-4671-6326-2
Hardcover ISBN 978-1-5402-9950-5

Published by Arcadia Publishing
Charleston, South Carolina

Printed in the United States of America

Library of Congress Control Number: 2025950278

For all general information, please contact Arcadia Publishing:
Telephone 843-853-2070
Fax 843-853-0044
E-mail sales@arcadiapublishing.com

Visit us on the Internet at www.arcadiapublishing.com

For that grasshopper weather vane, whose glassy eyes have seen a lot

Contents

Acknowledgments		6
Introduction		7
1.	Building Faneuil Hall	9
2.	Creating Quincy Market	43
3.	Revolution, Politics, and Social Justice	69
4.	Artwork, Monuments, and Mementos	97
5.	Reinventing Quincy Market	109
Bibliography		127

Acknowledgments

One of my favorite parts of digging into a new topic is meeting experts in the field. Writing *Faneuil Hall and Quincy Market* introduced me to historians, professors, and politicians—each of whom had a unique perspective on these landmark buildings and the people who shaped them.

Thank you to Eric Hanson Plass, who shared his deep knowledge of Peter Faneuil's Boston and his role in the city's slave economy. Thank you to Jonathan Beagle for insights into colonial Boston. I am grateful to Kenneth Turino, a fellow Arcadia author, who has expertise in Boston's historic markets, and to Joe Bagley, who offered his perspective as Boston's city archeologist. I had a wide-ranging conversation with former Boston City Councilor Lawrence S. DiCara. He cast one of the votes to authorize the transformation of Quincy Market and participated in the ribbon-cutting ceremony for North Market (and still has the scissors to prove it).

Thank you also to the rangers and guides at Boston's historic venues and to the many librarians and archivists who tracked down the historic photographs that illustrate this book. Thanks also to Alisa Capaldi, Bernadette McCarthy, Bill Buckley, Budington Press, Carol Berlin, Charlie Vasiliades, John Broderick, Peter Vanderwarker, Phil Creighton, Robert Shure, and Tom Palmer for leads, conversations, hot tips, photographs, books, and more.

Every author needs a support network, and I am indebted to David Dao, Liz Budington, Cindy Sragg, Nicki Rohloff, Gloria Leipzig, Co Sarkis, Richard Bregman, Fern Drillings, and Michael Bregman. Thanks, also, to my sweet pup, a fluffy distraction who somehow keeps me grounded. My team at Arcadia provided valuable advice and feedback; thanks to Caitrin Cunningham, Erin Vosgien, Maddison Potter, and Dani McGrath.

Many of the images in the book appear courtesy of the following archives and collections: Library of Congress, Prints and Photographs Division (LOC), Boston Public Library (BPL), Norman B. Leventhal Map and Education Center (BPL/Leventhal), Massachusetts Historical Society (MHS), and City of Boston Archives (BOS). Other credits are spelled out in the text.

INTRODUCTION

Every Bostonian has a story about Faneuil Hall or Quincy Market.

One friend remembered dining with her parents at Durgin-Park when a fire broke out in the kitchen. Nobody panicked, and no one was evacuated. Instead, diners and staff carried on as if nothing was happening, even while firefighters rushed into the North Market building, dragging unwieldy hoses up those historic wooden stairs, something that would be unthinkable today.

Naturalization ceremonies have become a treasured modern tradition at Faneuil Hall, and another friend shared his recollections from the day he became a US citizen in the historic Great Hall.

My story dates to my tenure at Boston City Hall. Working for the City of Boston as a transportation planner and policy analyst turned out to be my dream job, but it did not start out that way. It was probably my second week on the job, and the department's presence was required at multiple public meetings. My more experienced colleagues were assigned elsewhere, and my bosses sent me to a public hearing across the street. That sounded easy enough until I realized where I was going. While most Boston civic meetings are held in school auditoriums, church basements, and other low-key settings, I would be delivering remarks at Faneuil Hall in the shadow of great orators like Daniel Webster and Frederick Douglass. I no longer remember the topic or who wrote my testimony. All I remember was the stage fright. Somehow, I muddled through my prepared remarks, breathed a sigh of relief, and joined the patriots, presidents, protesters, and politicians who have spoken in that hallowed space.

Faneuil Hall opened in 1742, a gift to the town of Boston from wealthy merchant Peter Faneuil. The building was both a marketplace and a public forum, with stalls for food vendors on the ground floor and a meeting hall and municipal offices upstairs. A weather vane in the shape of a grasshopper sat atop a cupola. Bostonians met in the Great Hall, as the meeting space was known, in the years leading up to the Revolutionary War, and the building soon acquired the nickname "Cradle of Liberty." Faneuil Hall barely survived a fire in 1761, was rebuilt in 1763, and was enlarged in 1806 with a design by prominent architect Charles Bulfinch.

But even a larger Faneuil Hall could no longer serve the needs of a growing Boston by the 1820s, and Mayor Josiah Quincy III authorized construction of three new market buildings directly to the east of the historic structure. Architect and engineer Alexander Parris designed a monumental granite marketplace known as Faneuil Hall Market, flanked by the North and South Markets—two large structures holding shops and warehouses. Faneuil Hall Market officially opened on August 26, 1826.

The thriving center of New England commerce for over a century, the market buildings fell into disrepair and were all but abandoned by the 1950s. The City of Boston almost tore them down in the 1960s but instead transformed them into something new: a festival marketplace. Boston mayor Kevin H. White spearheaded the project, to be called Faneuil Hall Marketplace, and the city selected the Rouse Company as developer and Benjamin Thompson and Associates as architect. The revitalized Quincy Market building opened on August 26, 1976—exactly 150 years after the original Faneuil Hall Market welcomed its first customer—followed by the South and North Markets in 1977 and 1978, respectively. Today, Faneuil Hall and Faneuil Hall Marketplace attract some 20 million visitors a year.

Despite their popularity, no one can agree on what to call the market buildings. There is no ambiguity about Faneuil Hall, of course, although there is controversy. The building was named after its benefactor in 1742; the controversy stems from Peter Faneuil's connection to the slave trade. Faneuil made much of his fortune from the profits of slavery—mostly by trading in products like sugar and molasses that were produced by slave labor but also by trafficking enslaved Africans. That legacy has cast a shadow on Peter Faneuil and the building that carries his name, and some have called for renaming the historic marketplace.

Quincy Market is a different story. Mayor Quincy instructed the city council to name the central building Faneuil Hall Market, choosing to honor Peter Faneuil's original goal and not to aggrandize himself. But Bostonians have a habit of ignoring official building names (how many people still call the city's basketball and hockey arena Boston Garden regardless of corporate sponsorship?), and they soon dubbed the granite market Quincy's Market after the mayor. That morphed into Quincy Market by the mid-1800s, and that name stuck. (There was never confusion about the warehouses; they were known as the North and South Markets from the get-go.) Fast forward to 1976, when the three market buildings were transformed into the Faneuil Hall Marketplace (which did not include Faneuil Hall, despite its name). By then, the Quincy Market appellation was firmly embedded in the popular imagination, and gilt letters spelling "Quincy Market" were affixed to the front and rear entrances of the central market building in 1989, along with companion signs for the North and South Markets.

But whatever you call them, both Faneuil Hall and Faneuil Hall Marketplace are perfect metaphors for Boston. They embody tradition and reinvention, commerce and conscience, freedom and hardship, and joy and sorrow. Together, these historic buildings reflect Boston's layered and complicated past.

For the sake of consistency, this book calls the central market building Faneuil Hall Market and Quincy Market interchangeably from the 1800s into the 1970s and Quincy Market thereafter. Faneuil Hall, North Market, and South Market are called by their historic and still current names. Faneuil Hall Marketplace will refer to the present-day festival marketplace that includes Quincy, North, and South Markets. In addition, the text identifies Boston as a town from 1630 to 1822, when it was incorporated, and as a city from 1822 to the present day. Dates reflect the modern calendar, although it was not adopted until a decade after Peter Faneuil's death.

One

Building Faneuil Hall

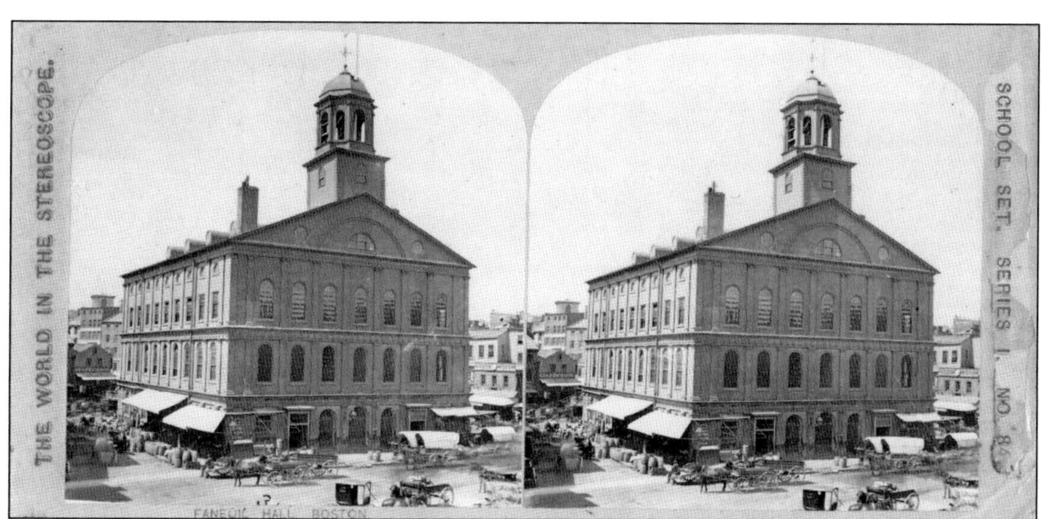

Merchant, philanthropist, bachelor, slave trafficker—these are some of the words used to describe Peter Faneuil. One of Boston's wealthiest residents in the 1700s, Faneuil presented Boston with a building that still bears his name. He built much of his wealth on the institution of slavery, which some say tarnishes his legacy. (BPL.)

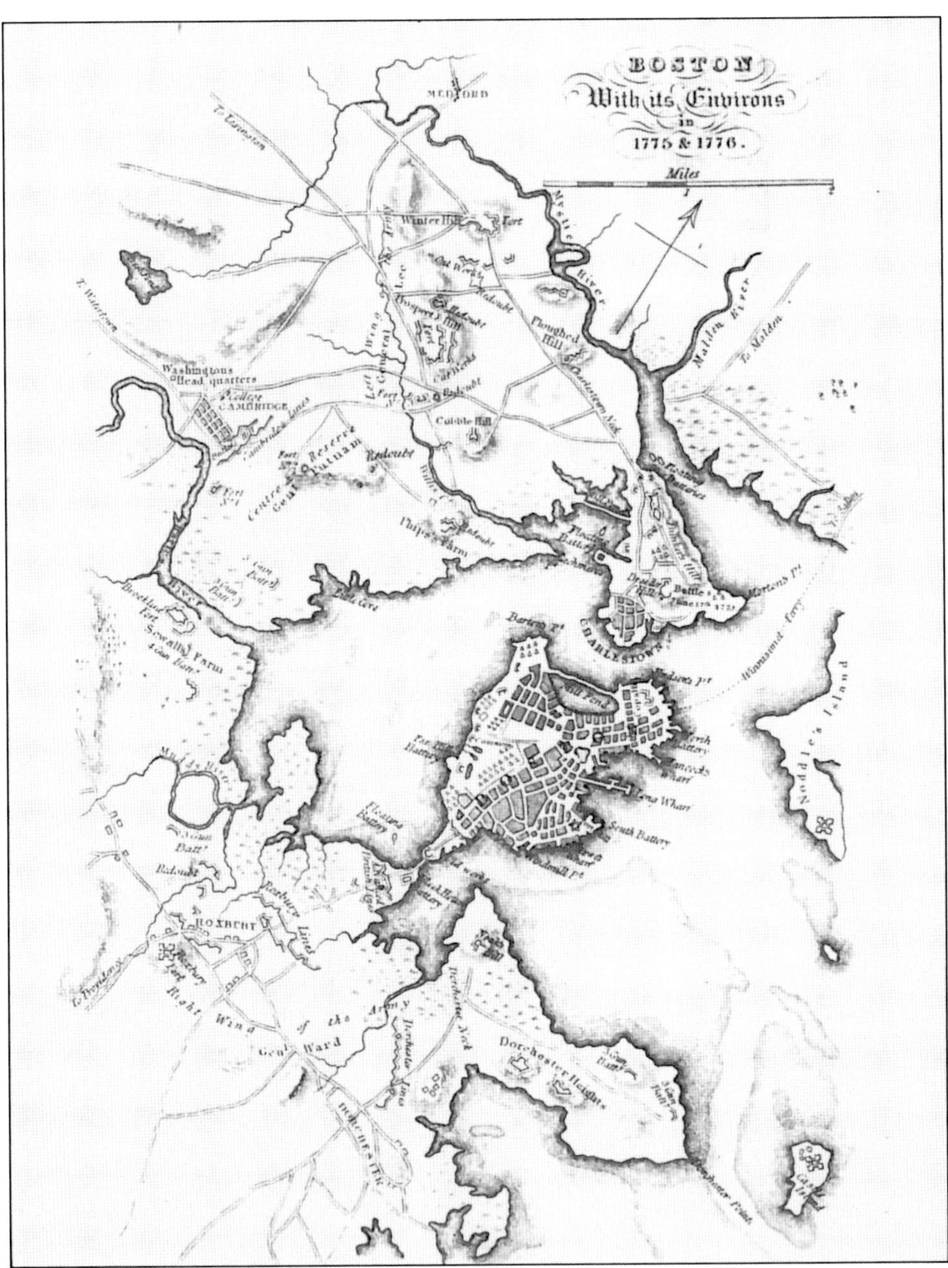

The original Boston settlement was on the Shawmut Peninsula, which took its name from a native Algonquin word. The landmass was surrounded by water on three sides: the Charles River to the west, the Mystic River to the north, and the Boston Main Channel to the east. A narrow isthmus connected the peninsula to the mainland. "The Neck," as colonists later called the land bridge, ran along today's Washington Street into Roxbury. Rev. William Blackstone (also spelled Blaxton) was the first European to settle in present-day Boston. He arrived from England around 1625 and lived alone near Beacon Hill until 1630, when John Winthrop and his Puritan followers settled nearby. They named their community Boston after their English home. Blackstone grew disaffected with his new neighbors and moved to Rhode Island in 1635; he built a home near the river that later bore his name. (National Archives.)

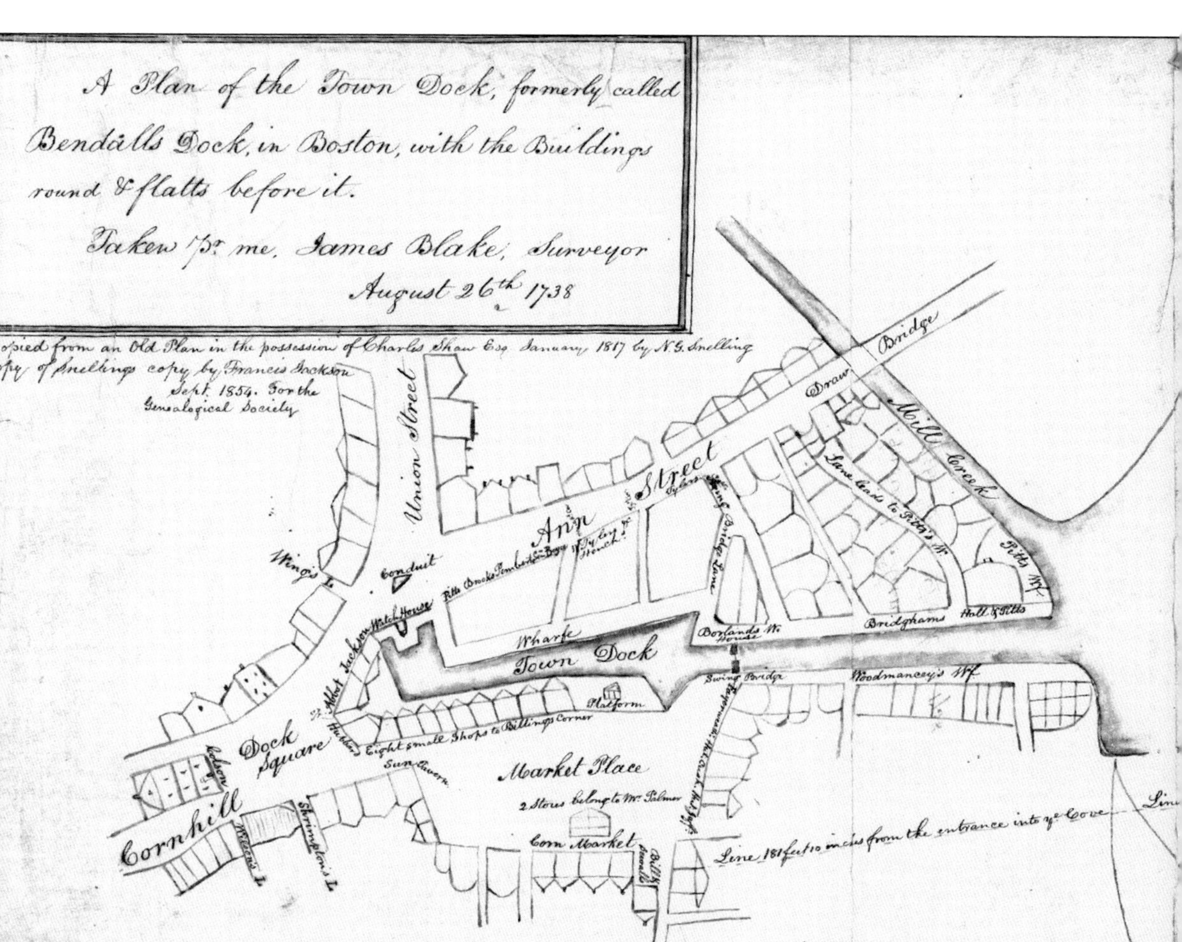

Early Bostonians mostly settled on the eastern side of the Shawmut Peninsula near the Town Dock. The dock was mostly enclosed by land in the 1640s, which provided protection for ships, and a swing bridge was constructed at its entrance in the 1670s. (The word "dock" once meant a protected area of water between wharves.) The adjacent streets—where Faneuil Hall is today—became known as Dock Square. North of the dock, Mill Pond was created in 1643 by damming part of the Charles River to support a water-powered gristmill. The pond covered much of the North End and West End sections of Boston, and Mill Creek was created to connect the pond with the dock. The dock was filled in around 1784, and Mill Pond was filled in the early 1800s. (BPL/Leventhal.)

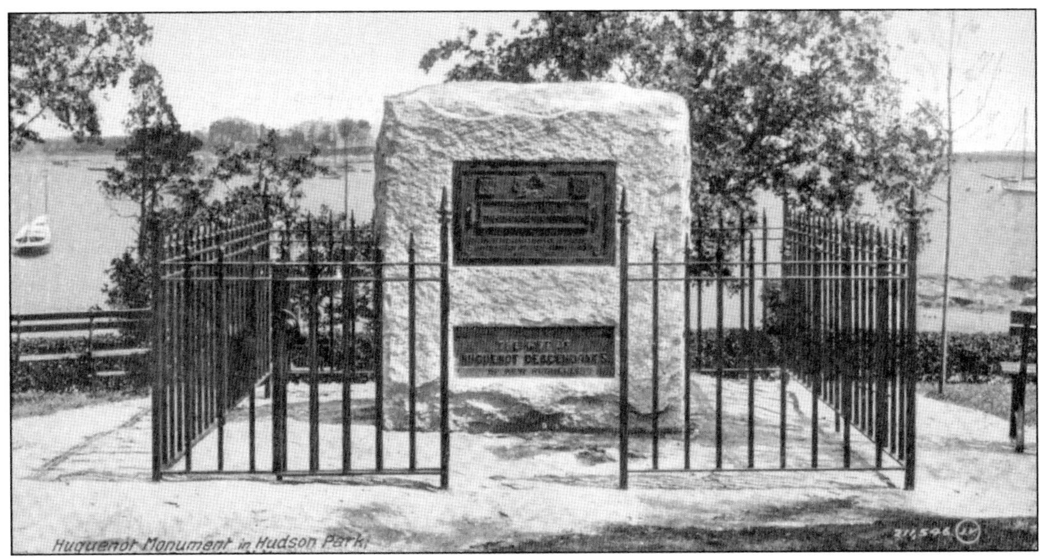

Benjamin Faneuil and Anne Bureau were Huguenots who fled France in the late 1600s to escape religious persecution. They settled in New Rochelle, New York, where their son Peter was born in 1700. Peter was originally named Pierre, and his first language was French. At least six Faneuil siblings survived to adulthood: Peter, Benjamin, Mary Anne, Mary, Anne, and Susannah. Shown here is the Huguenot monument in New Rochelle. (LOC.)

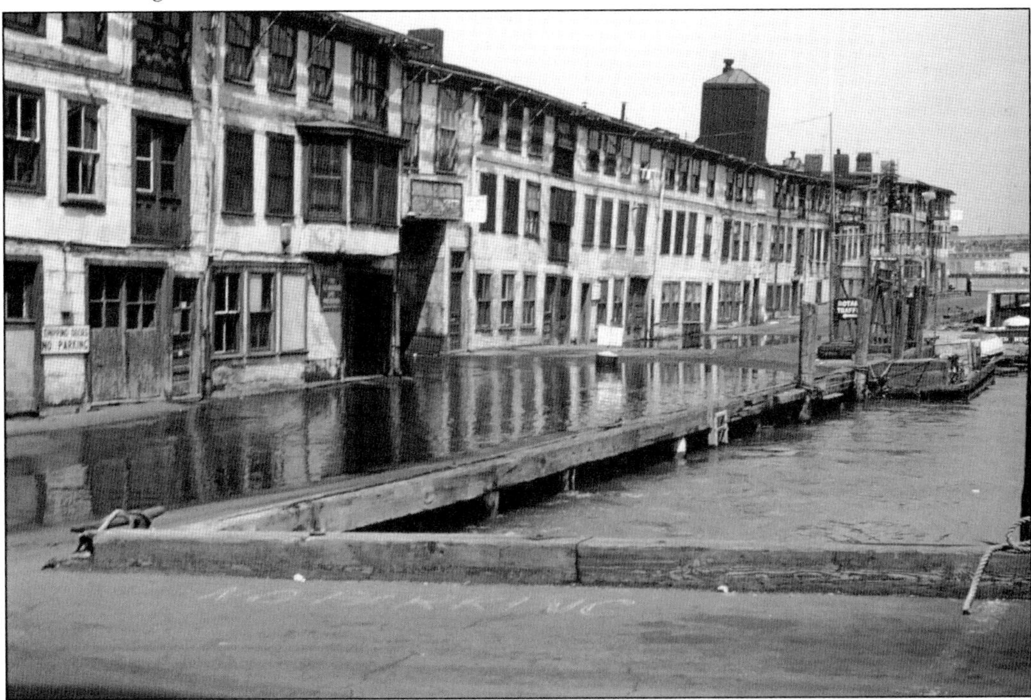

Nineteen-year-old Peter and his younger brother, Benjamin, moved to Boston after their father died in 1719. They apprenticed with their father's brother, Andrew Faneuil. The elder Faneuil was a wealthy businessman—trading in rum, molasses, sugar, timber, and enslaved Africans—and he reportedly owned a warehouse on Merchants Row and held a financial interest in T Wharf, shown here in 1961. (Photograph by Edmund L. Mitchell, BPL.)

Not much is known about Peter's early years in Boston, but one incident suggests strong connections with family in France. In July 1728, Benjamin Woodbridge was mortally wounded in a duel with Henry Phillips on the Boston Common. Wanted for murder, the well-connected Phillips (whose brother Gillam was married to Faneuil's sister Mary) fled Massachusetts and lived out the rest of his life with Faneuil's relatives in France. (Photograph by Leon H. Abdalian, BPL.)

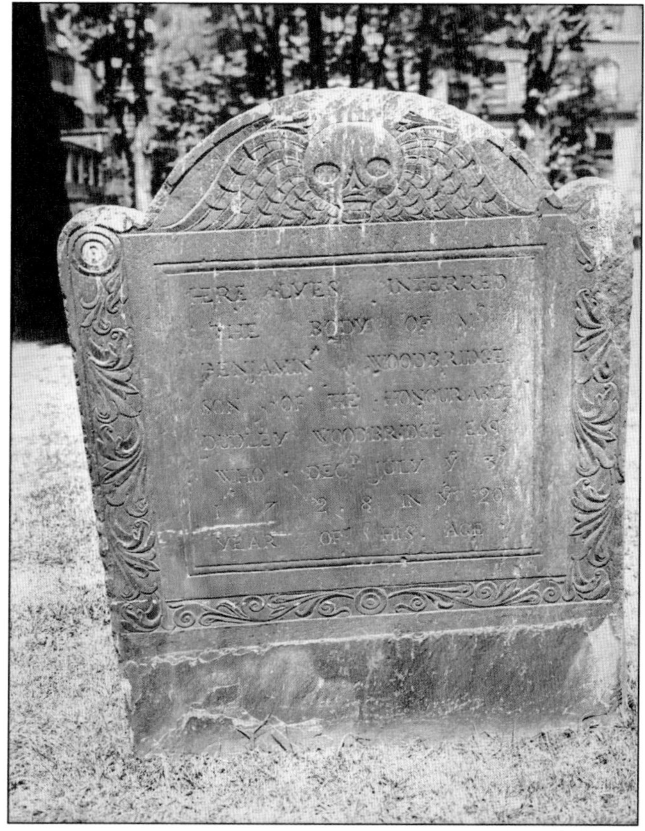

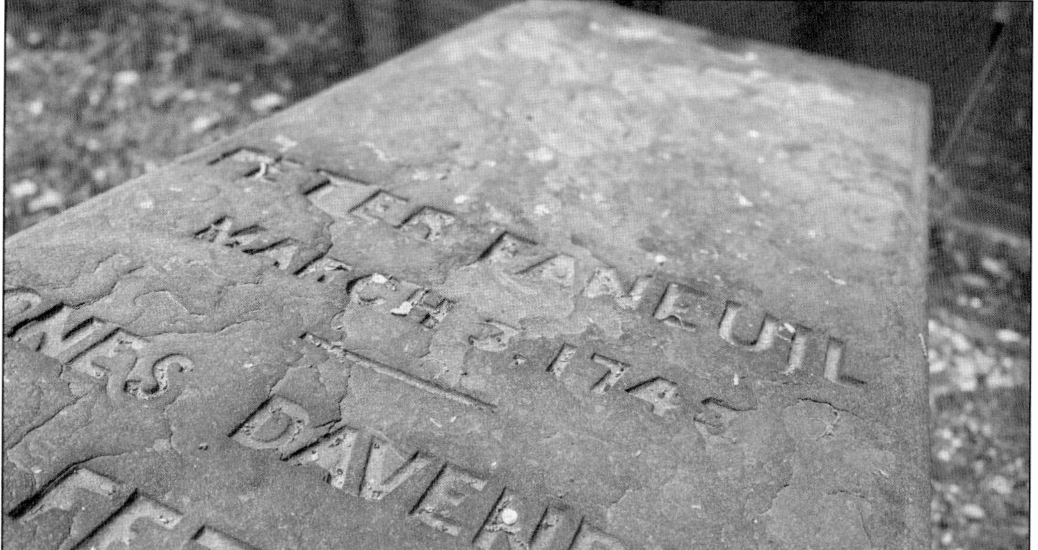

The proper pronunciation of "Faneuil" has been debated since Peter Faneuil was alive. Despite the name's French origins, he was said to prefer "Fan-nel" (to rhyme with "flannel"). In the 1825 novel *Lionel Lincoln*, James Fenimore Cooper used eye dialect to suggest that some Bostonians rhymed the name with "funnel." Today, many stick with "Fan-nel," but others attempt a phonetic pronunciation and say "Fan-yule" or "Fan-yu-ell." (Author's collection.)

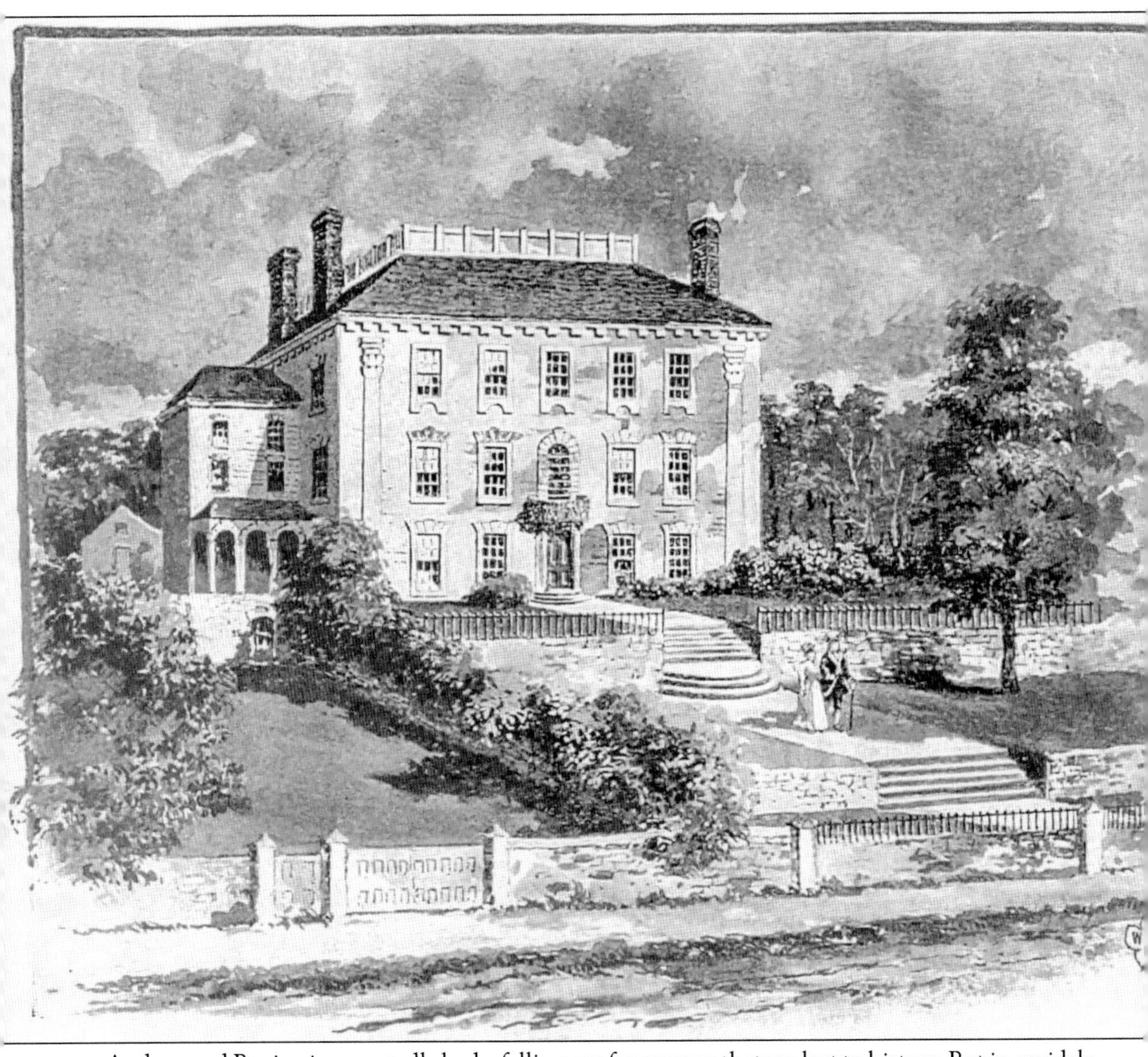

Andrew and Benjamin reportedly had a falling out for reasons that are lost to history. But in a widely repeated (although never verified) story, Andrew reportedly insisted that his nephews remained single. When Benjamin married Mary Cutler, Andrew cut him out of the business and turned his focus to Peter. Reaping the rewards of singlehood, Peter inherited most of Andrew's considerable estate upon the latter's death in 1738, including a mansion on Tremont Street in Boston (shown here). The four Faneuil sisters also benefited under their uncle's will, while Benjamin received "five shillings and no more." Peter wasted no time enjoying (and perhaps flaunting) his new wealth. The 38-year-old bachelor moved into the Tremont Street property and embraced his new circumstances, quickly importing household goods, wine, a chariot, and other luxuries from Europe. "He was fond of display and good living, and the customs of the times encouraged him in the fullest indulgence of his inclinations," Abram English Brown wrote in his book *Faneuil Hall and Faneuil Hall Market*. This image is from the book. (Internet Archive.)

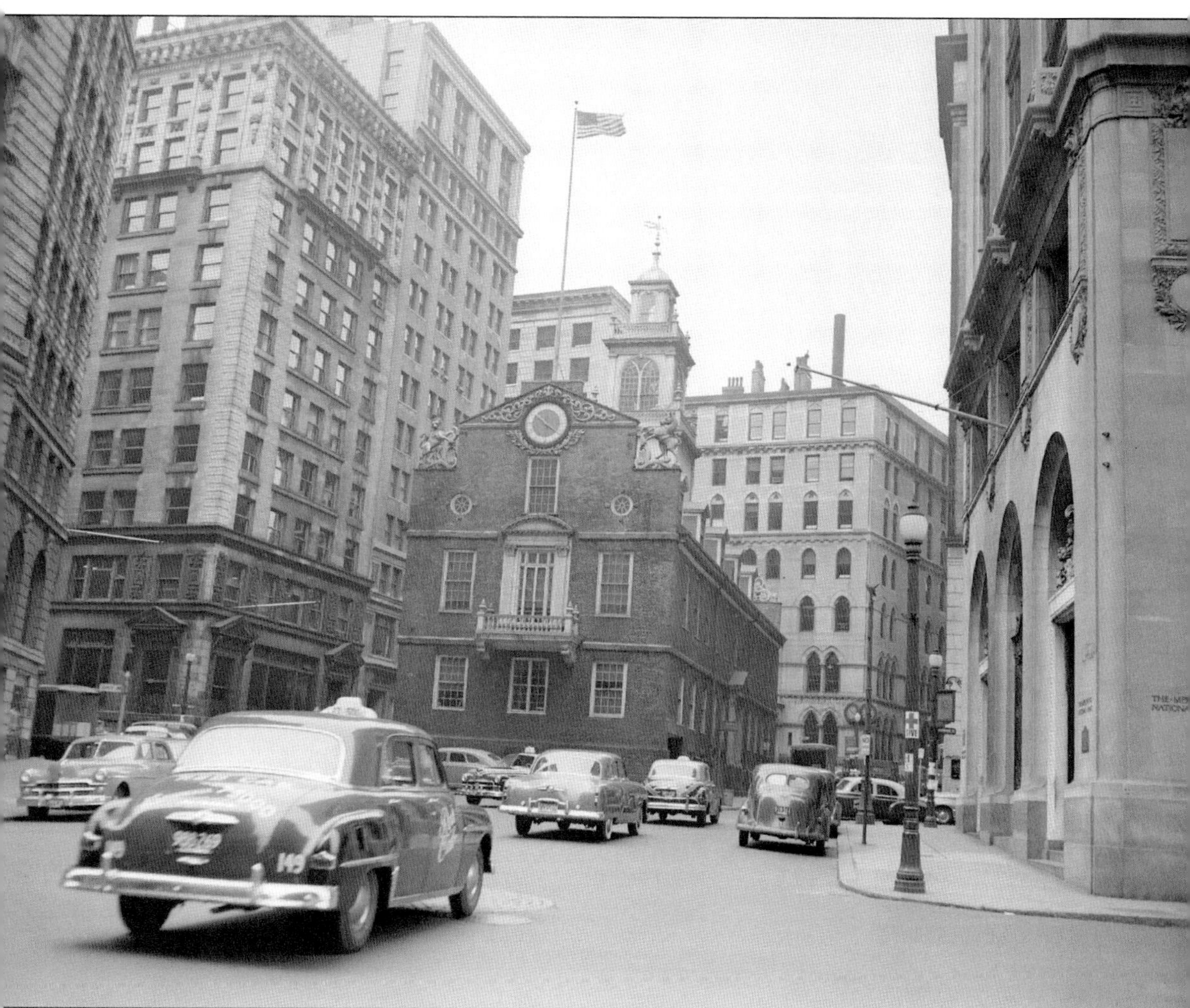

Bostonians had a complicated relationship with formal marketplaces. Many preferred to buy their necessities from peddlers who sold food and household goods door-to-door. Boston's first outdoor market was established in a field near the Town Dock in the 1630s and was variously known as Dock Market and Corn Market. The Town House followed in 1658. The two-story wooden structure was built at King and Cornhill Streets (now State and Washington Streets) and housed a market on the ground floor and government offices upstairs. The building was destroyed in a fire in 1711 and rebuilt in 1713, this time with brick. A merchants' exchange replaced the ground-floor marketplace, and the royal governor, the Massachusetts legislature, the state court, and Boston town meetings all operated from upstairs rooms. Today, the brick structure is known as the Old State House. (Photograph by Leon H. Abdalian, BPL.)

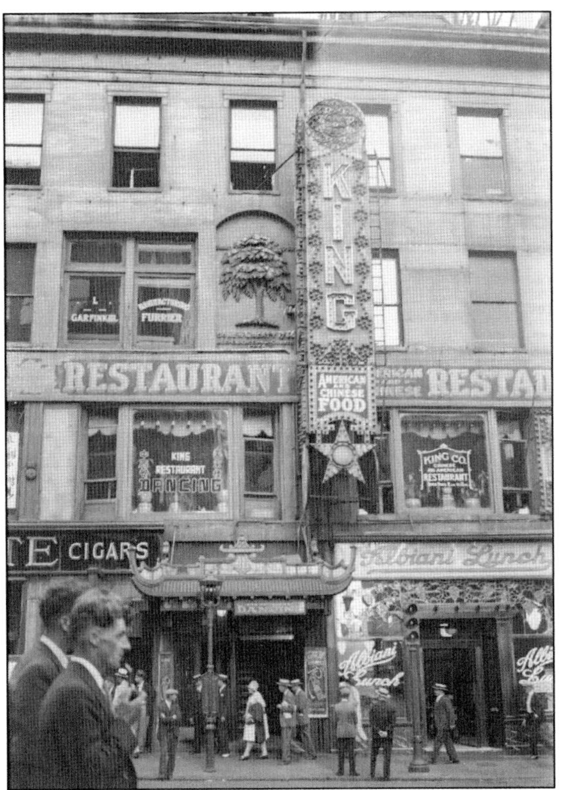

With the Town House market gone, market advocates tried again in 1734. This time, the town voted 517-399 to establish three public market buildings. North Market was in today's North End neighborhood, Centre Market was in Dock Square, and South Market was near the Liberty Tree by the current intersection of Boylston and Washington Streets (later marked by the Liberty Tree Building, shown here). But antimarket sentiment was still strong, and the new markets were gone three years later, with two abandoned and one destroyed by a mob. (BPL.)

Boston was still without a centralized marketplace in 1740—and decades from the ones pictured here—when Peter Faneuil made an unusual offer. He would pay for a new market and donate it to his adopted hometown. But the offer came with an important contingency: approval from a townwide vote. (LOC.)

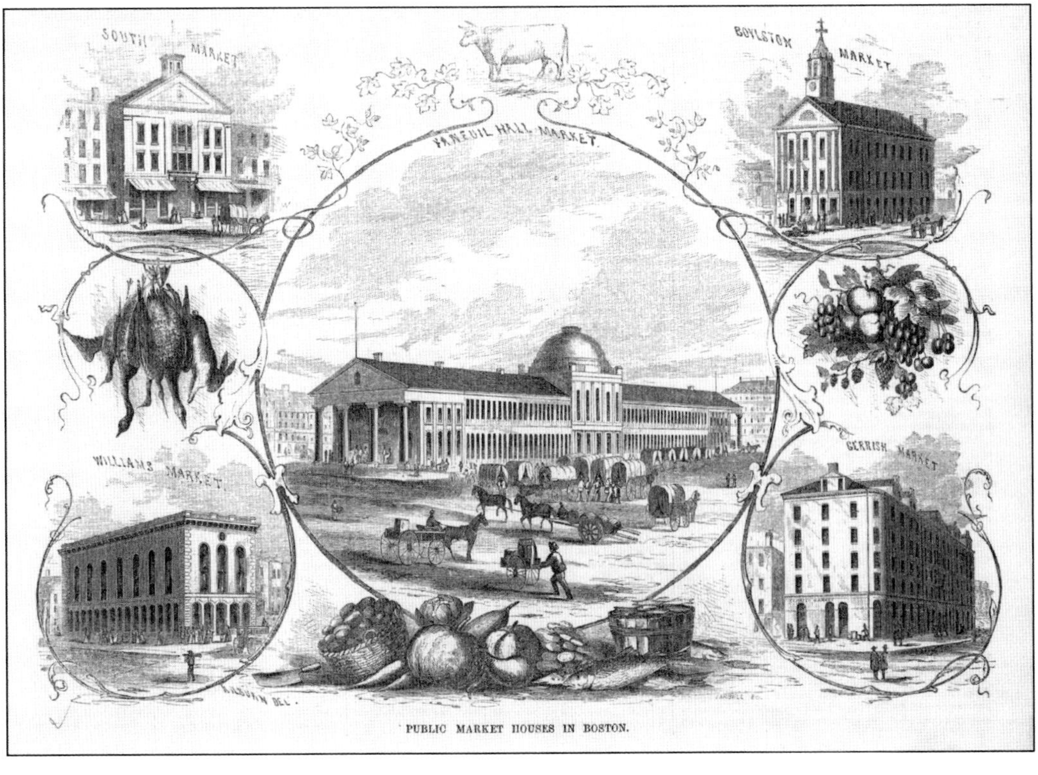

PUBLIC MARKET HOUSES IN BOSTON.

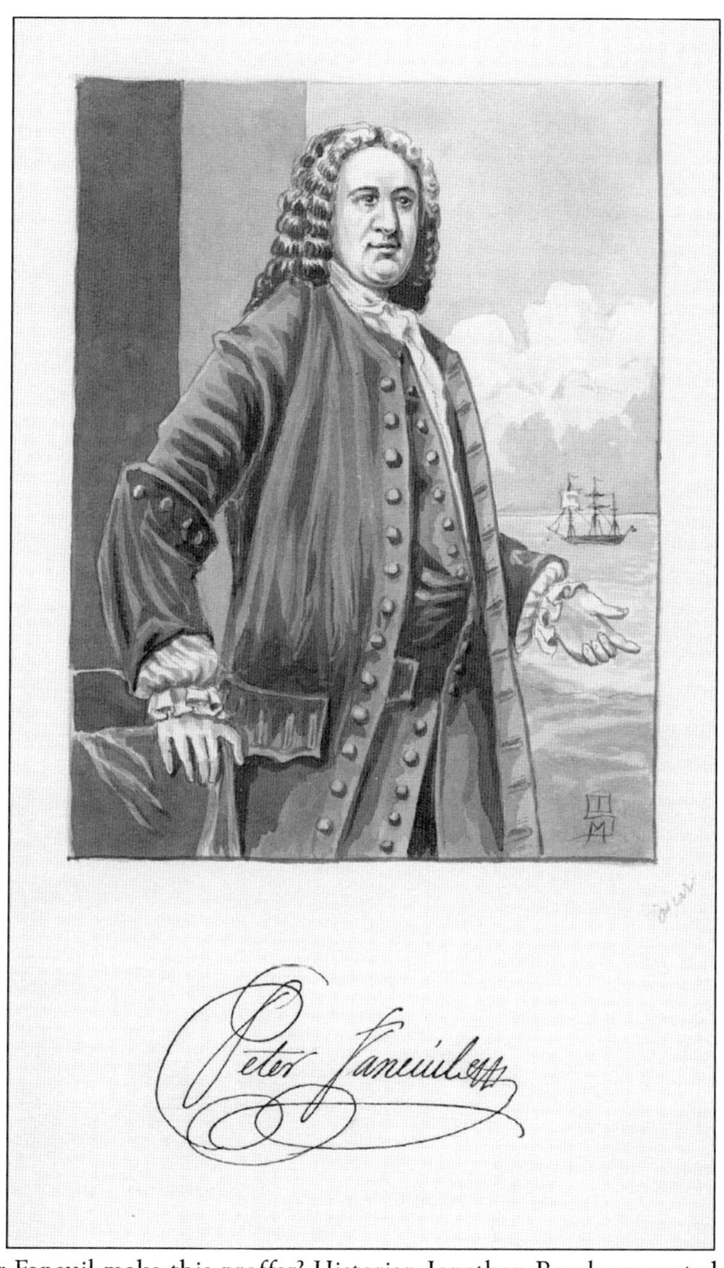

Why did Peter Faneuil make this proffer? Historian Jonathan Beagle suggested that Faneuil's display of generosity and public-spiritedness was intended both to burnish his reputation as a benevolent gentleman and to better integrate himself into his adopted community. Public historian Eric Hanson Plass speculated that Faneuil's desire to leave a legacy, perhaps made more urgent by a sense of mortality, may have influenced the offer. After all, he was still unmarried and had no heirs. Regardless of motivation, the offer changed the dynamics of the ongoing debate about a centralized marketplace. A yes vote was hardly a sure thing in this skeptical environment, but positioning the market as a gift to the town, Beagle said, "took a little bit of the teeth out of the opposition." And, sweetening the deal, Faneuil assured Bostonians that the new market would not interfere with the door-to-door peddlers many still preferred. (New York Public Library.)

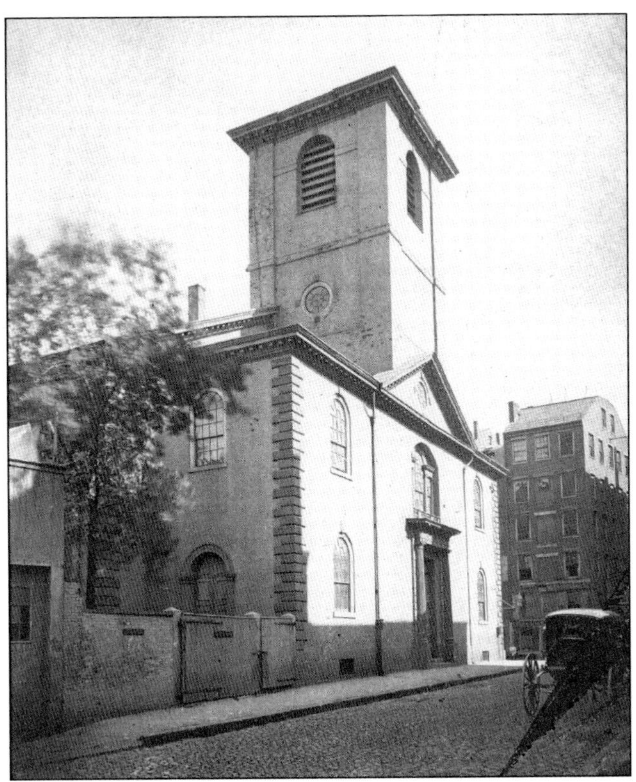

Faneuil's market proposal came up for a vote on July 14, 1740. Interest was so intense that the meeting was moved from the Town House to the larger Brattle Street Church to accommodate the crowd. The vote was conducted by paper ballot to ensure accuracy, and voting qualifications were strictly enforced. This disqualified some men who had voted in the past, and the close 367-360 vote in favor of the market stirred up "a whole heap of controversy," as Jonathan Beagle wrote. Protests were filed after the tally but without success. (BPL.)

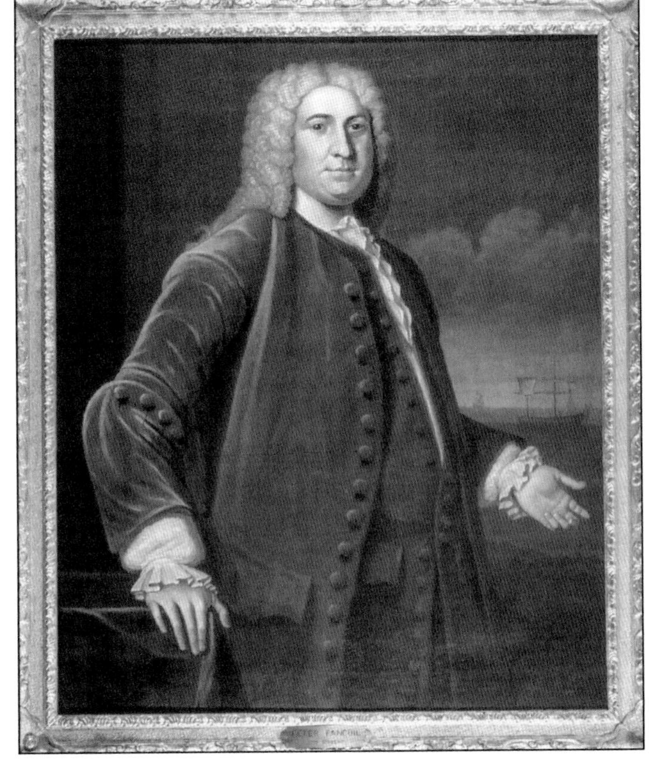

With construction complete, members of the Boston town meeting voted on September 13, 1742, to "Accept this most Generous and Noble Benefaction" and, a few days later, to name the "hall over the market-place" Faneuil Hall. And in a final burst of gratitude, the town freeholders agreed to install a full-length portrait of Peter Faneuil in the meeting hall at the town's expense. Artist John Smibert did the honors. (MHS.)

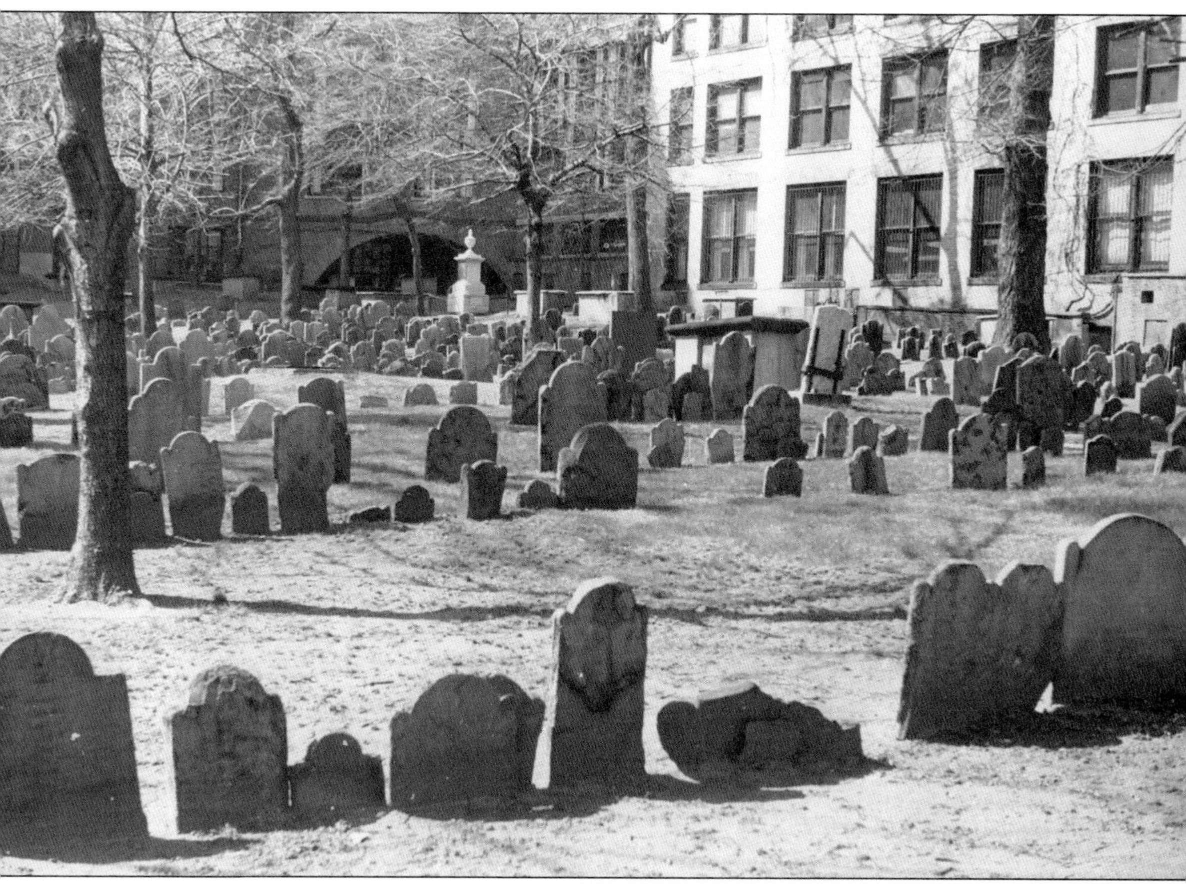

Peter Faneuil died of dropsy (now called edema) on March 3, 1743, at the age of 42, just six months after Faneuil Hall opened. He had outlived his uncle by only five years and was interred in Boston's Granary Burying Ground in the family tomb. John Lovell delivered the funeral oration on March 14. Fittingly, it was the first public address given in the structure Faneuil built. Lovell, who was headmaster of the South Grammar School (later known as Boston Latin School), praised Faneuil's private acts of charity ("so secret and unbounded") and public gifts. "This building erected by him at an immense charge, for the convenience and ornament of the town, is incomparably the greatest benefaction ever yet known to our western shore," he said. Note that early printed versions of Lovell's address were dated March 14, 1742, likely because Great Britain and its colonies did not adopt the modern Gregorian or "New Style" calendar until 1752. (BOS.)

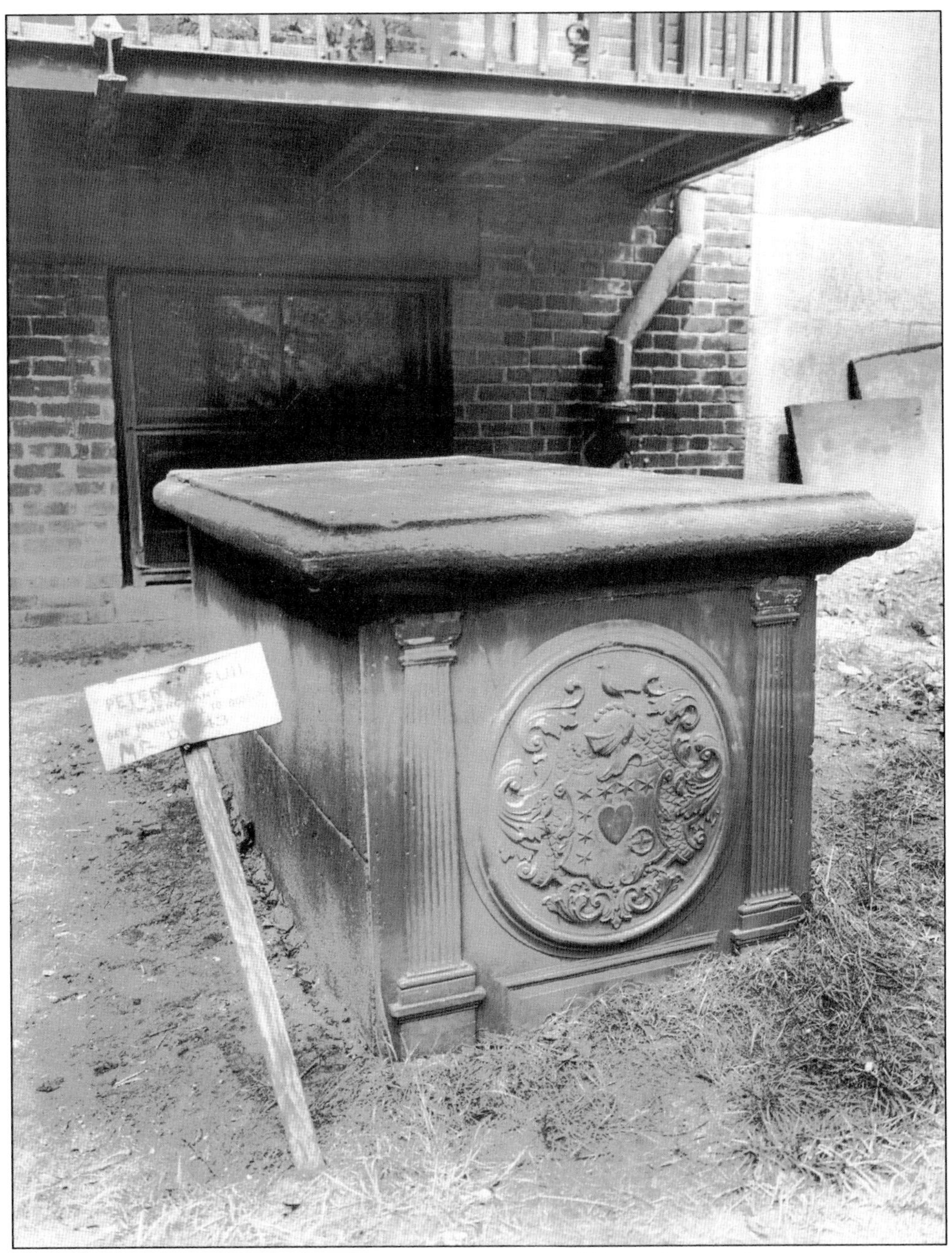

Chroniclers of the time offered a fascinating portrait of Faneuil upon learning of his death, acknowledging his good deeds while describing his appearance in less than flattering terms. Abram English Brown quoted Benjamin Walker's journal on the occasion of Faneuil's death: "He was a fat, squat, Lame, hip short, went with high heeled shoe (In my opinion a great loss too This Town, aged 42, 8m.) & I think by what I have heard has done more charitable deeds than any man yt, ever liv'd in this Town & for whom I am very sorry." According to historian J.L. Bell, "hip short" was probably a variation of "hipshot," an 18th-century term for a sprained or dislocated hip. He concluded that Faneuil was likely born with one leg shorter than the other and wore special shoes to compensate. (Photograph by Leon H. Abdalian, BPL.)

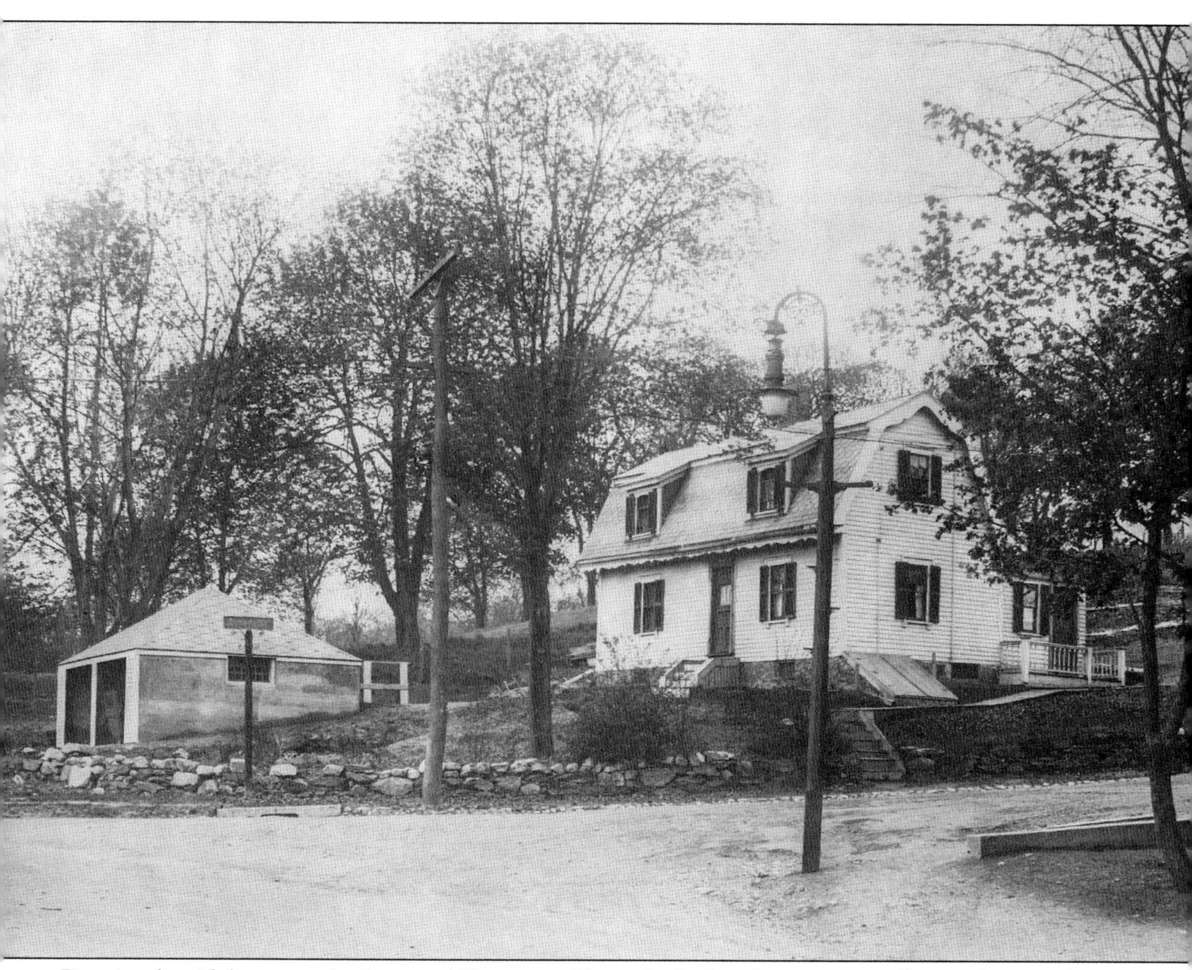

Despite the rift between Andrew and Benjamin Faneuil, the brothers apparently stayed in touch. And when Peter Faneuil died without a will, Benjamin inherited his fortune. In 1760, the younger Faneuil purchased a 70-acre estate on Bigelow Hill in Cambridge (now in the Brighton neighborhood of Boston). The gatekeeper's house (pictured here) is the last surviving part of the Faneuil estate. Benjamin's two sons sided with the British Crown and left Boston during the Revolution. Benjamin Jr. was a consignee (or tax collector) for the tea shipments at the center of the Boston Tea Party. He fled to Nova Scotia when the British evacuated Boston and lived out the rest of his life in England. Peter spent some time in the West Indies but returned to Boston to live with his sister Mary, who inherited the Brighton property after their father's death in 1785. (Brighton-Allston Historical Society.)

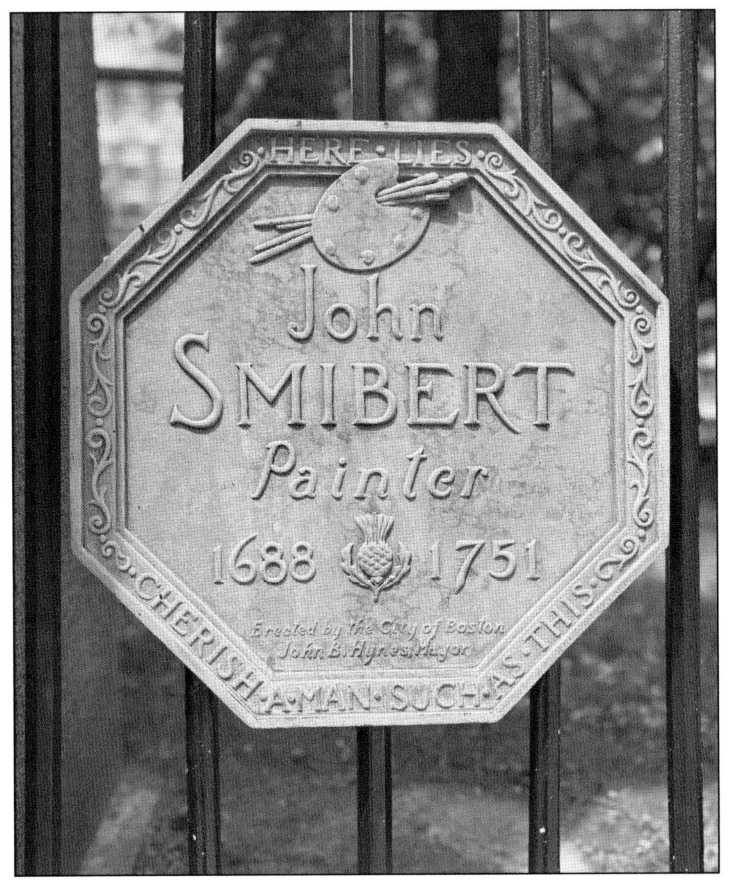

Better known as a portraitist, Scotland-born John Smibert created the original design for Faneuil Hall. Built in the Georgian style, Faneuil Hall was two stories high, three bays wide (40 feet), and nine bays long (100 feet). The exterior was red brick, and the roof was topped with a central cupola and a weather vane in the form of a grasshopper. The ground floor had stalls for vendors, and the second floor held town offices and a public meeting hall (dubbed the Great Hall) that could hold 1,000 people. Windows and market arcades were arched; pilasters separated the openings. (Left, author's collection; below, engraving by Samuel Hill, LOC.)

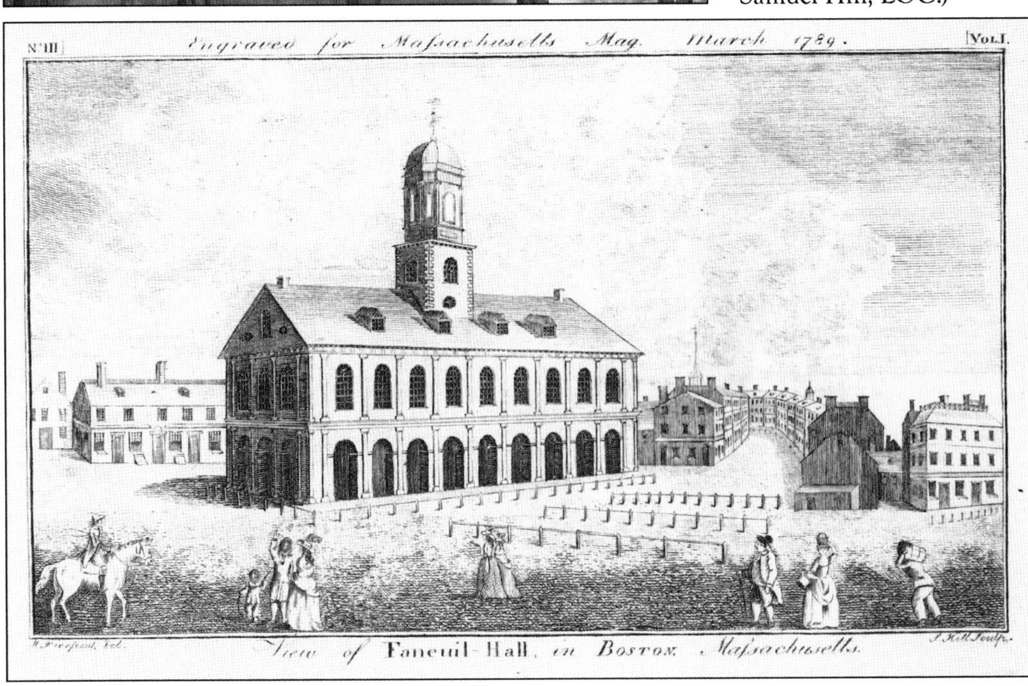

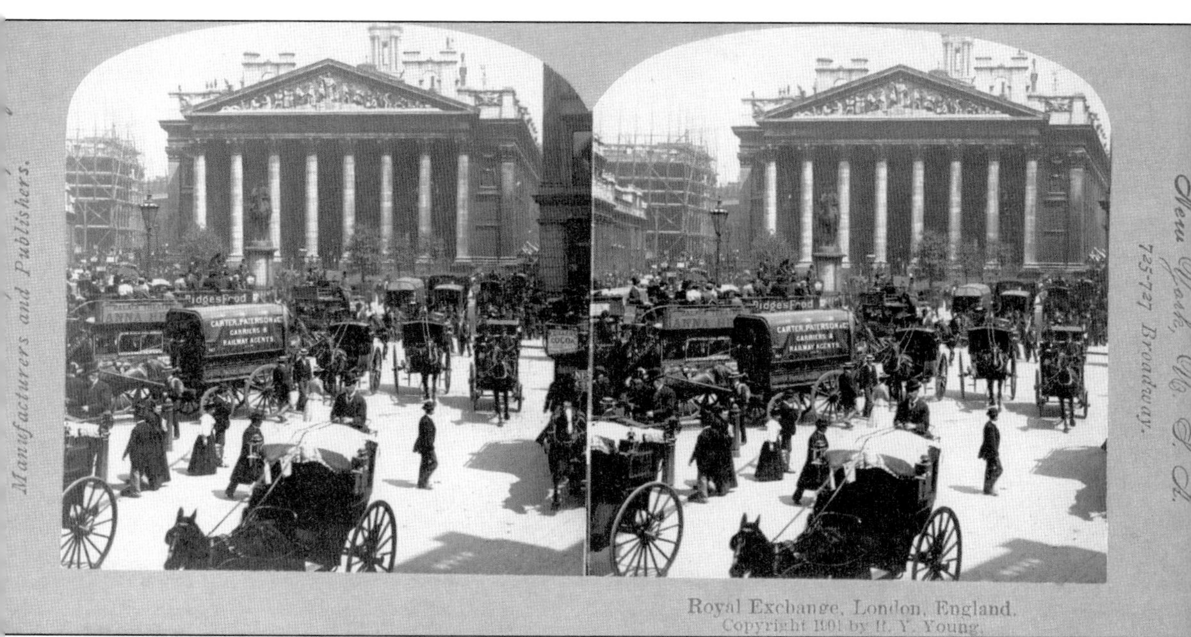

Deacon Shem Drowne fashioned the 38-pound grasshopper weather vane from copper and gold leaf. The eyes were glass, and metal antennae caught the wind. The vane was said to reference the grasshopper atop the Royal Exchange in London, which was founded by Sir Thomas Gresham in the 1500s. By mirroring its counterpart across the Atlantic, the grasshopper embodied Peter Faneuil's desire for Boston to take its place alongside other major cities. (LOC.)

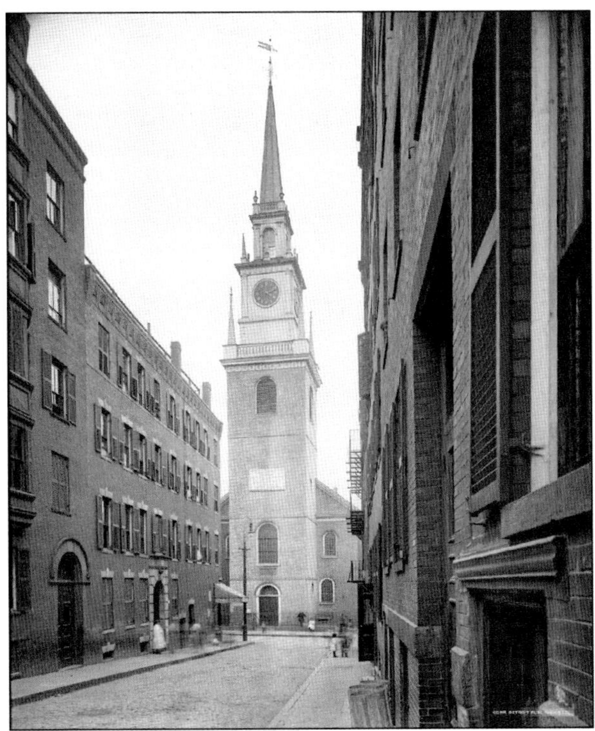

Before creating his most famous work, Drowne fashioned weather vanes for other prominent buildings in colonial Boston. He crafted a gilded Native American archer for the residence of the royal governor, a rooster-shaped weather vane for the New Brick Church, and the six-foot-long swallowtail banner that sits atop the Old North Church, shown here. (LOC.)

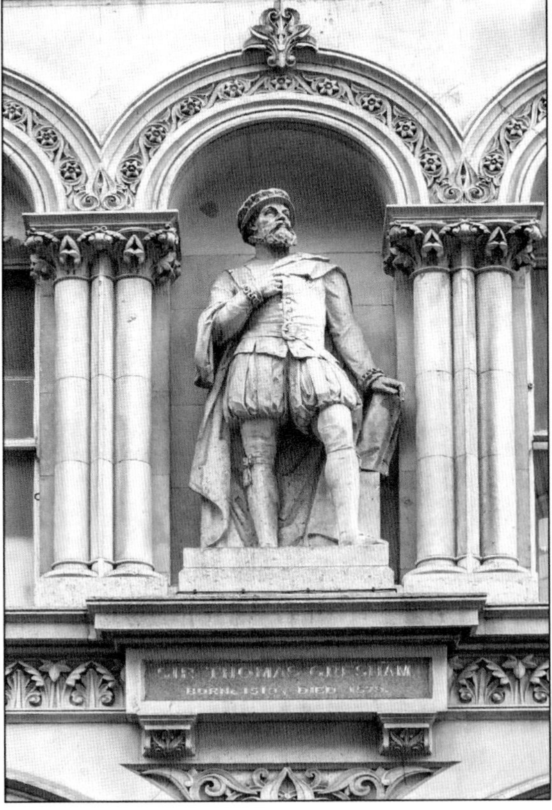

Why was there a grasshopper at the Royal Exchange? Credit goes to the Gresham legacy. According to legend, a woman found an abandoned baby around 1290 when she heard some grasshoppers chirping in a field. She took him in, and that 13th-century foundling grew up to be family patriarch Roger de Gresham. A more prosaic (and likelier) explanation is that the grasshopper connection is a play on the Gresham name, with "grass" sounding like "gres." No matter what the true story is, the Gresham name became closely linked to the insect. A grasshopper appears in the crest above Sir John Gresham's coat of arms, and statues of grasshoppers are scattered across London. Shown here is a statue of Sir Thomas Gresham on the Holborn Viaduct in London. (Gresham College.)

Not to be outdone, Shem Drowne had a story, too. As a young man, the fanciful tale goes, Drowne was napping in a field when a boy chasing a grasshopper ran by. Drowne befriended the lad and was eventually adopted by the boy's wealthy parents. The grasshopper weather vane was said to commemorate this turning point in Drowne's life. (Robert Shure.)

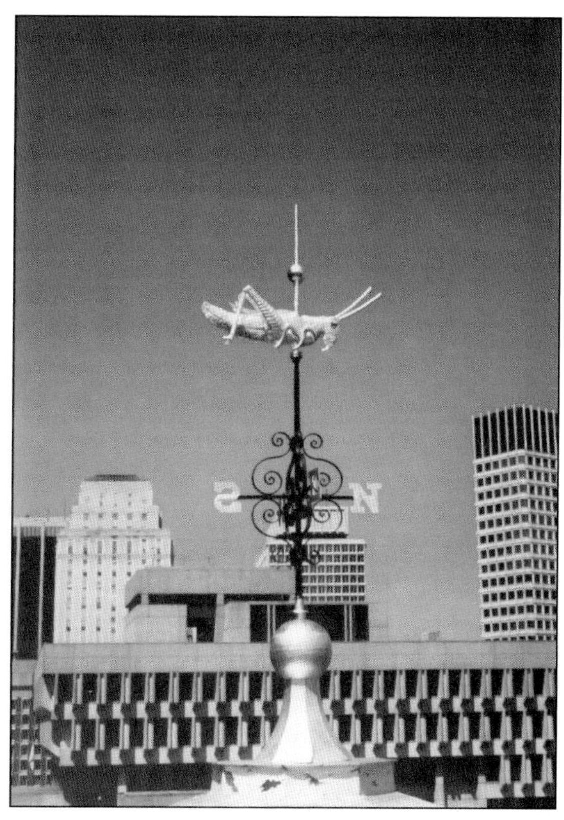

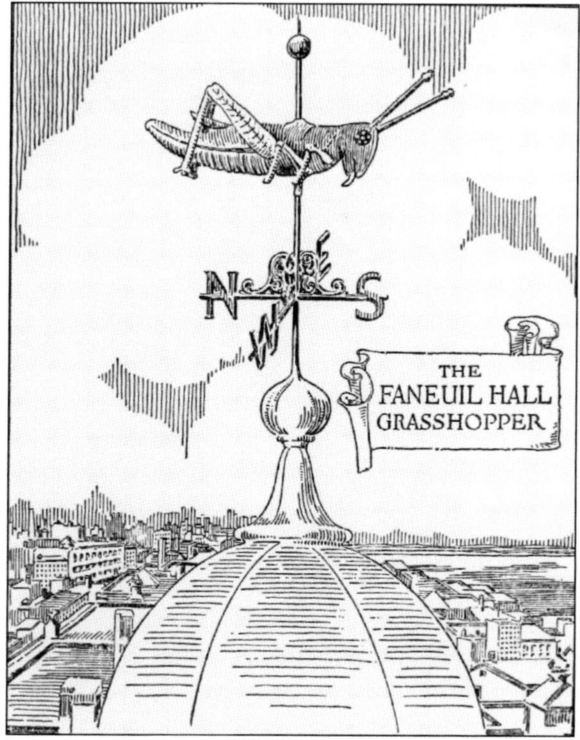

During the Revolutionary War and the War of 1812, the grasshopper served as an informal lie detector. Patriots asked suspected spies what was on top of Faneuil Hall. True Bostonians knew the answer; traitors did not. This image is from *I'm from Boston: Scenes from the Living Past* by Mark Antony De Wolfe. (LOC.)

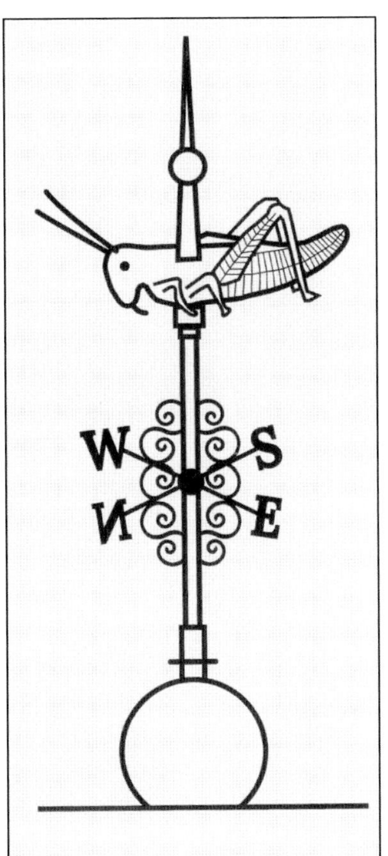

The grasshopper had many ups and downs over the years. When an earthquake toppled the bug in 1755, the Town of Boston hired Shem Drowne's son to make the repairs. Thomas Drowne fixed a broken leg and placed a note inside the weather vane. The dates are a bit off, but the note read, in part: "To my brethren and fellow grasshoppers, Fell in ye year 1753, November 13, early in ye morning by a great earthquake by my Old Master above." (Boston Landmarks Commission.)

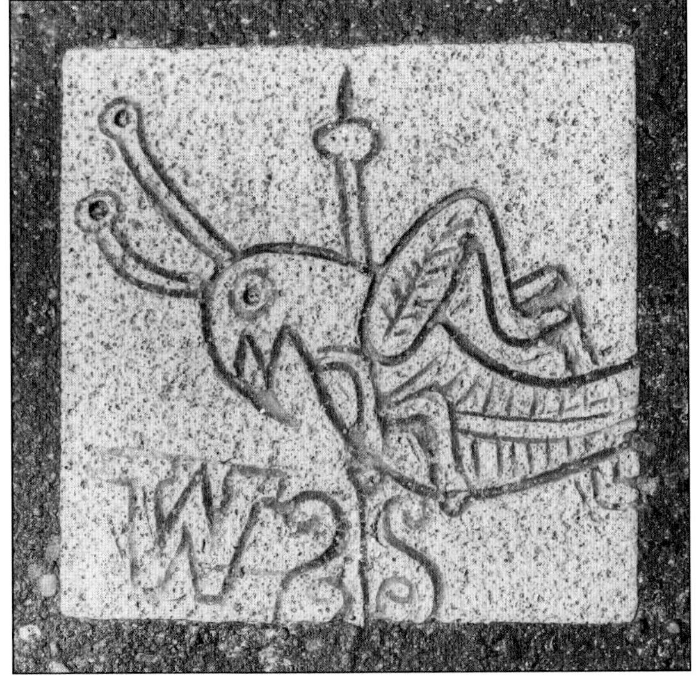

The bug survived the 1761 fire that nearly destroyed Faneuil Hall but was accidentally knocked down in 1889. The vane was periodically removed for maintenance and regilding, and a time capsule was added in 1852. The creature was stolen (and recovered) in 1974 and briefly displayed at Boston's Museum of Fine Arts in the early 1990s after a restoration. (National Park Service.)

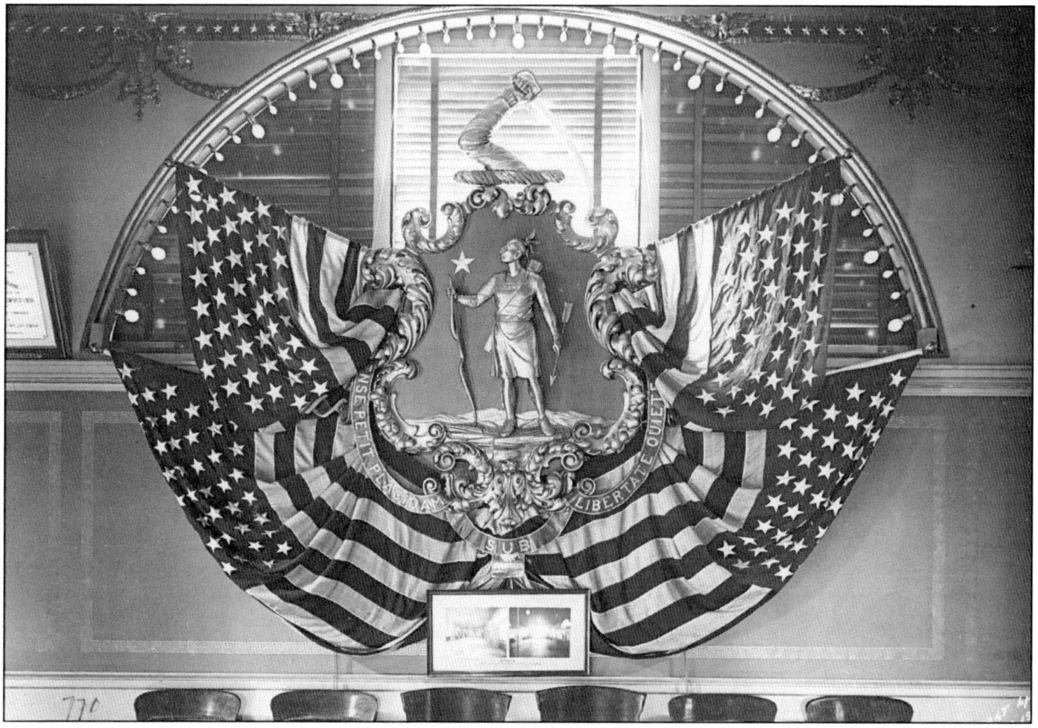

The Ancient and Honorable Artillery Company (sometimes called the Ancients) was chartered in 1638 by the Great and General Court of Massachusetts Bay to train officers serving in local militias. The organization moved into Faneuil Hall in 1746 and today maintains an armory, library, and museum on the fourth floor. (Photograph by Thomas E. Marr, BPL.)

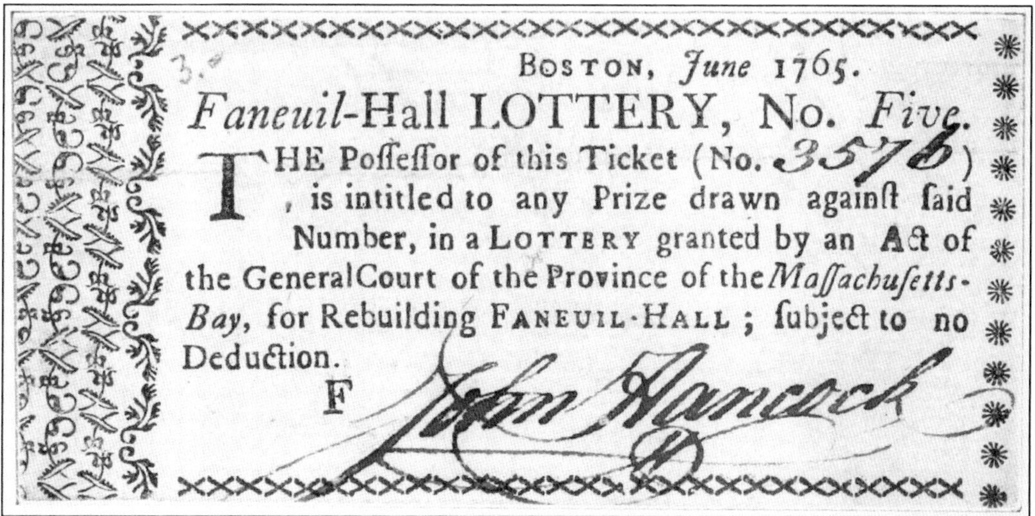

3.

BOSTON, *June* 1765.

Faneuil-Hall LOTTERY, No. *Five*.

THE Poſſeſſor of this Ticket (No. 3576), is intitled to any Prize drawn againſt ſaid Number, in a LOTTERY granted by an Act of the General Court of the Province of the *Maſſachuſetts-Bay*, for Rebuilding FANEUIL-HALL; ſubject to no Deduction.

F John Hancock

Faneuil Hall burned down on January 13, 1761; only the brick exterior walls and the weather vane remained. The market was firmly established within the Boston community by then (after closing three times between 1747 and 1759), and the town authorized funding through a public lottery to rebuild the marketplace. Selectman John Hancock sponsored the lottery, and some of the tickets bore his soon-to-be-famous signature. The rebuilt market opened on March 14, 1763. (New York Public Library.)

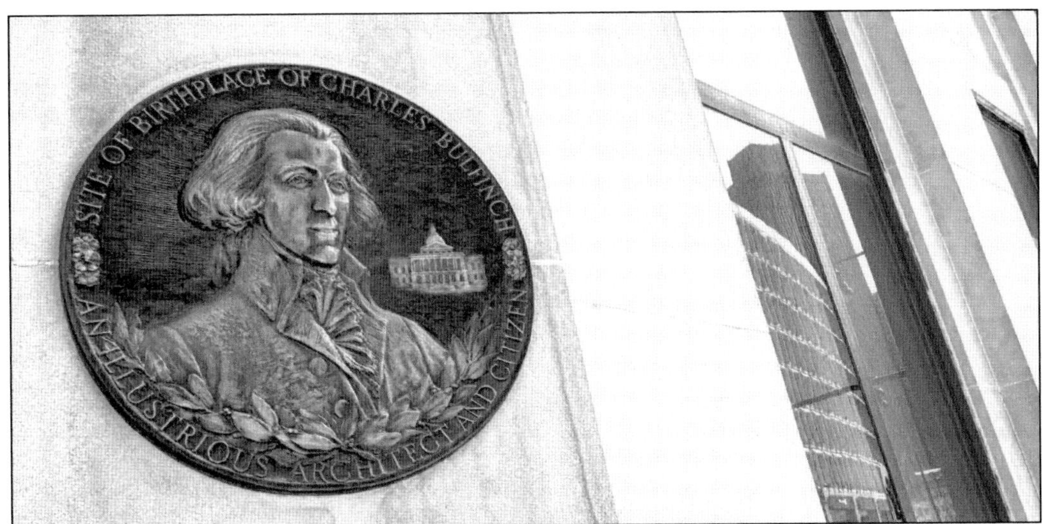

The Faneuil Hall of today began to take shape in 1806. By the end of the 18th century, neither the meeting hall nor the marketplace could support a growing Boston, and the town's selectmen accepted a proposal to enlarge Faneuil Hall from one of their own, Charles Bulfinch, who was both an architect and a fellow selectman. (Author's collection.)

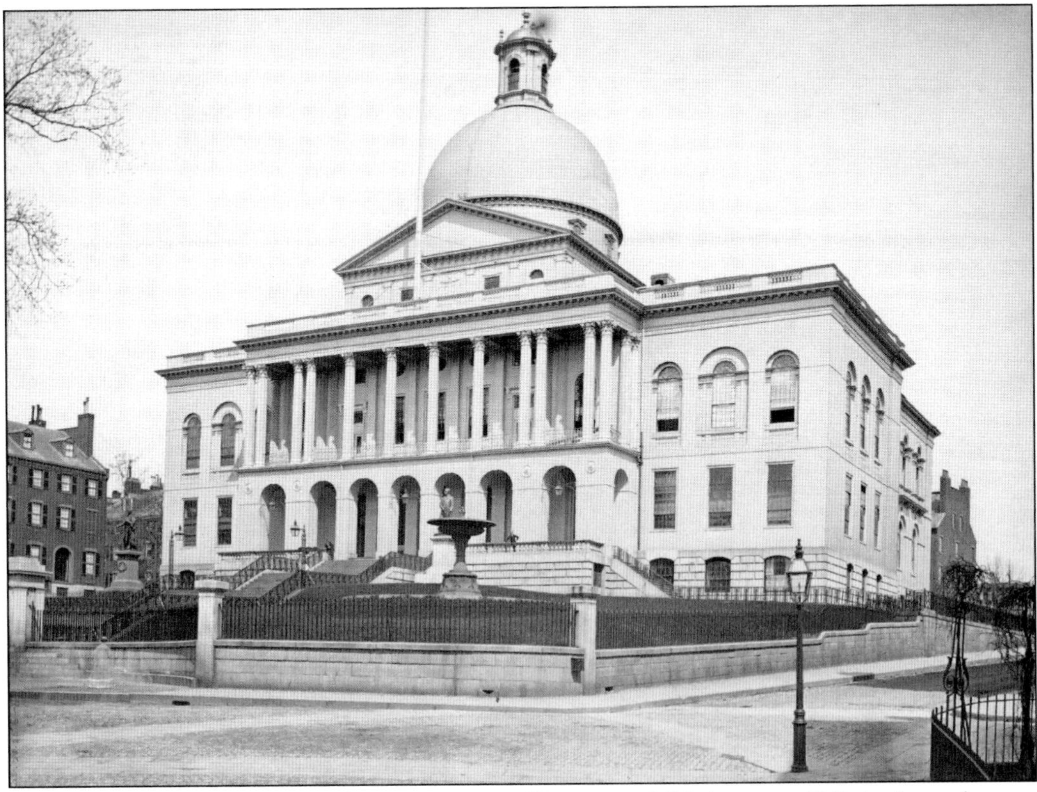

Charles Bulfinch helped shape the streetscapes of Boston and Washington, DC, in the early years of the country. Besides Faneuil Hall, he is known for designing the Massachusetts State House (shown here), India Wharf, and the US Capitol. He also laid out a new commercial district on the site of the former Mill Pond, now called the Bulfinch Triangle. (BPL.)

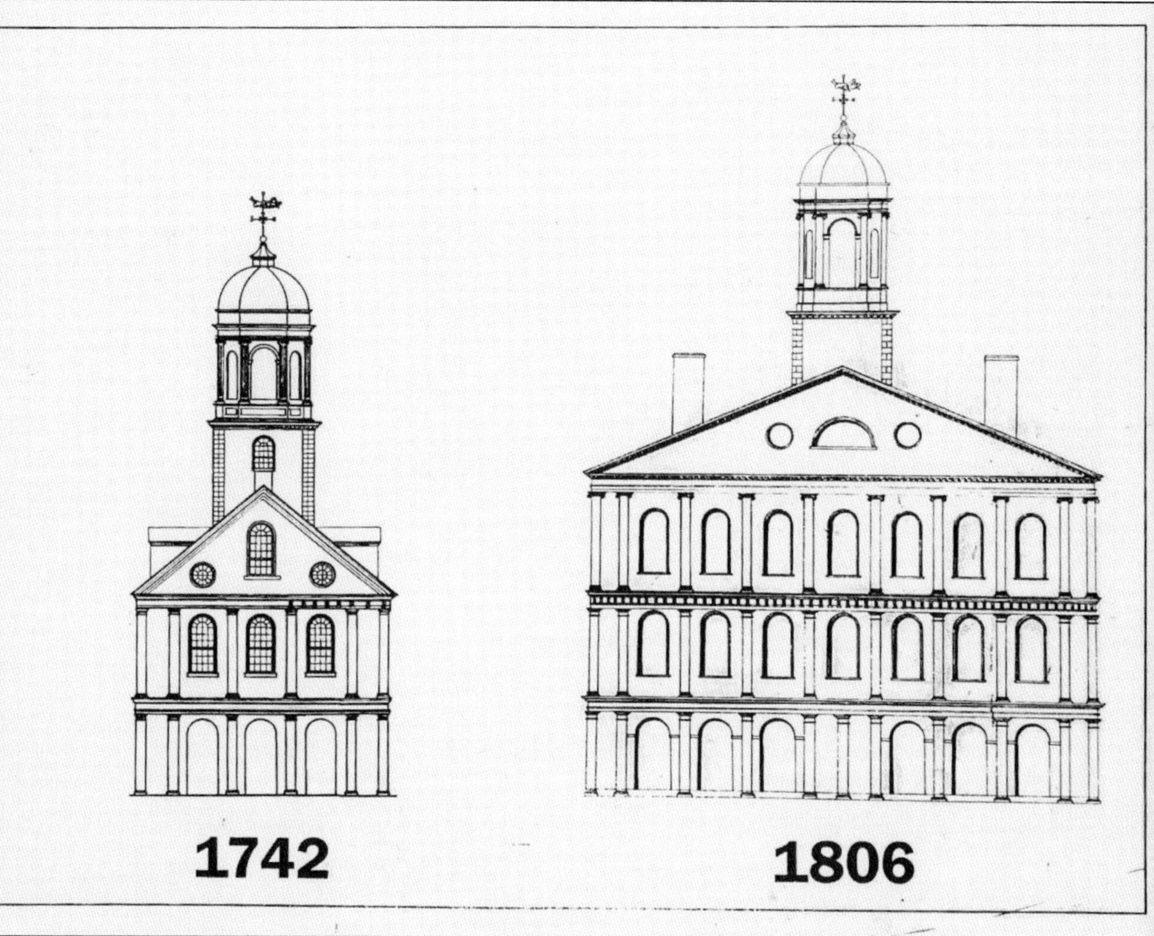

Bulfinch expanded Faneuil Hall at a cost to the town of about $58,000. The renovation added one-and-a-half stories and doubled the width from 40 feet to 80 feet through an addition on the north side of the building. The enlarged structure was nine bays deep (no change) and seven bays wide. The update also added cellar space, enclosed the first-floor stalls, and moved the cupola (including the weather vane) to the eastern edge of the building to better relate to its main entrance and to the harbor. (With Quincy Market 20 years away, Faneuil Hall still had a waterfront location.) A seating gallery was added on three sides of the Great Hall to accommodate larger meetings. Bulfinch added a grand staircase to the Great Hall as well as offices for town officials. Space was carved out on the fourth floor for the Ancients. Shown here is a comparison of the original 1742 design with the 1806 update. (National Park Service.)

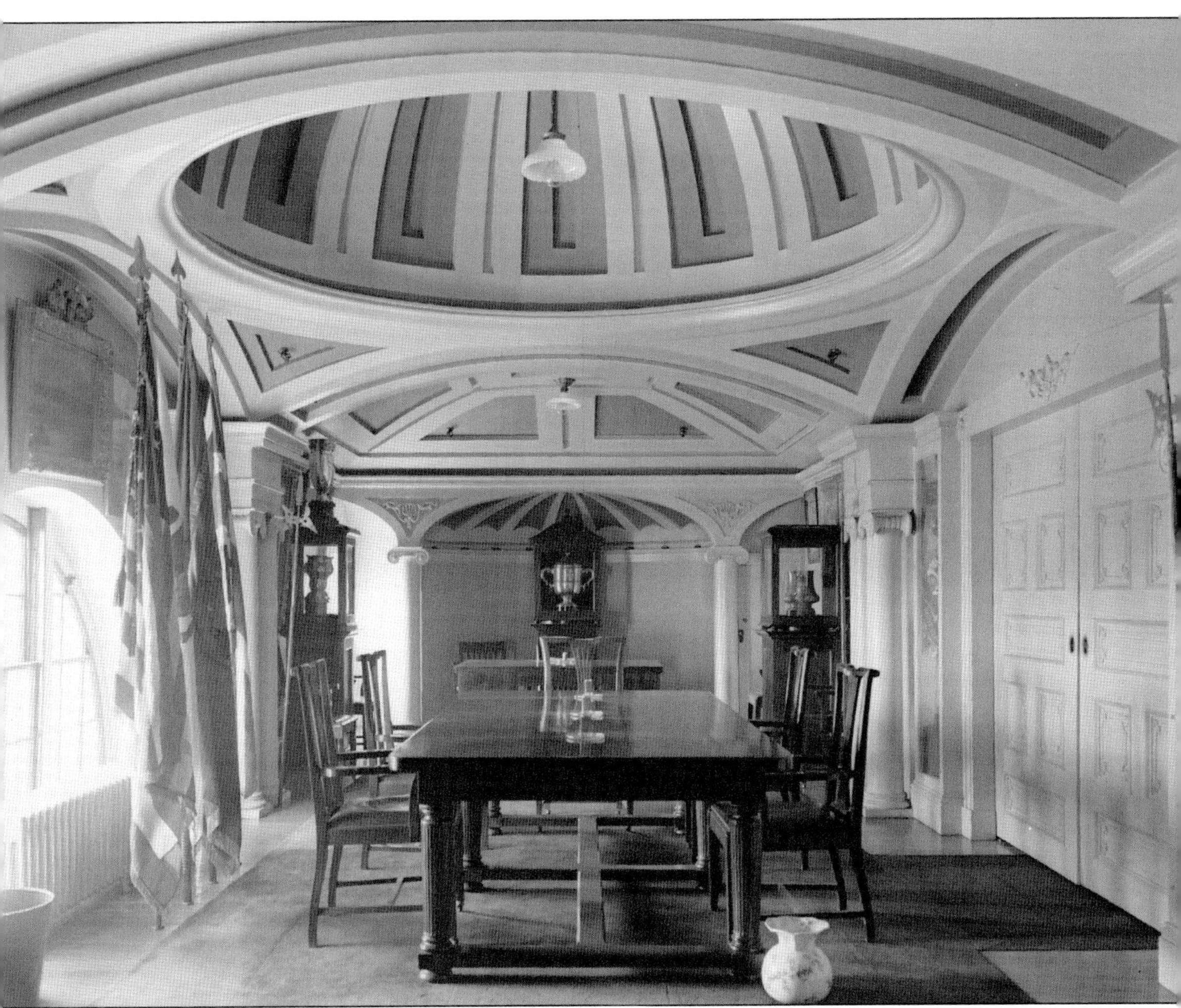

Faneuil Hall has undergone multiple updates and renovations since the Bulfinch expansion. Fresh off the Faneuil Hall Market project, Alexander Parris oversaw the first update in 1827. He created a new arched entrance on the east side of the building and widened the staircase leading to the Great Hall. But his most significant contribution was the Commandery Room, a ceremonial space beneath the cupola used by the Ancients; his Greek Revival scheme incorporated a coffered domed ceiling, Ionic columns, and shell niches. Parris may also have been responsible for painting the exterior brick to a "light Portland stone color," as noted in *Bowen's Picture of Boston*, to better complement Quincy Market. In 1858, Gridley Bryant built a spiral staircase that linked the Great Hall rostrum to the market floor. (Bryant was also known for developing a horse-drawn railroad to transport granite blocks from a quarry in Quincy to the construction site for the Bunker Hill Monument.) (LOC.)

An extensive 1898 update improved Faneuil Hall's fire safety. With oversight from architects Frank W. Howard and Francis W. Chandler, wood elements were removed and replaced with iron, steel, and stone replicas to reduce the risk of fire. The cupola was shored up with steel supports, and the space occupied by the Ancients received safety upgrades. (LOC.)

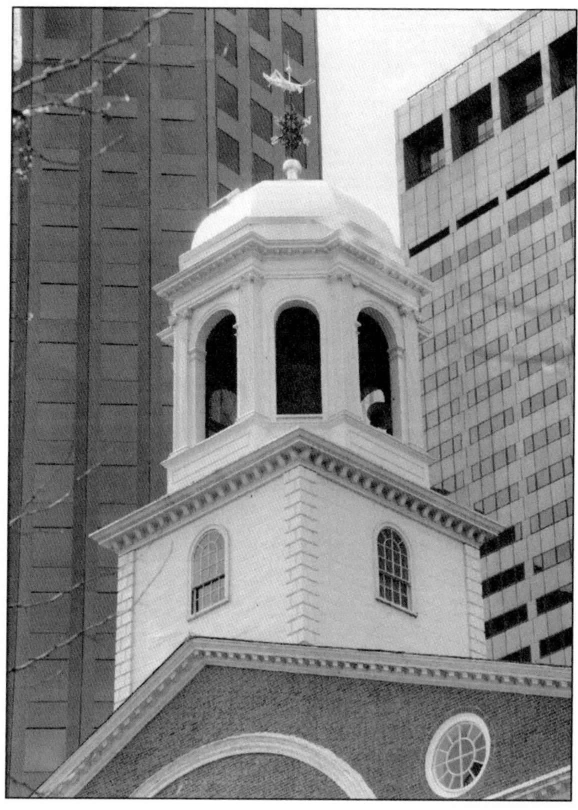

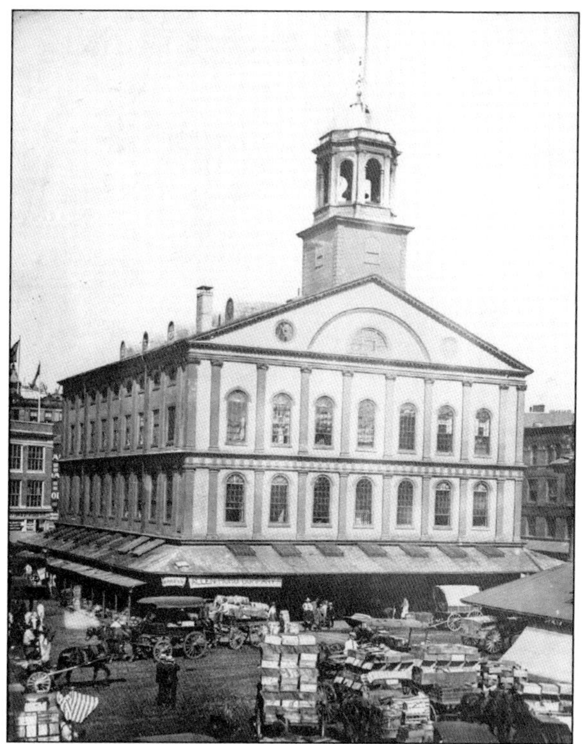

In 1923, the architecture firm of Cram and Ferguson used sandblasting to remove several layers of exterior paint from Faneuil Hall. Although this was a common practice at the time, contemporary historians believe the technique damaged the protective coating of the bricks and left them vulnerable to the weather. More recently, a renovation in the 1990s by architectural firm Goody, Clancy & Associates in cooperation with the National Park Service updated the building's mechanical systems. (BPL.)

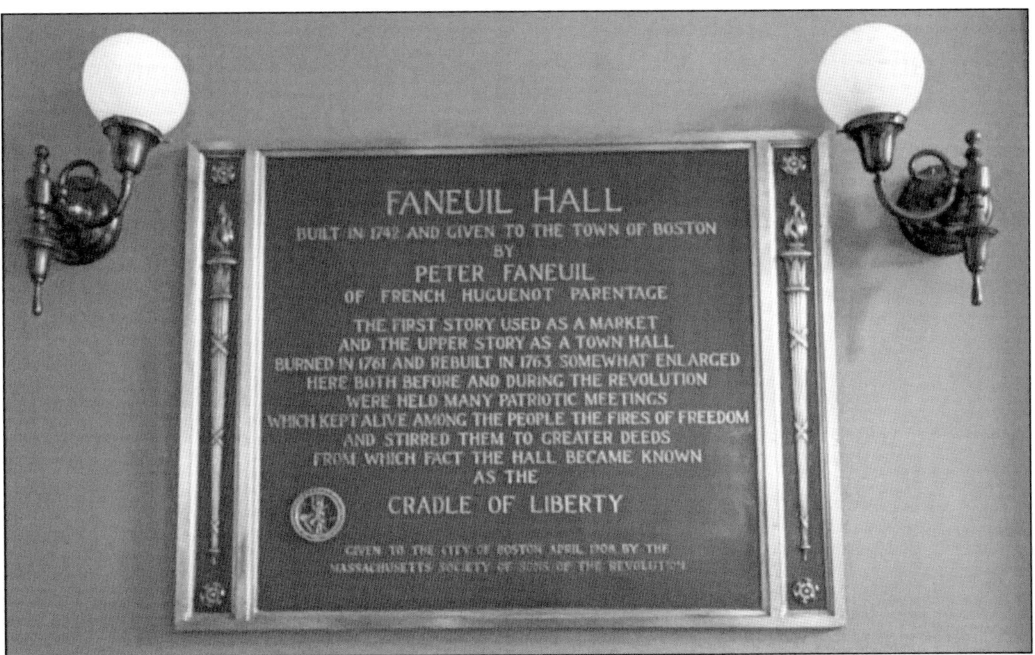

In 1908, the Massachusetts Society of Sons of the Revolution installed a bronze tablet in Faneuil Hall. The inscription read, in part, "Here both before and during the Revolution / Were held many patriotic meetings / Which kept alive among the people the fires of freedom / And stirred them to greater deeds." The plaque sits outside the Great Hall. (Author's collection.)

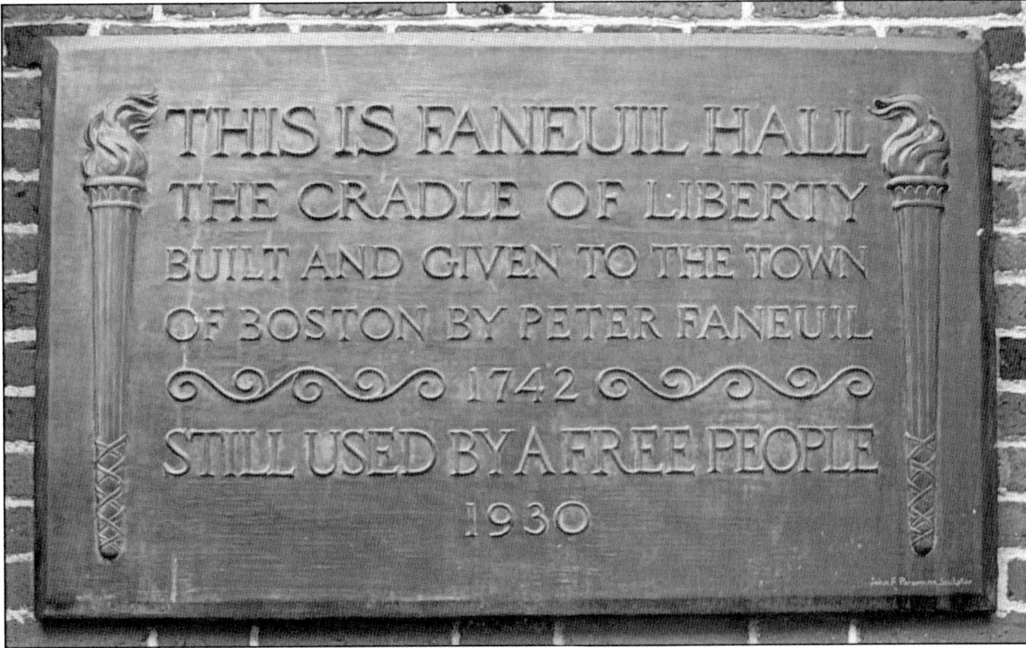

A plaque was installed on the exterior of Faneuil Hall in 1930, probably for the 300th anniversary of the founding of Boston. The marker was engraved with the following message: "This is Faneuil Hall / The Cradle of Liberty / Built and given to the town / of Boston by Peter Faneuil / 1742 / Still used by a free people / 1930." (Author's collection.)

After the Revolutionary War, Faneuil Hall and its association with American independence took on almost mythological status in the minds of Bostonians. In August 1797, a newspaper reporting on an event to honor Pres. John Adams described Faneuil Hall as the "cradle of American liberty." The nickname stuck, and Faneuil Hall was widely known as the Cradle of Liberty by the early 1800s. But the moniker was not unique to Boston—or even to the new country. The name was also applied to Independence Hall in Philadelphia, and some trace the metaphor to the 1789 French Revolution. (Right, Budington Press; below, LOC.)

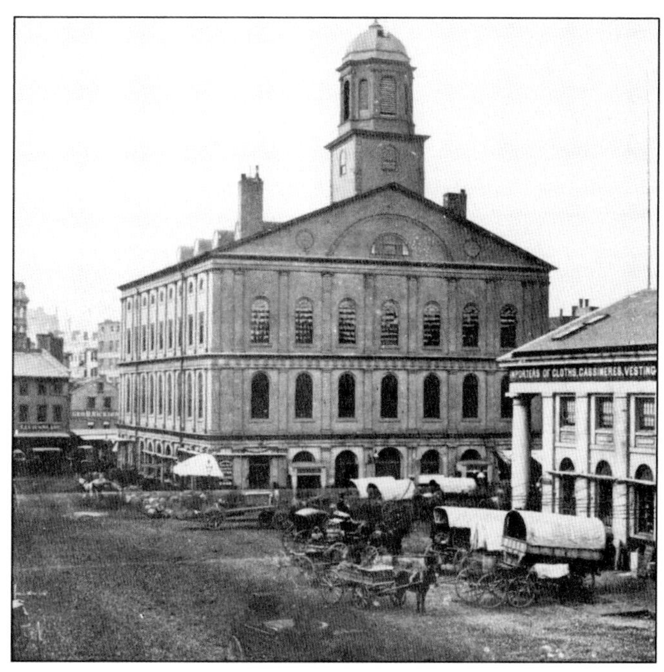

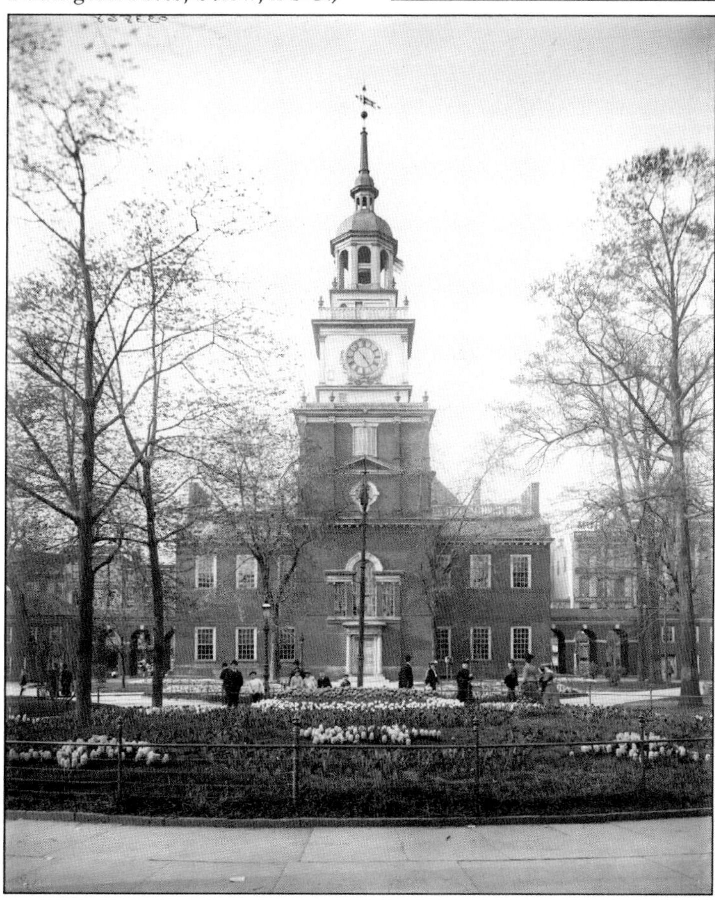

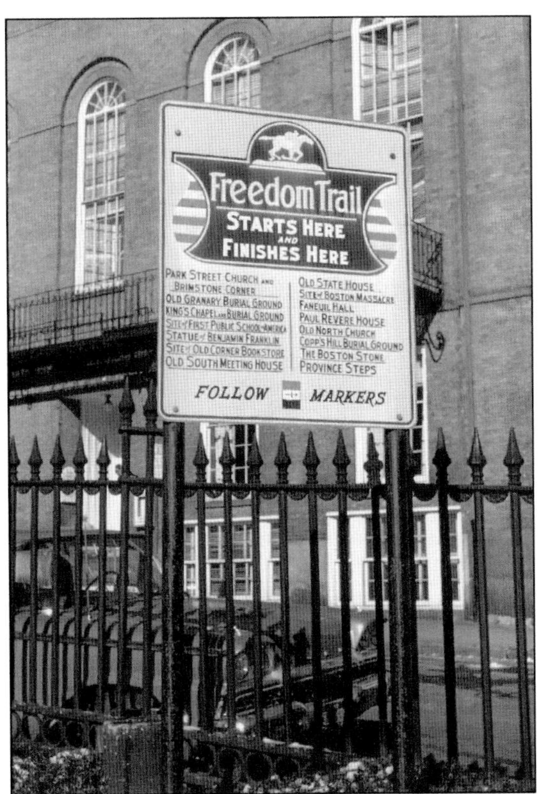

The Freedom Trail is a 2.5-mile walking path through Boston designated by a red line on sidewalks that guides visitors to 16 historic sites. The collection of museums, churches, meetinghouses, burying grounds, parks, historic markers, and a ship—and, of course, Faneuil Hall—documents the city's Revolutionary history and more. (Photograph by Edmund L. Mitchell, BPL.)

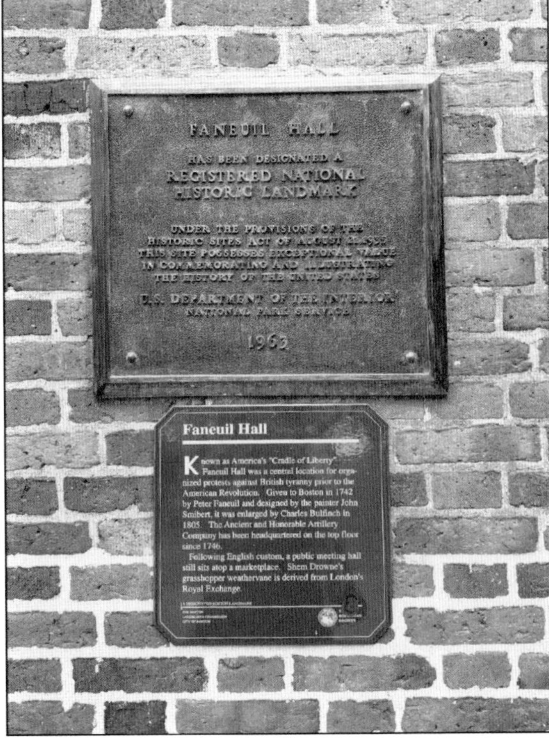

Faneuil Hall was designated a national historic landmark in 1960 and added to the National Register of Historic Places in 1966. Designation as a Boston landmark followed in 1994. Still owned by the City of Boston, the building is also part of the Boston National Historical Park. (Author's collection.)

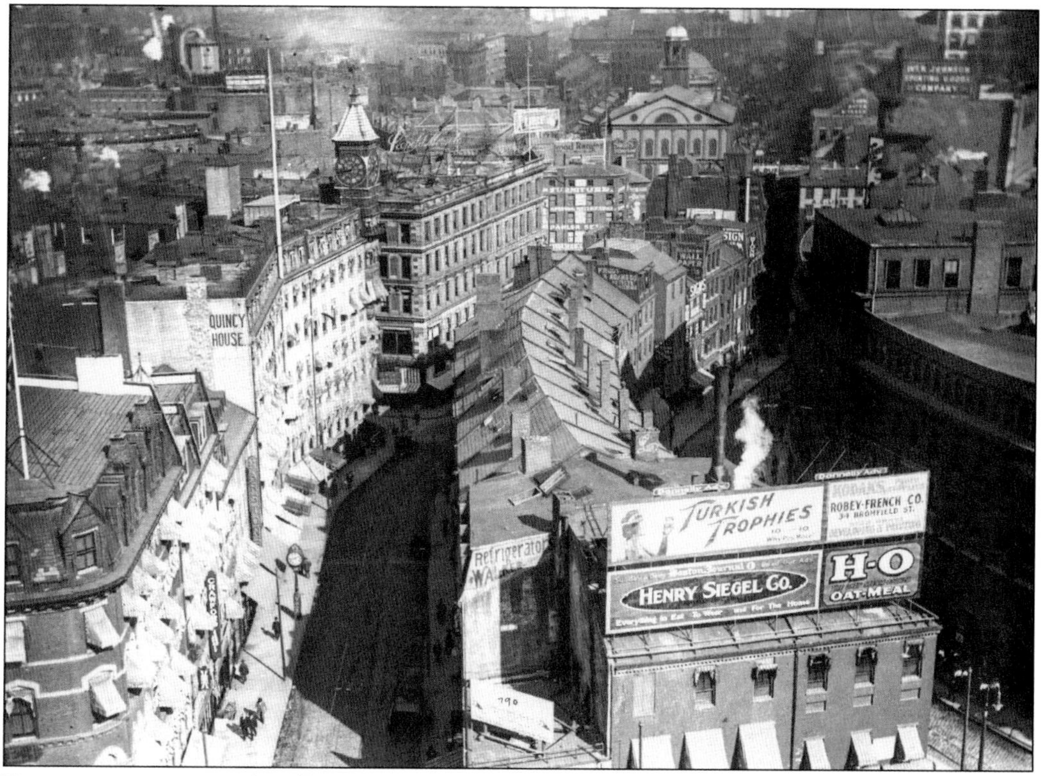

For many years, Faneuil Hall sat chock-a-block with other shops, part of the everyday jumble in a densely developed market district. This view along Brattle Street shows Faneuil Hall surrounded by all types of businesses, such as purveyors of furniture, art supplies, signs, sporting goods, and wallpaper. The scene is undated but is likely from the early 20th century, before the paint was sandblasted off the building's bricks. (BPL.)

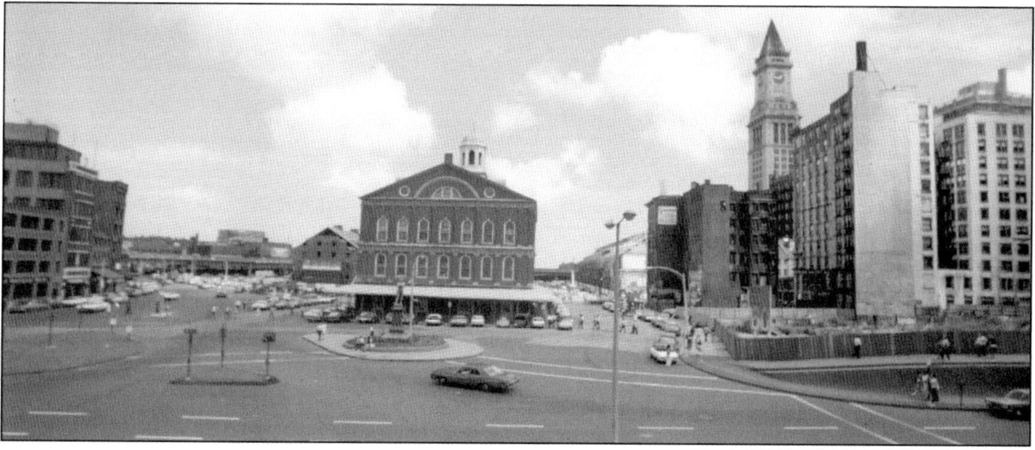

Many of these buildings were demolished and streets were eliminated by the early 1960s (including Brattle Street) as part of the urban renewal project to create Government Center. In the *Boston Globe's* Cityscapes column in 2005, Robert Campbell and Peter Vanderwarker wrote, "Today Faneuil looks less like a congenial piece of the city and more like a solo star on an empty stage." Here is Faneuil Hall in 1973, after Government Center was built but before Dock Square was transformed into a park. (Photograph by Edmund L. Mitchell, BPL.)

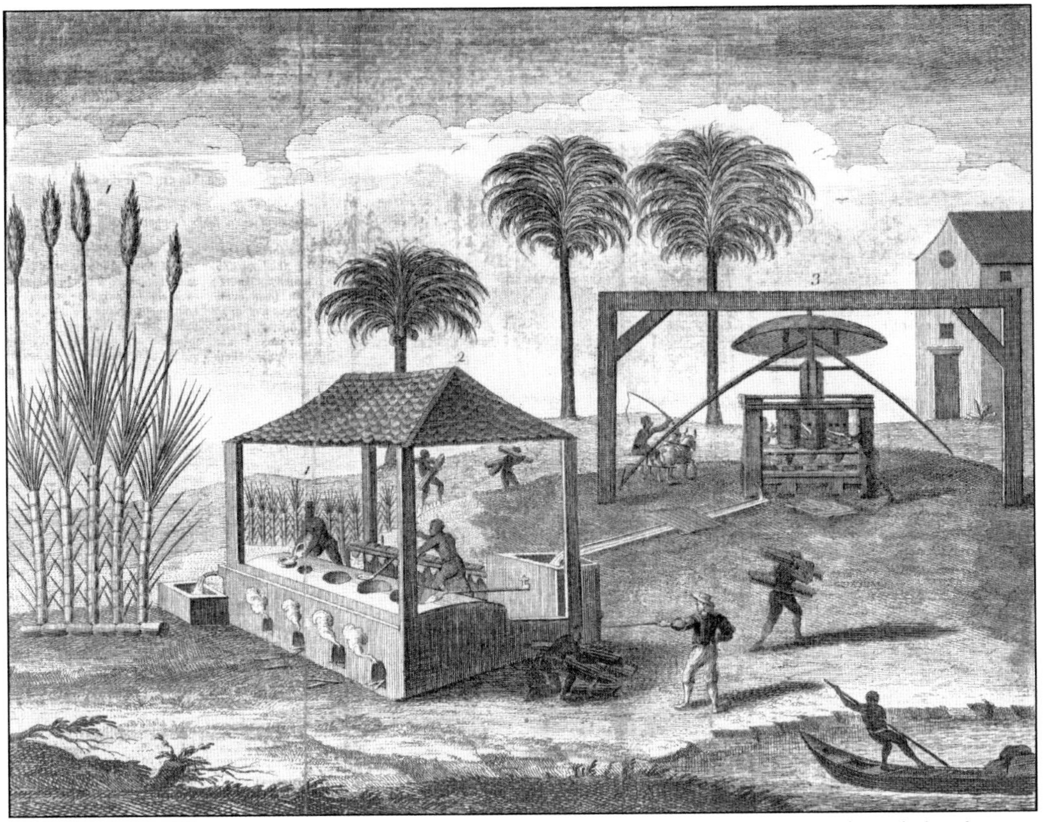

Boston's economy was built on the sea, and Peter Faneuil (and his uncle before him) made his fortune in the lucrative trans-Atlantic trade. He imported sugar and molasses produced by enslaved workers on Caribbean plantations, and he provided those plantations with low-grade fish, referred to as "refuse grade," intended as sustenance for the laborers. And, most troubling to modern observers, Faneuil bought and sold human beings. (LOC.)

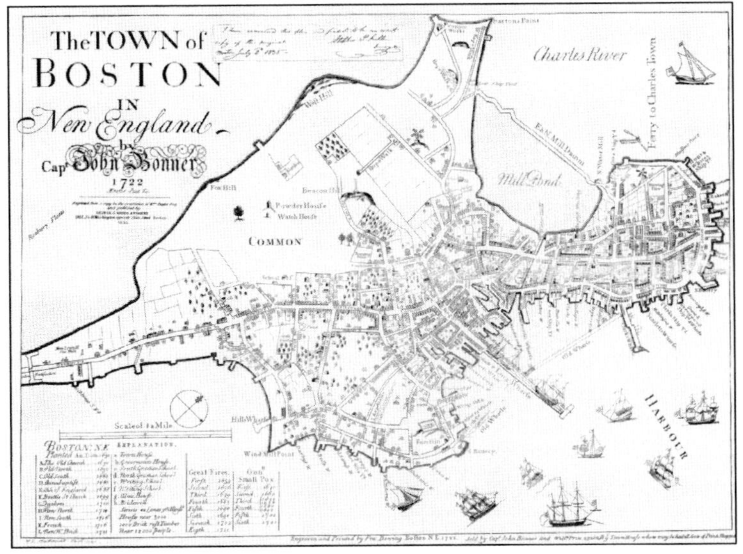

Bostonians relied on the labor of enslaved workers from the town's earliest days. The first enslaved Africans arrived in 1638 on a ship called the *Desire*, and Massachusetts legalized slavery in 1641. By 1720, shortly after the Faneuil brothers moved to Boston, enslaved Africans made up about 10 percent of the local population. Most labored as household servants, artisans, or sailors. (LOC.)

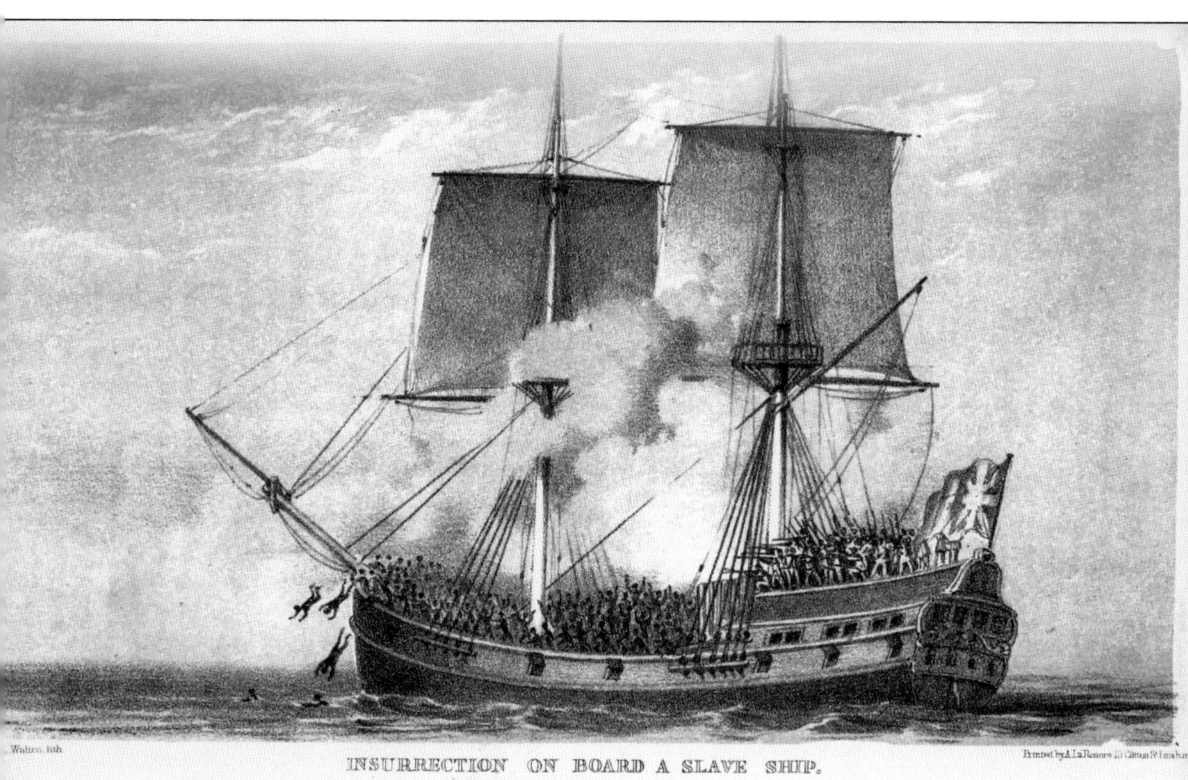

Records are sketchy, but Peter Faneuil financed at least two trips to West Africa in the last years of his life to engage in slave trafficking. John Cutler (brother to Benjamin Faneuil's wife, Mary) captained both trips, the *Mary Anne* in 1739 and the *Jolly Batchelor* in 1741. The former ship honored Faneuil's sister, who lived with him in the Tremont Street estate, and the latter was likely a wry reference to his own unmarried state. The *Mary Anne* sailed to Sierra Leone, where Cutler negotiated with European and African middlemen to purchase kidnapped Africans. The ship returned to North America with about 80 enslaved Africans. Arriving in Virginia in 1740, Cutler sold his human cargo and purchased corn and wheat with the proceeds. (Lithograph by W.L. Walton, Library Company of Philadelphia.)

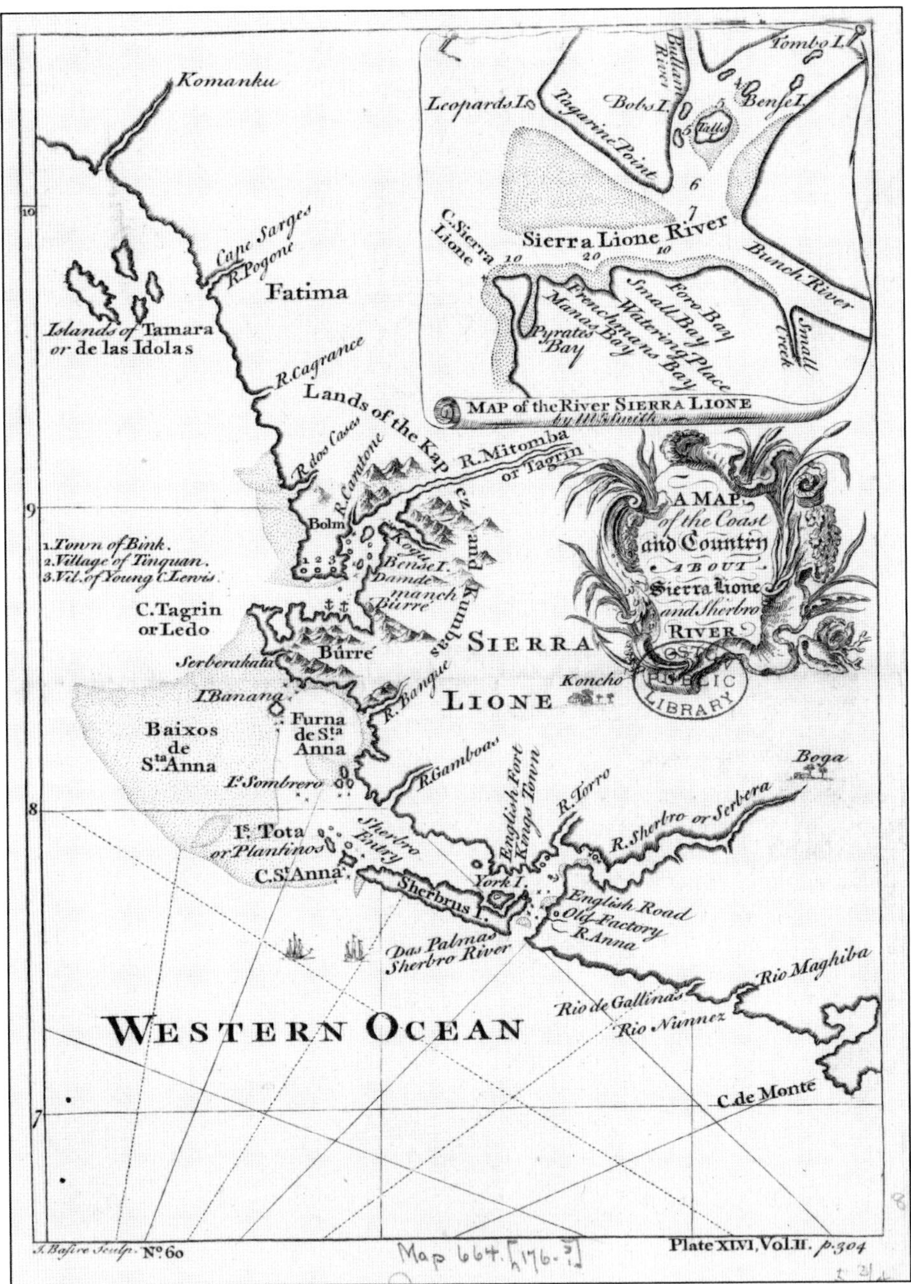

Cutler set sail for Boston but was blown way off course to Madeira, where he sold his cargo for a substantial (and unexpected) profit before returning to Boston in 1741. Buoyed by the financial success of the voyage of the *Mary Anne*, Cutler set sail for Sierra Leone again; this time, he helmed the *Jolly Batchelor*. He arrived in 1742 and purchased 84 kidnapped Africans. But before the *Jolly Batchelor* could return to America, the ship was attacked by pirates who killed Cutler, crippled the vessel, and took the captive Africans to be sold again. European traders recaptured 34 twice-kidnapped Africans, sold 12 to pay for repairs to the ship, and arrived in Newport, Rhode Island, in the summer of 1743 with 20 surviving Africans on board. By then, Peter Faneuil had died. (BPL/Leventhal.)

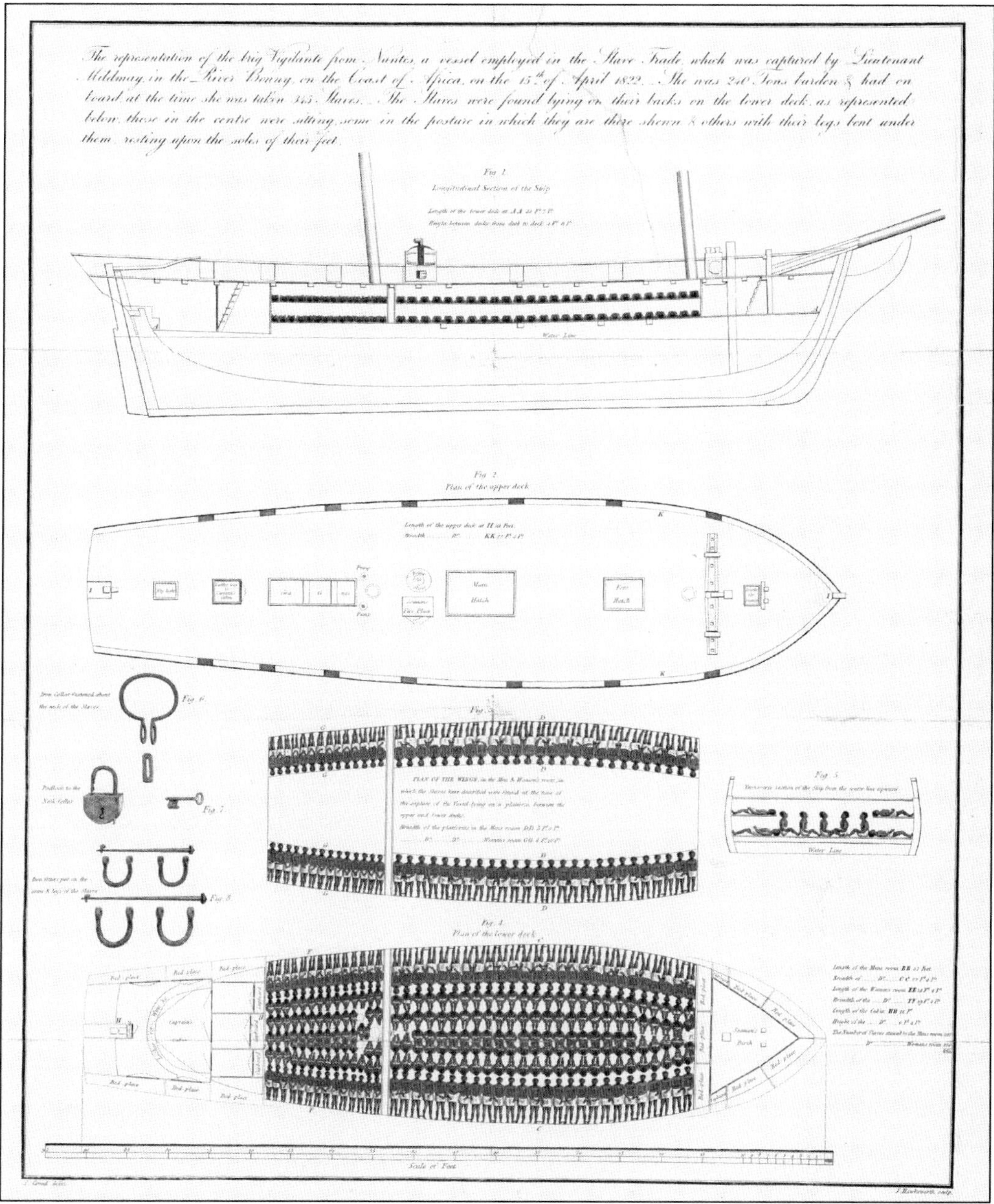

The historical record does not indicate how extensively Faneuil participated in slave trafficking beyond the trips of the *Mary Anne* and *Jolly Batchelor*. Historian Eric Hanson Plass uncovered a possible connection to a vessel partially owned by Gulian Verplanck, Faneuil's agent in New York. The *Ranger* carried dozens of enslaved individuals from Antigua to New Jersey in 1740, and fragmentary records suggest that Faneuil showed an interest in the voyage. Moreover, surviving letters document Faneuil's efforts to acquire an enslaved household servant in 1738. Writing to a sea captain who was transporting goods to Antigua, Faneuil instructed him to sell the cargo and to "purchase for me, for the use of my house, as likely a strait negro lad as possibly you can, about the age from twelve to fifteen years." Faneuil was known to have five enslaved workers in his household at the time of his death. Shown here is a rendering of a French slave ship. (LOC.)

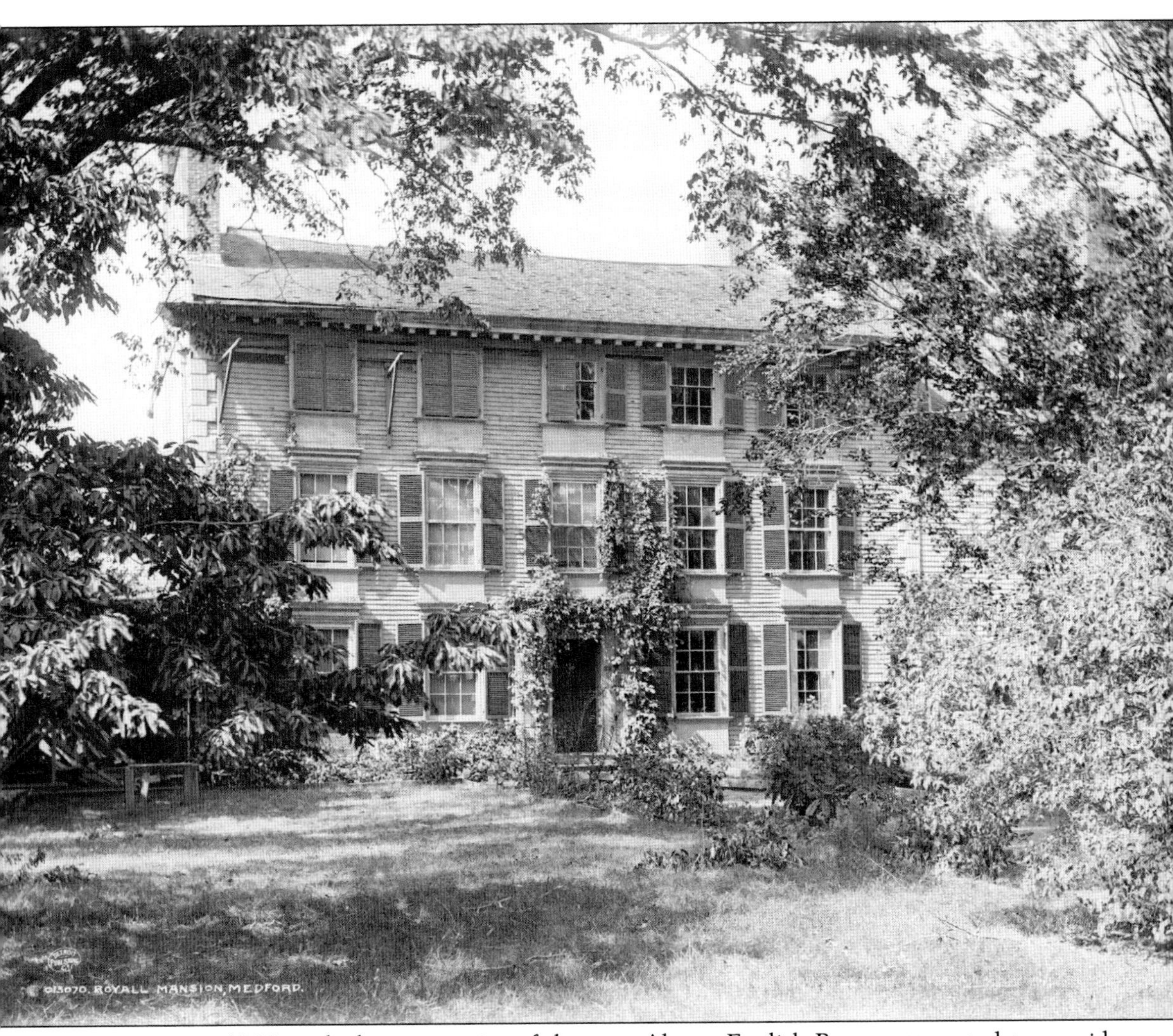

Writing in 1900, with the perspective of that era, Abram English Brown attempted to provide a context for Faneuil's participation in the slave trade. "It was the common practice of the time, believed to be right," he wrote in his book *Faneuil Hall and Faneuil Hall Market*. "None knew the enormity of the offence, and consequently to them it was not a crime." But looking through a modern lens, many scholars, elected officials, and citizens do not share Brown's opinion. Since 2018, religious leaders and community activists have pressured Boston officials to address the role of slavery in the city's history and to change the name of Faneuil Hall. They have raised awareness through acts of civil disobedience—even chaining themselves to the building—and gathered more than 3,000 signatures for a petition supporting the name change. Shown here is the Royall Mansion in Medford, Massachusetts, now a museum but once home to more than 60 enslaved men, women, and children. (LOC.)

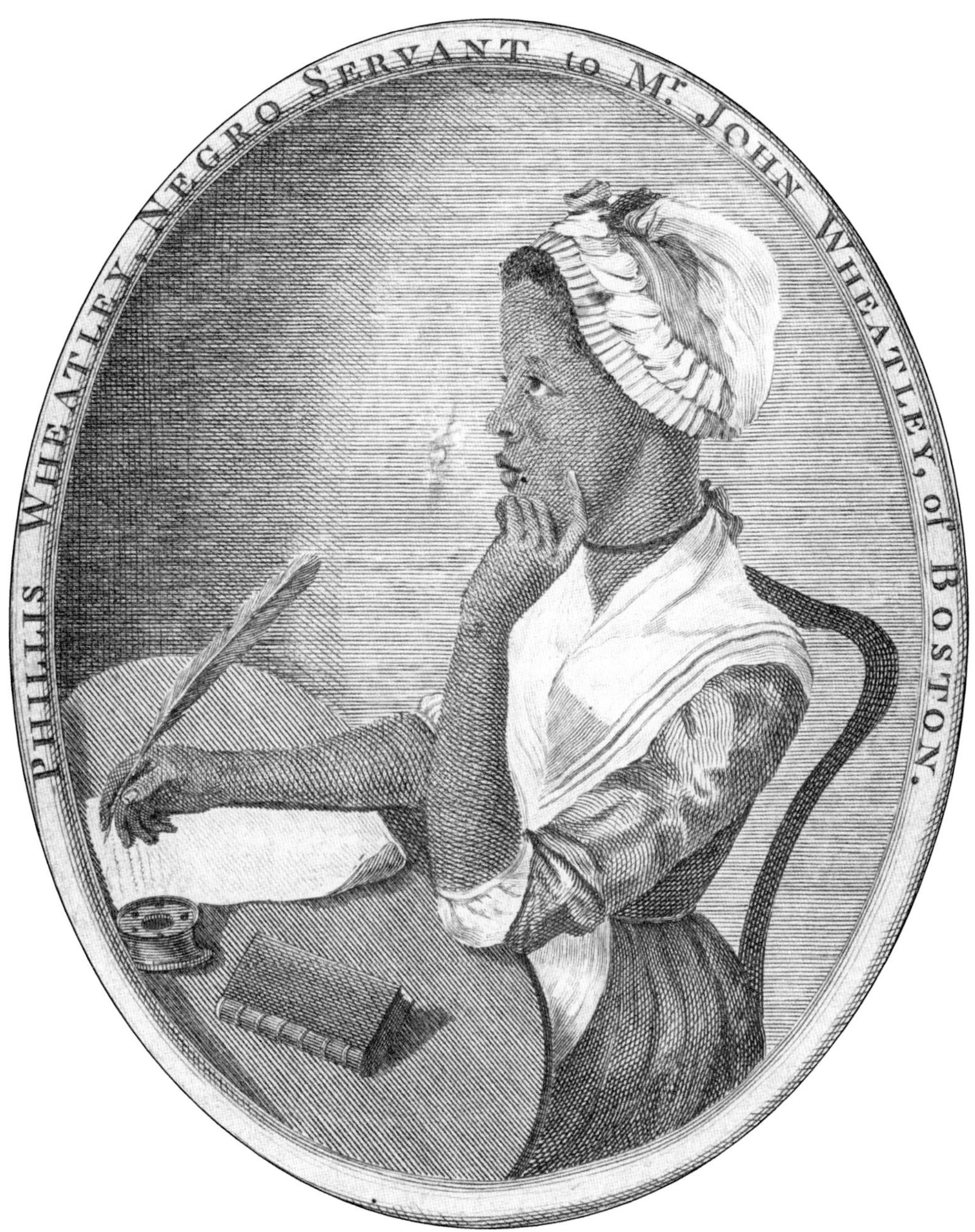

In June 2023, an exhibition about the history of slavery in Boston opened in Faneuil Hall. As described on the city's website, the exhibit "reveals the lives of individual enslaved people: the persistence of their community, their fight for freedom, and how the struggle for freedom continues today." Protesters objected to the location. "We do not object to this exhibit being placed at another site," said Rev. Kevin C. Peterson, speaking on behalf of the New Democracy Coalition. "History tells us that Peter Faneuil was a bigot. His name should not adorn a publicly owned building." In response to calls for renaming Faneuil Hall, Mayor Michelle Wu issued a statement that read, in part, "As we work to build an equitable Boston for everyone, the city is committed to advancing racial justice and learning from our past and right wrongs." Poet Phillis Wheatley, enslaved in Boston, is pictured here. (Metropolitan Museum of Art.)

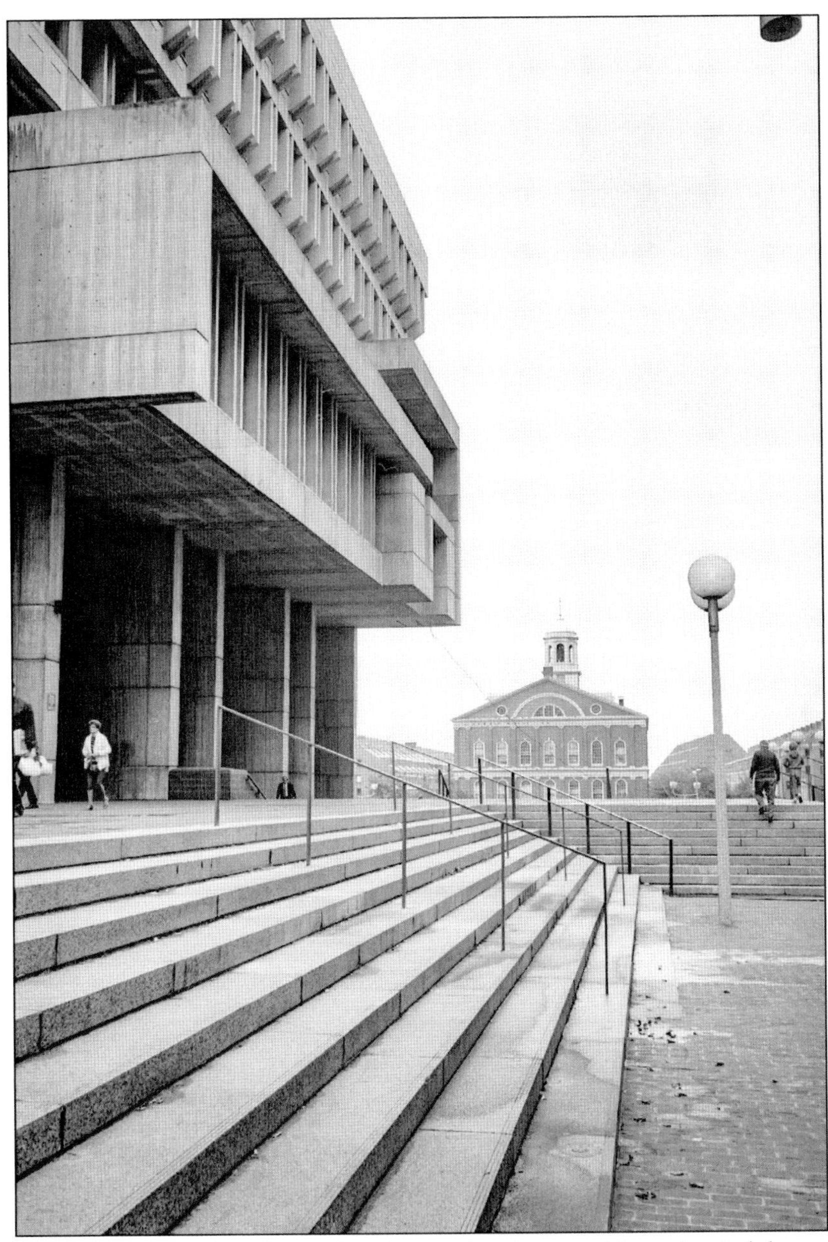

Starting in 2022, the Boston City Council took several actions to address the city's legacy of slavery. On June 15, 2022, councilors passed a resolution to "acknowledge, condemn, and apologize for the role played by the City of Boston in the trans-Atlantic slave trade." Later that year, the council also passed an ordinance to establish a task force on reparations. Finally, the council adopted a resolution in October 2023 by a 10-3 vote to rename Faneuil Hall. The text described Peter Faneuil as a "white supremacist, a slave trader, and a slave owner who contributed nothing recognizable to the ideal of democracy." The resolution acknowledged that a name change would not erase the past but instead would "place history in its proper perspective." Suggested alternative namesakes included Crispus Attucks, Elizabeth Freeman, and Frederick Douglass; other proposed options were Freedom Hall and Liberty Hall. The city council does not have the authority to rename a public building, and no changes have been made to date. (LOC.)

Two

Creating Quincy Market

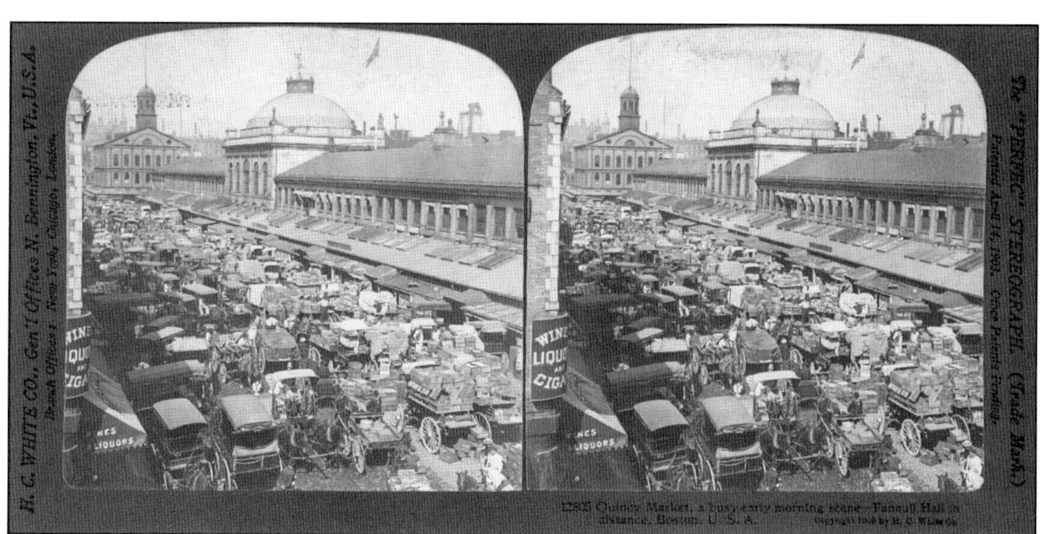

By the 1820s, Faneuil Hall could not meet the needs of a growing Boston, and Mayor Josiah Quincy III envisioned a new public marketplace adjacent to the historic structure. Quincy spearheaded the project—widely considered one of the first urban renewal projects in the country—and Quincy Market opened on August 26, 1826. (LOC.)

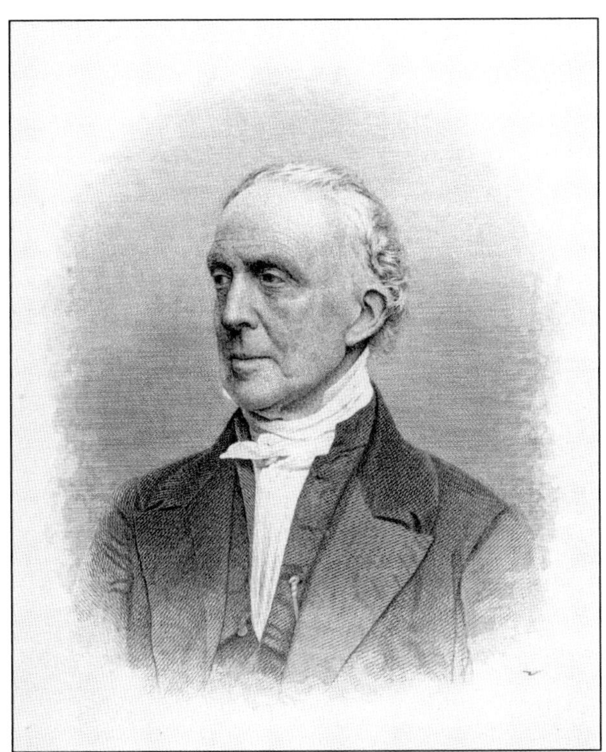

An accomplished political and academic leader, Josiah Quincy III served in the Massachusetts state legislature and the US House of Representatives before he was elected as mayor of Boston in 1823. After six one-year terms as mayor, he left elective politics and was president of Harvard University from 1829 to 1845. (BOS.)

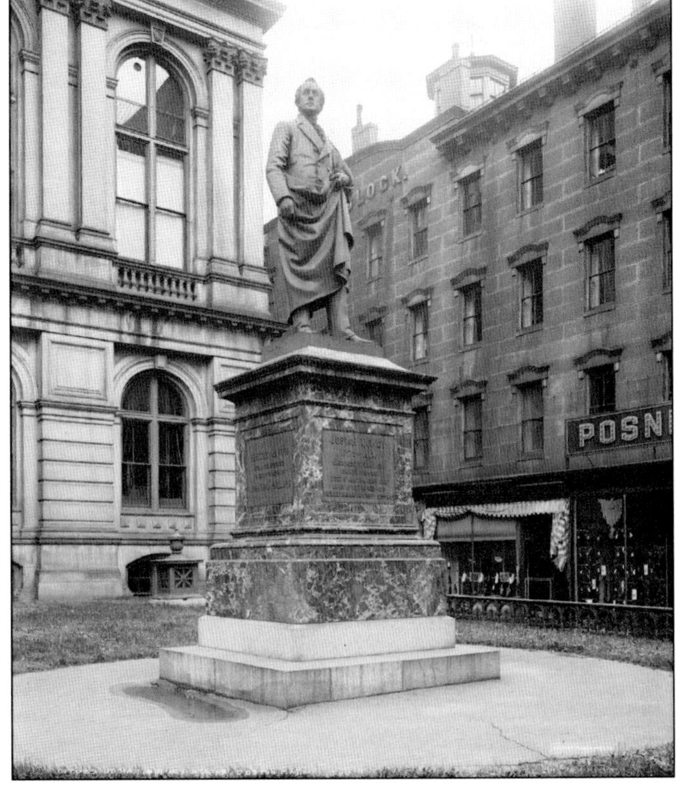

Boston was newly incorporated as a city in 1822, and Quincy was its second mayor. Upon taking office, Quincy established financial controls, implemented a street-sweeping program, cleaned up the water and sewer systems, and modernized the city's fire-fighting capabilities. A bronze sculpture of the "Great Mayor," as Quincy was known, was installed outside Boston's Old City Hall in 1879. (LOC.)

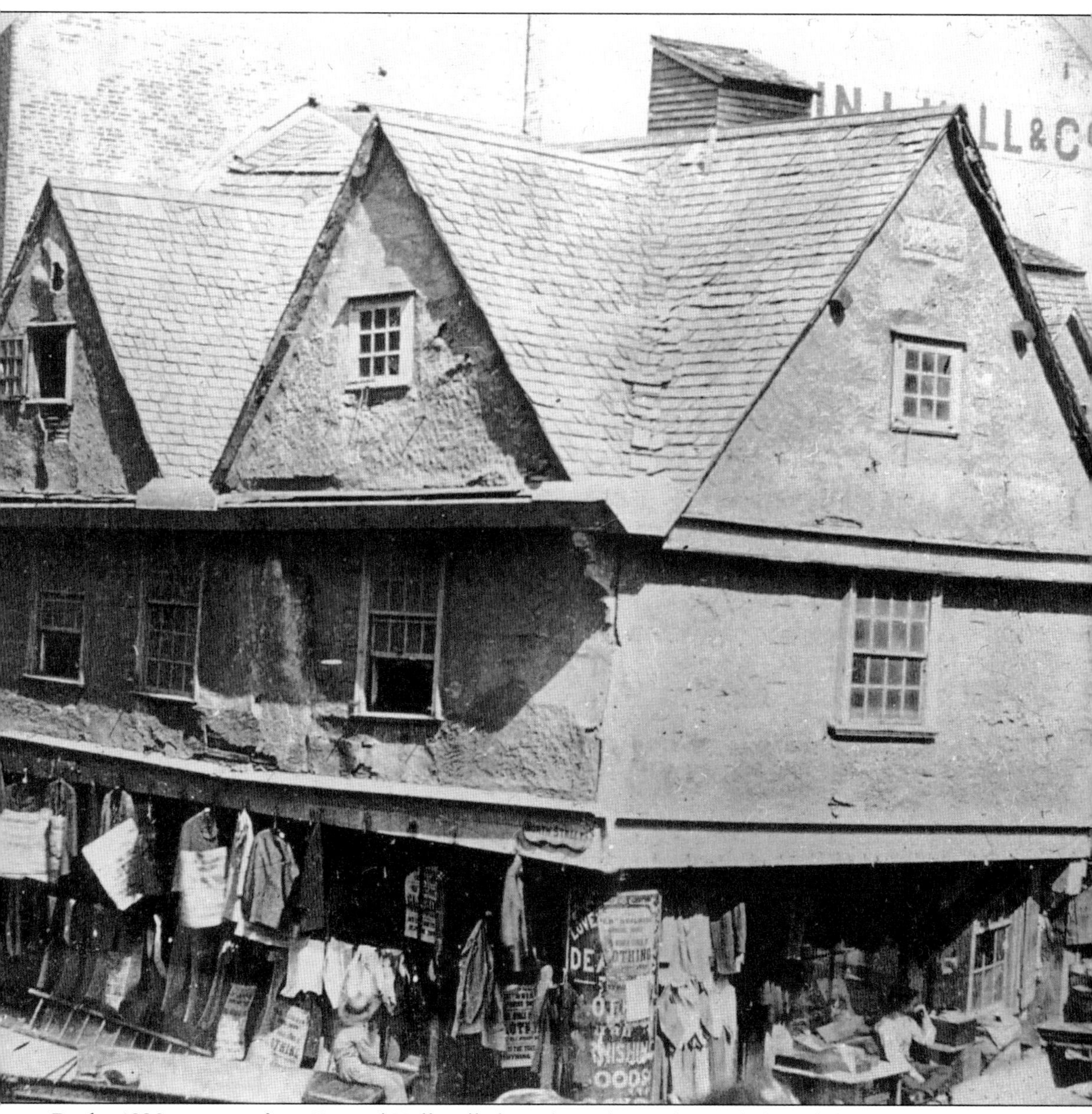

By the 1820s, activity from Faneuil Hall spilled out from the market and choked the narrow streets surrounding the Town Dock. Making things worse, the stench from the city's main sewer outflow was appalling. "Noxious effluvia," Quincy reportedly called the polluted harbor and the lingering odor as he observed the crowded market district from his office in Faneuil Hall. (No doubt his view included the Old Feather Store, shown here, built in 1680 at the water's edge.) Quincy formed a committee to identify solutions for his market problem; the group called for a produce market on the north side of Faneuil Hall, measuring a modest 36 feet wide by 180 feet long. The city council approved the project in 1823 and allocated $15,000 for construction, but Quincy had something grander in mind. (BPL.)

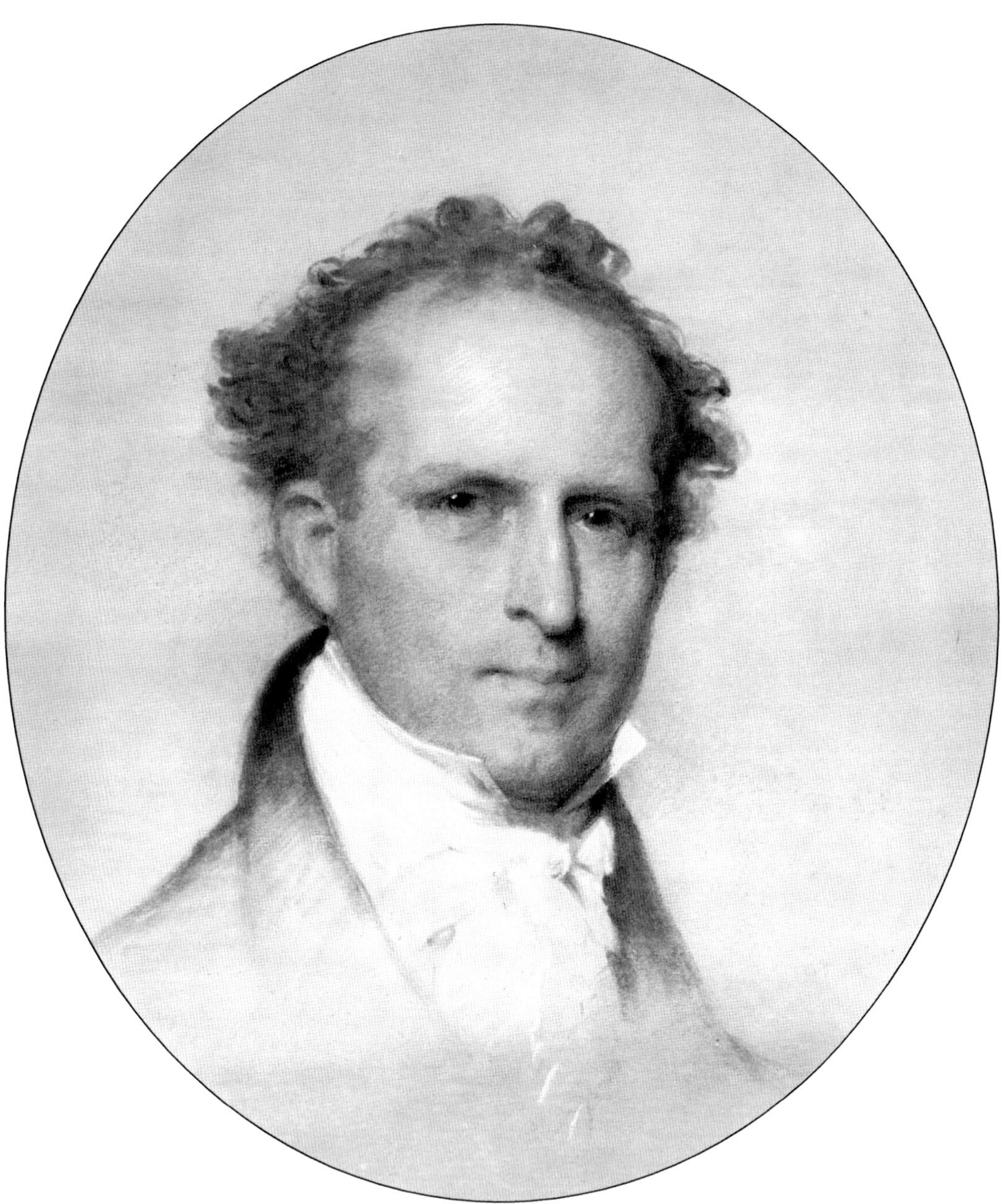

Mayor Quincy (above) created a new market committee, which included architect and city alderman Asher Benjamin, and directed members to develop plans for a larger market to the east of Faneuil Hall. Benjamin created a master plan for a new market district, with support from architect Alexander Parris. In January 1824, Benjamin presented the work-in-progress at a town meeting. The preliminary proposal called for a single-story wooden building, 50 feet wide by 420 feet long, flanked by two brick warehouses that were three-and-a-half stories tall. The central building would have no walls, windows, or doors; only the roof would provide protection from the elements. Six streets would be created, and the entire project would be built on land still underwater. Despite initial opposition to what some called "Quincy's Folly," the mayor was persuasive and secured approval from the town meeting members. This detail from a painting by Gilbert Stuart was produced by William Henry Furness Jr. (Harvard University Portrait Collection.)

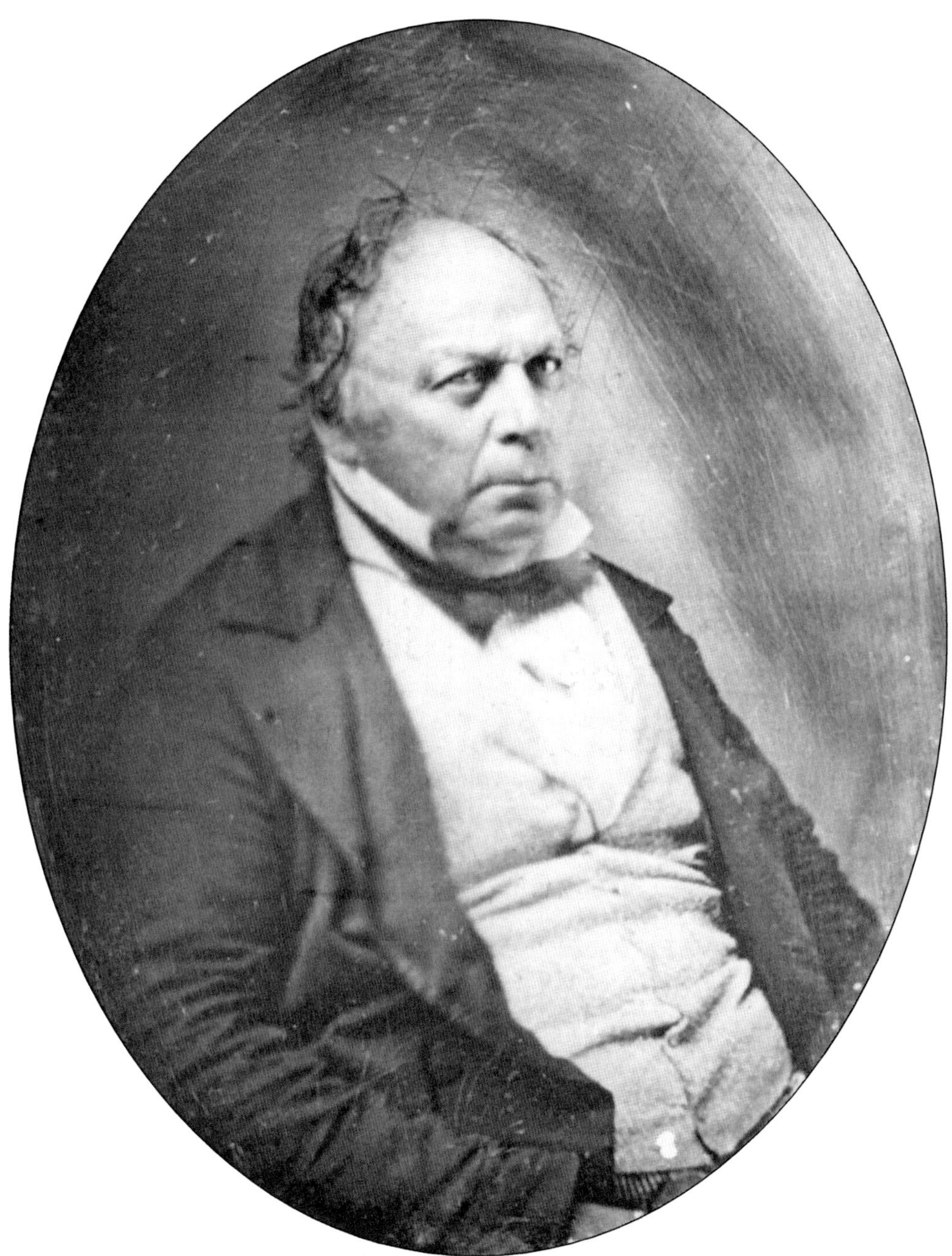

Benjamin withdrew from Quincy's market project in 1824, citing personal financial problems, and he recommended Alexander Parris as the new architect. Born in Halifax, Massachusetts, Parris (shown here) trained as a housewright but acquired engineering expertise when serving in the US Army during the War of 1812. He settled in Boston in 1815 and began working for Charles Bulfinch. After his mentor left Boston in 1817 to work on the US Capitol, Parris emerged as one of the city's preeminent architects. He was best known for his buildings in the Greek Revival style and his innovative use of granite; Quincy Market showcased both. He spent the last 20 years of his career working for the federal government and became the chief civil engineer for the Boston Naval Shipyard. (Photograph by Warren S. Parker, Thomas Crane Public Library.)

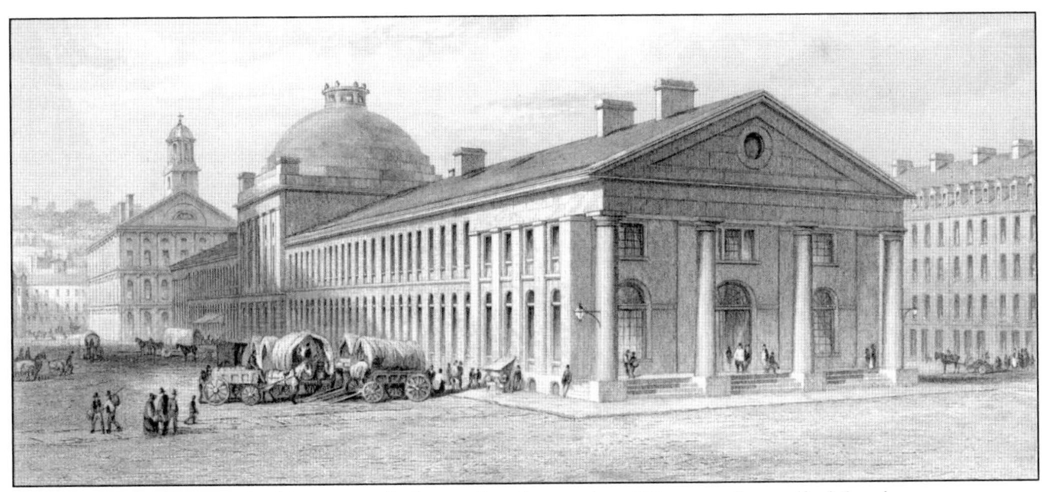

Parris completely reworked Benjamin's design for the market. His new plan called for three structures: a central granite market house, later called Quincy Market, flanked by two brick-and-granite buildings known as the North Market and South Market. The Boston City Council allocated $150,000 for the updated central market project, but the North and South Market buildings were to be privately owned and constructed, following the example of India Wharf. (New York Public Library.)

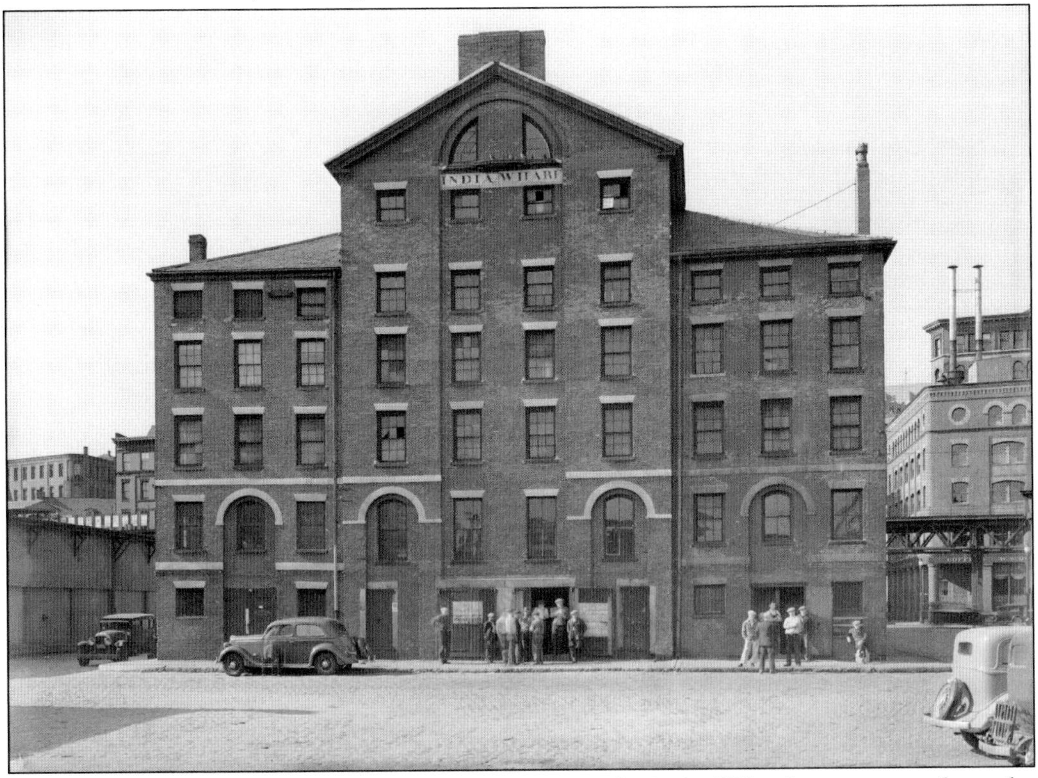

Predating Quincy's market proposal by some 20 years, the India Wharf project transformed a rundown section of Boston's waterfront into "an efficient wharf system," as described by John Quincy Jr. The privately funded India Building, designed by Charles Bulfinch, consisted of 32 five-story individual brick warehouses that appeared as a single structure—a model that the North and South Markets would replicate. (LOC.)

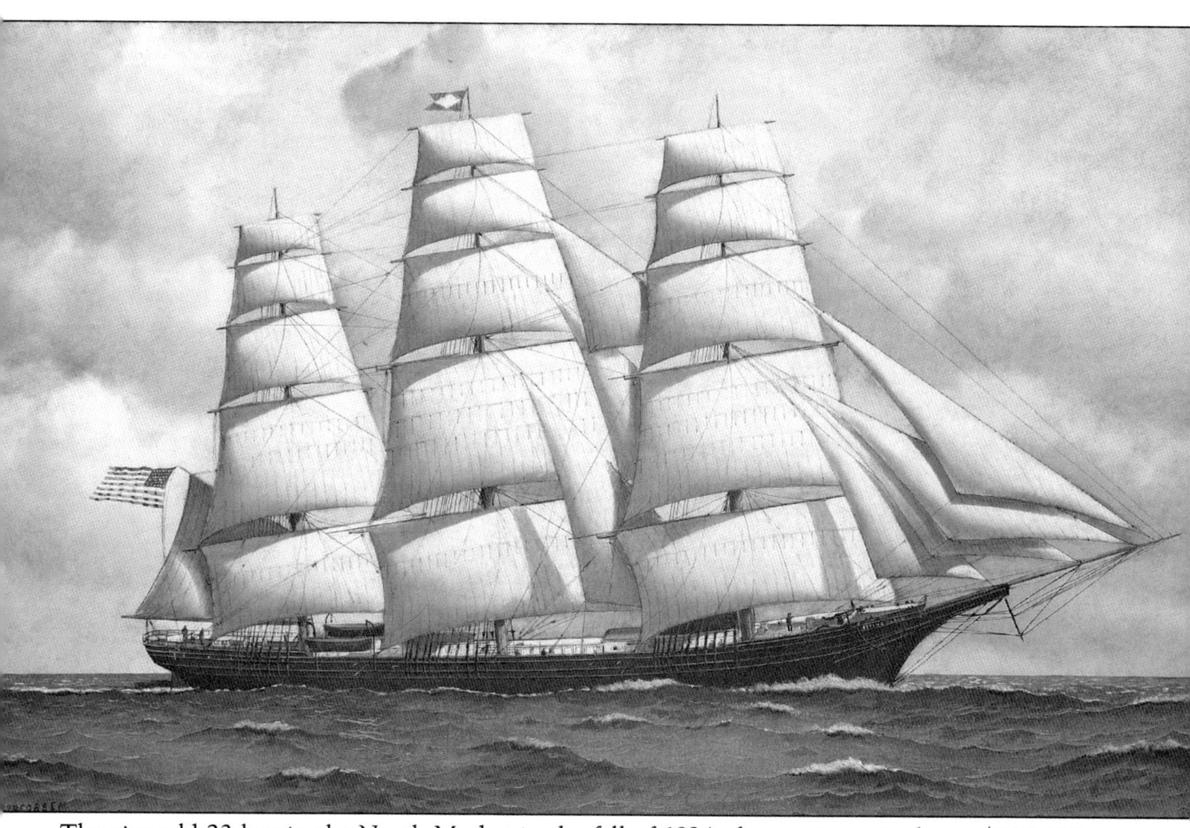

The city sold 23 lots in the North Market in the fall of 1824; the auction raised over $300,000. Two lots adjacent to the North Market but separated from the other 23 by Merchants Row had been previously sold for $32,000. Another 22 lots in the South Market were sold the next spring, yielding more than $400,000. Alexander Parris developed design guidelines to ensure consistency among the three market houses. A 1996 report from the Boston Landmarks Commission described the market investors as the "apex of Boston society." They included textile manufacturers Amos and Abbott Lawrence, after whom the mill city of Lawrence, Massachusetts, was named; Enoch Train, who commissioned and then sold the *Flying Cloud*, the fastest clipper ship at the time; and millionaire Robert Gould Shaw, whose namesake grandson was the well-known Civil War colonel. Seen here is a print of *Flying Cloud* from a painting by Antonio Jacobsen.

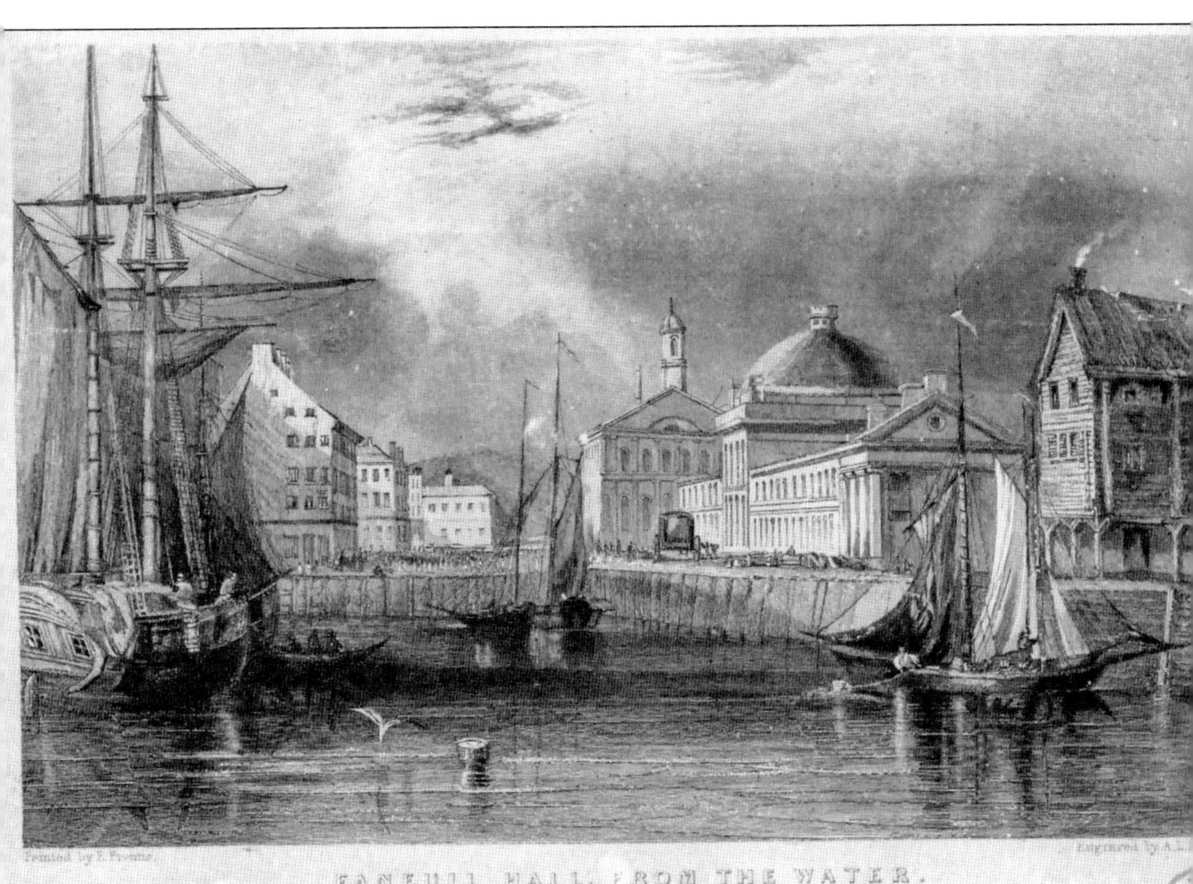

After the city acquired the necessary land from multiple property owners—some willing and some not—construction began in 1824. Directly east of Faneuil Hall, the footprint for the new buildings covered the Town Dock and a series of wharves. So the first step was one that would be repeated many times in Boston's history: making new land. Workers built a structure around the target area and dumped in fill until the new ground reached above the high-tide line. Trash was often used as fill in the 17th and 18th centuries, but gravel and earth were the preferred materials when the markets were built. "Word was spread by handbills of the need for laborers to haul earth for the new landfill," John Quincy Jr. wrote in *Quincy's Market*. "Individuals who owned tipcarts, heavy wagons, or stone trucks were hired, as were truck companies with their own fleets of heavy wagons and stone trucks." This engraving of E. Prentis's painting was produced by A.L. Dick. (BPL.)

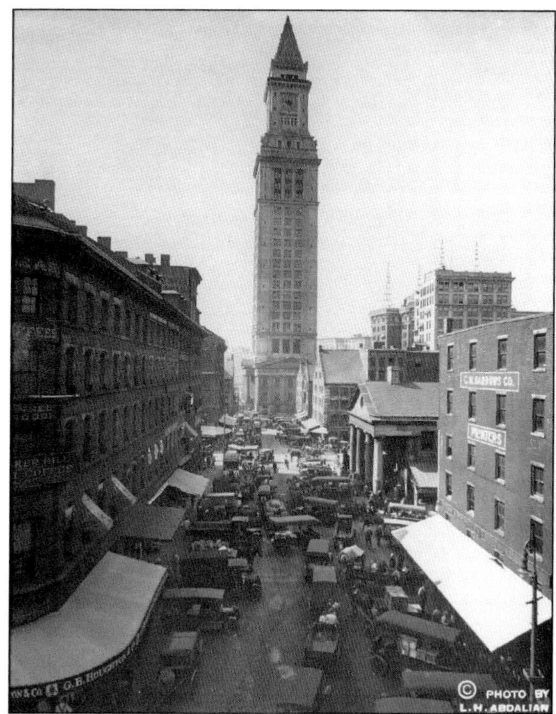

Six new streets were added to handle the market traffic: North Market, South Market, Clinton, Chatham, and Commercial Streets and the extension of Merchants Row. Commercial Street (originally called Marginal Street and shown here around 1920) was later extended into the North End neighborhood. (Photograph by Leon H. Abdalian, BPL.)

Quincy's original plans called for lining up the central market building with Faneuil Hall and for the two market streets to be of equal width. But the site plans were adjusted to accommodate a few property owners who refused to sell out. After some political maneuvering whereby South Market Street was widened to 102 feet and North Market Street was narrowed to 65 feet, the city seized the remaining parcels and moved forward with the project. This 1929 photograph shows the asymmetrical layout. (BPL.)

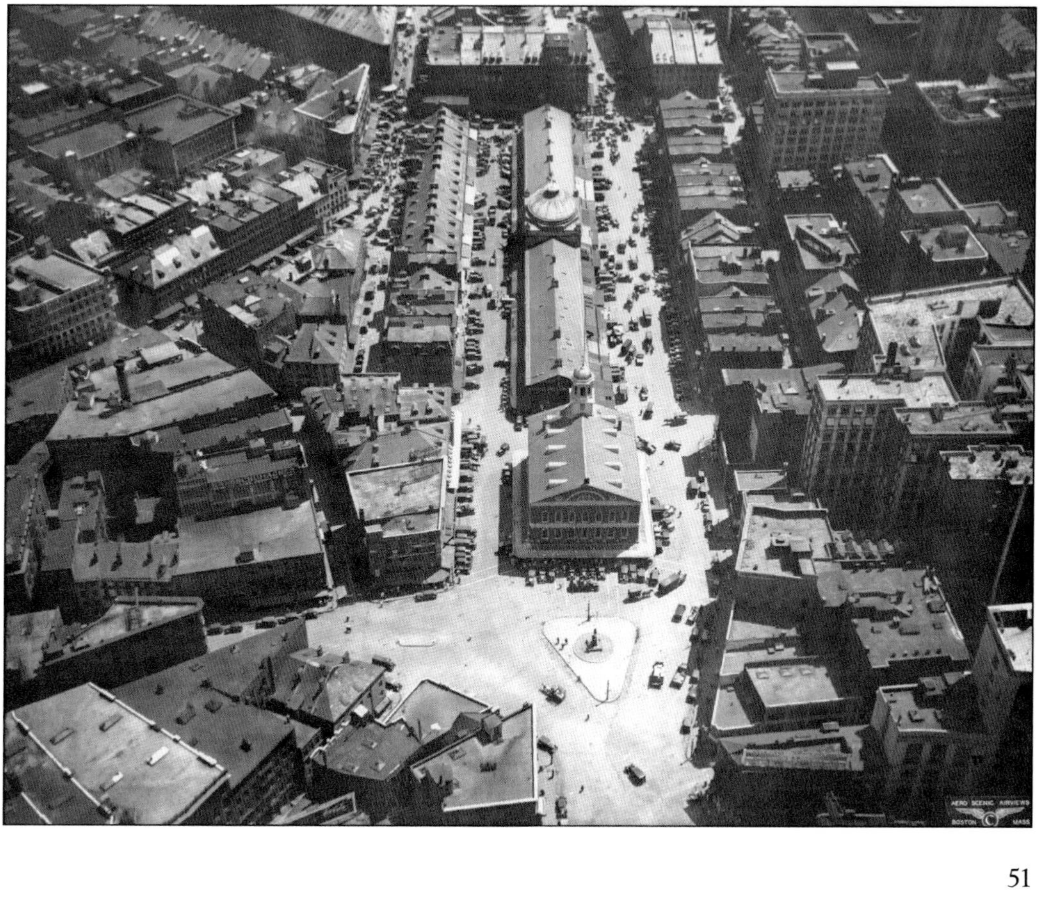

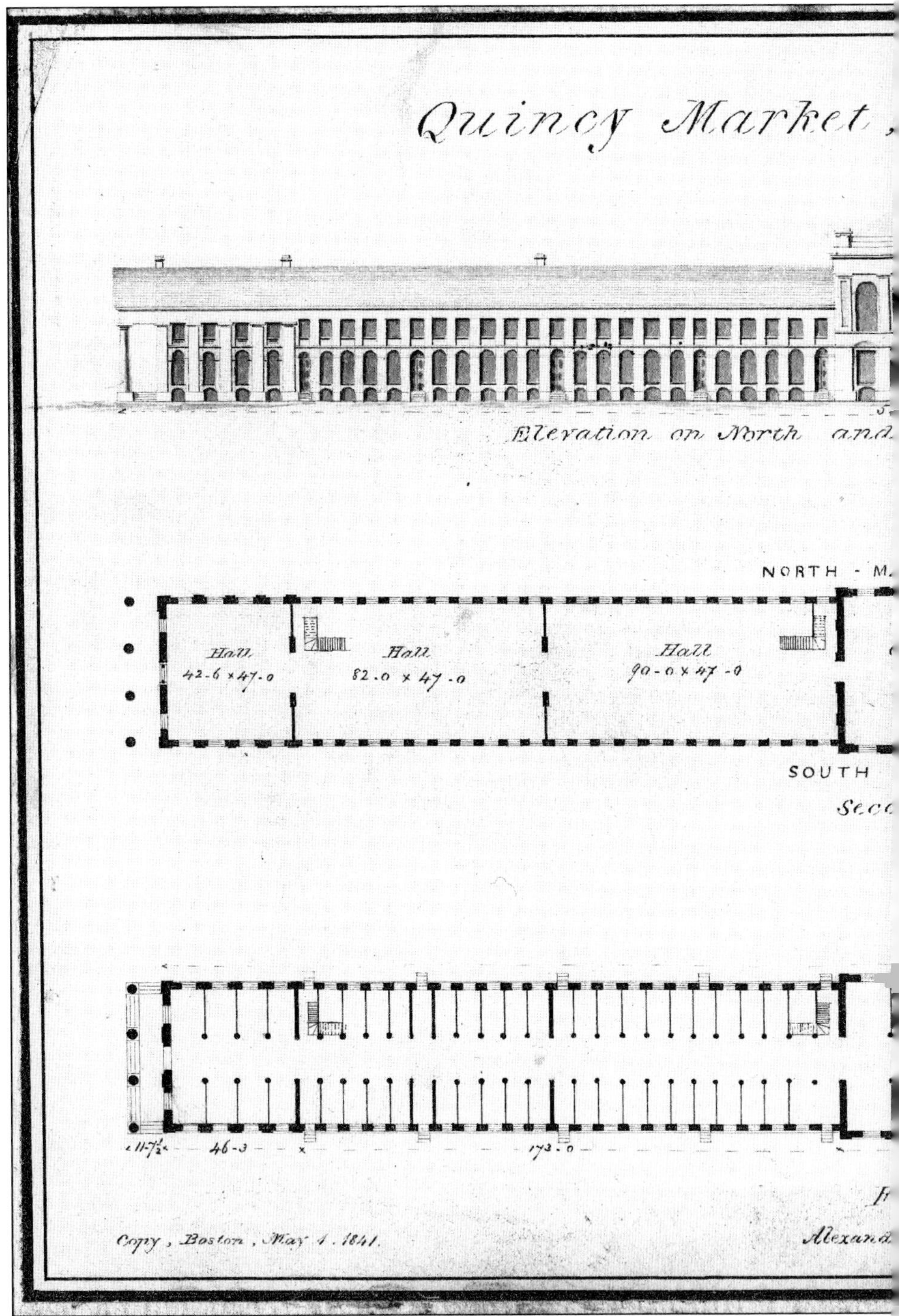

The central market house was 535 feet long and 50 feet wide. The two-story granite structure comprised a central domed pavilion with two wings. Porticos at the east and west entrances were supported by four monolithic granite Doric columns and topped by a pediment with a round window. The copper-sheathed elliptical dome supported a cupola containing a lantern and topped by a weather vane in the shape of a bull (which may have come later). The first-floor windows and

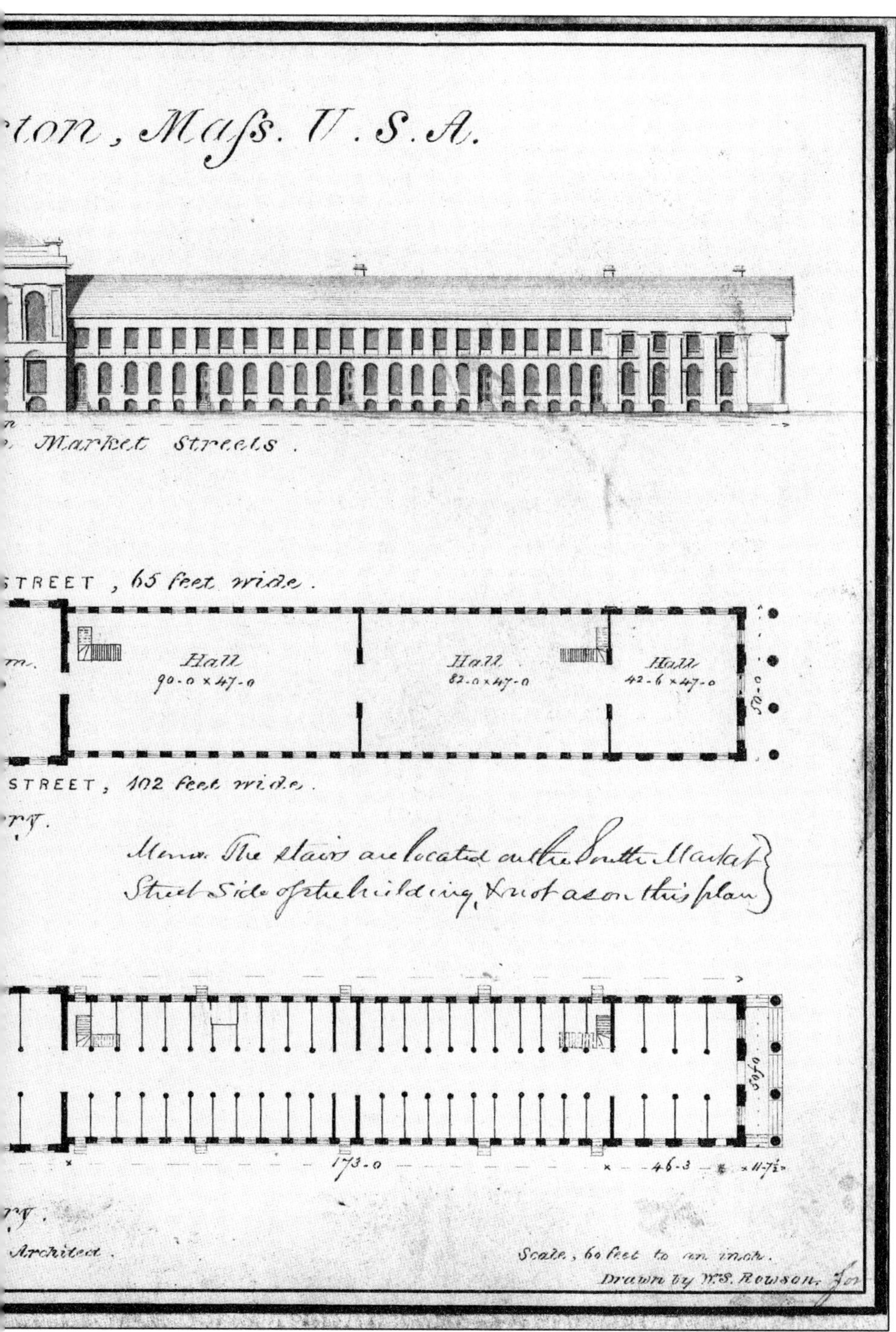

doors had round arches. Second-floor windows were rectangular, except in the pavilion, where they were topped with arches. The first floor was divided into 128 vendor stalls separated by columns and arranged along a 12-foot-wide central aisle. The second-floor hall originally served as a meeting and exhibition space but was subdivided into offices in 1913. (Revolutionary Spaces.)

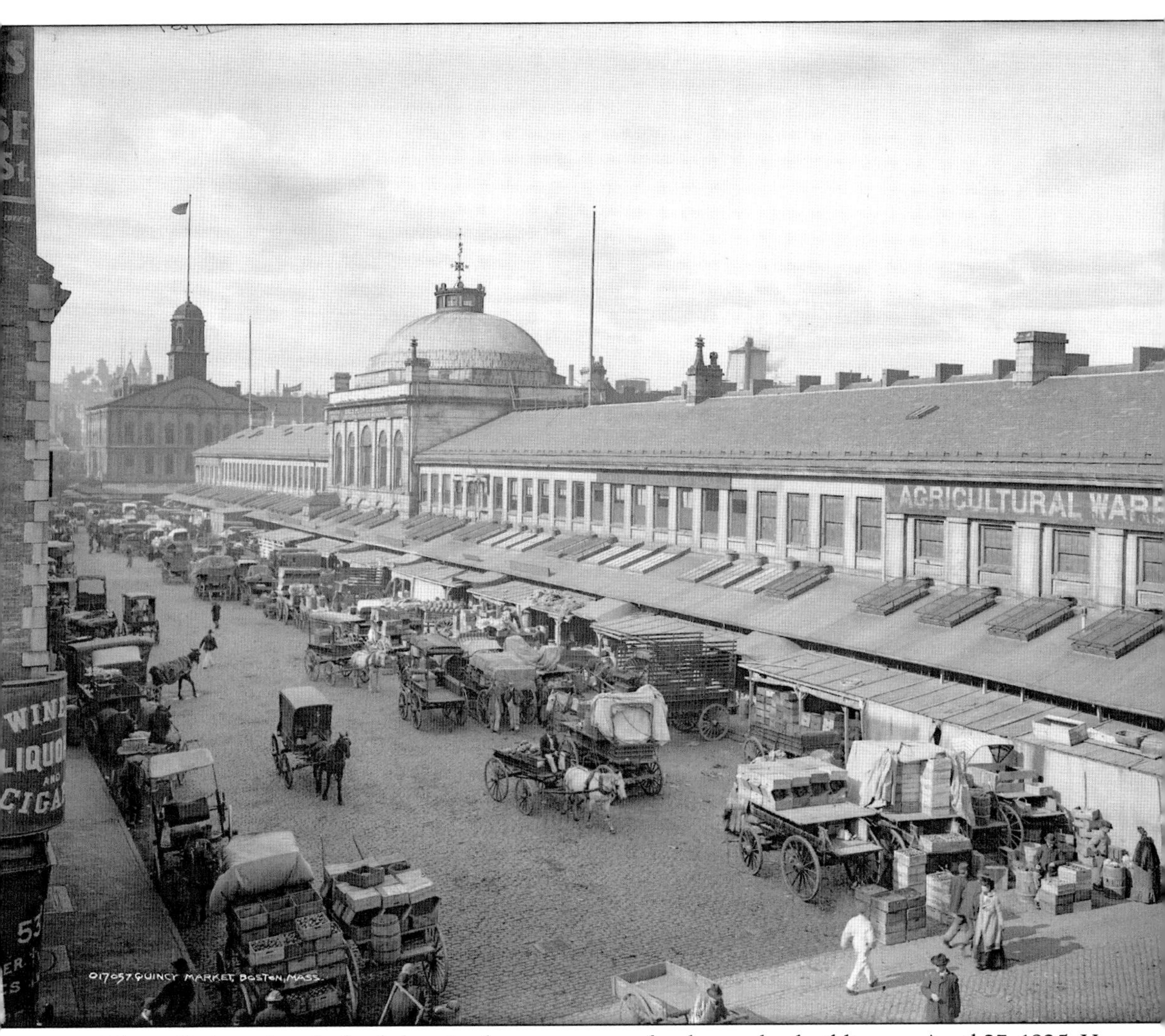

Mayor Quincy placed a lead chest in the cornerstone for the market building on April 27, 1825. He lavished praise on the structure at the ceremony, calling it "an ornament to the city, a convenience for its inhabitants, a blessing to the poor, an accommodation to the rich, and an object of pleasure to the whole community." The chest contained maps and plans, city rules and regulations, recent newspapers, eight copies of *A History of Boston* by Caleb Snow, a cache of coins, and an engraved silver plate memorializing the event. Despite his pride in the project, the mayor did not want the market to carry his name. Instead, he instructed the city council to use the name Faneuil Hall Market for the central structure. The council obliged but bestowed the name Quincy Hall on the second-floor meeting space under the dome. As meat and produce vendors moved to the new market, the council restricted Faneuil Hall to meeting spaces, city offices, and a handful of dry goods retailers. (LOC.)

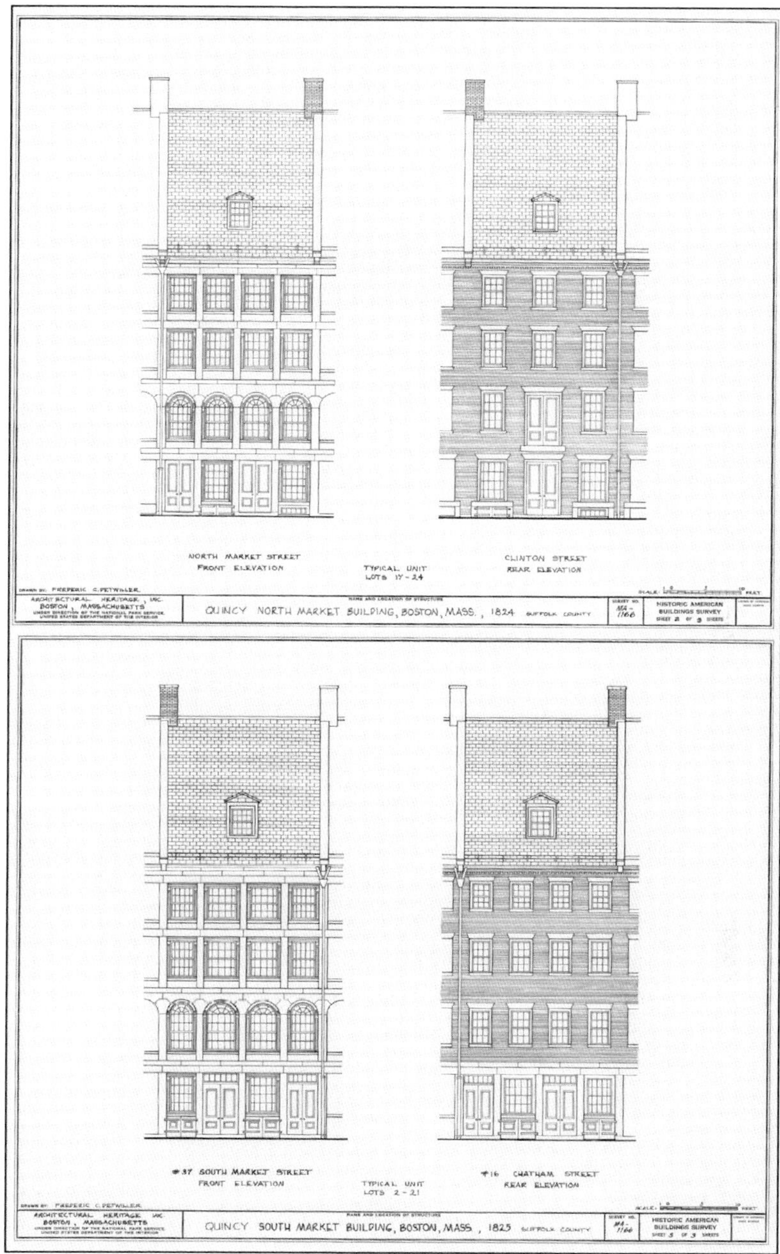

Flanking Faneuil Hall Market, the North and South Markets were built to conform to guidelines prepared by Alexander Parris. Each structure was four-and-a-half stories tall with a gabled roof. The front facades and first floors of the east and west ends were granite. The rear walls differed slightly, with solid brick for the North Market and brick above a granite first floor for the South Market. The consistent facades incorporated storefronts on the ground floor, arched windows on the second floor, and rectangular windows above. Opened in 1825, the North Market included 23 privately owned attached buildings and measured 520 feet long and 50 feet wide. The South Market was completed in 1826; the structure was 530 feet long and 65 feet wide and contained 22 privately owned buildings sharing brick party walls. An open passageway bisected each building to connect North Market Street with Clinton Street and South Market Street with Chatham Street. (LOC.)

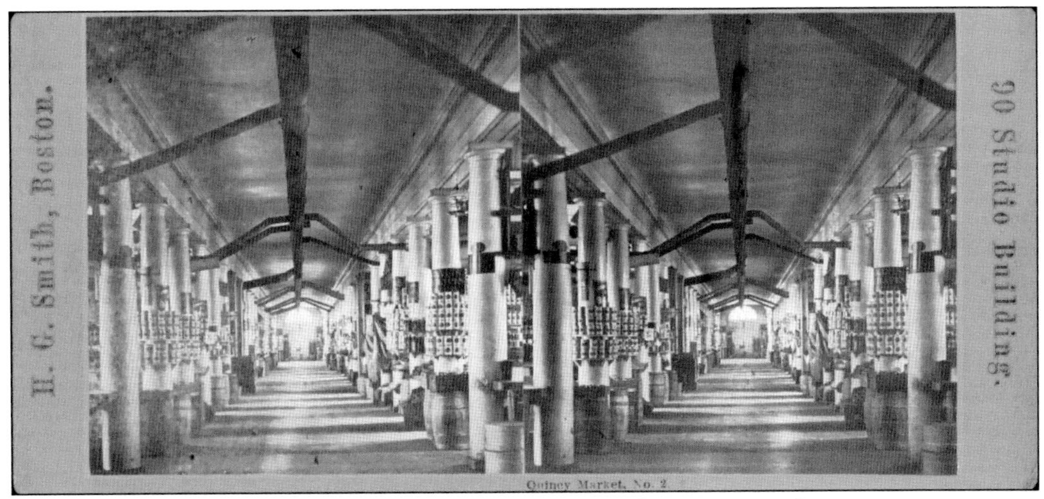

Quincy Market was notable for its early use of iron structural components. Iron compression posts were hidden in 48 of the market's 118 wooden Doric columns. Two flat trusses ran the length of the building and bore the weight of the second floor. The trusses used 15-foot iron hanger rods to support the weight of the central corridor. (New York Public Library.)

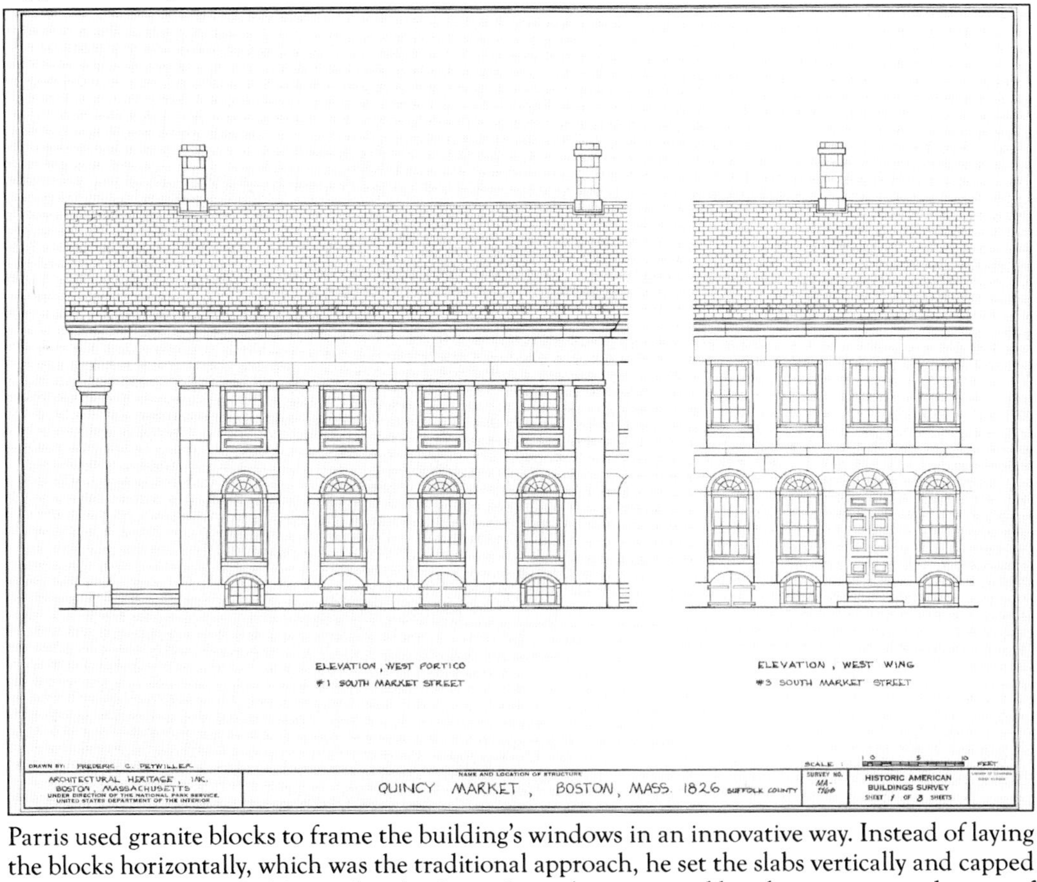

ELEVATION, WEST PORTICO
#1 SOUTH MARKET STREET

ELEVATION, WEST WING
#3 SOUTH MARKET STREET

DRAWN BY: FREDERIC C. PETWILLER

ARCHITECTURAL HERITAGE, INC.
BOSTON, MASSACHUSETTS
UNDER DIRECTION OF THE NATIONAL PARK SERVICE
UNITED STATES DEPARTMENT OF THE INTERIOR

NAME AND LOCATION OF STRUCTURE
QUINCY MARKET, BOSTON, MASS. 1826 SUFFOLK COUNTY

SURVEY NO. MA-1160

HISTORIC AMERICAN BUILDINGS SURVEY
SHEET 1 OF 8 SHEETS

Parris used granite blocks to frame the building's windows in an innovative way. Instead of laying the blocks horizontally, which was the traditional approach, he set the slabs vertically and capped them with a horizontal slab as a lintel. This trabeated, or post-and-lintel, system created a row of narrow windows which opened the market to light. (LOC.)

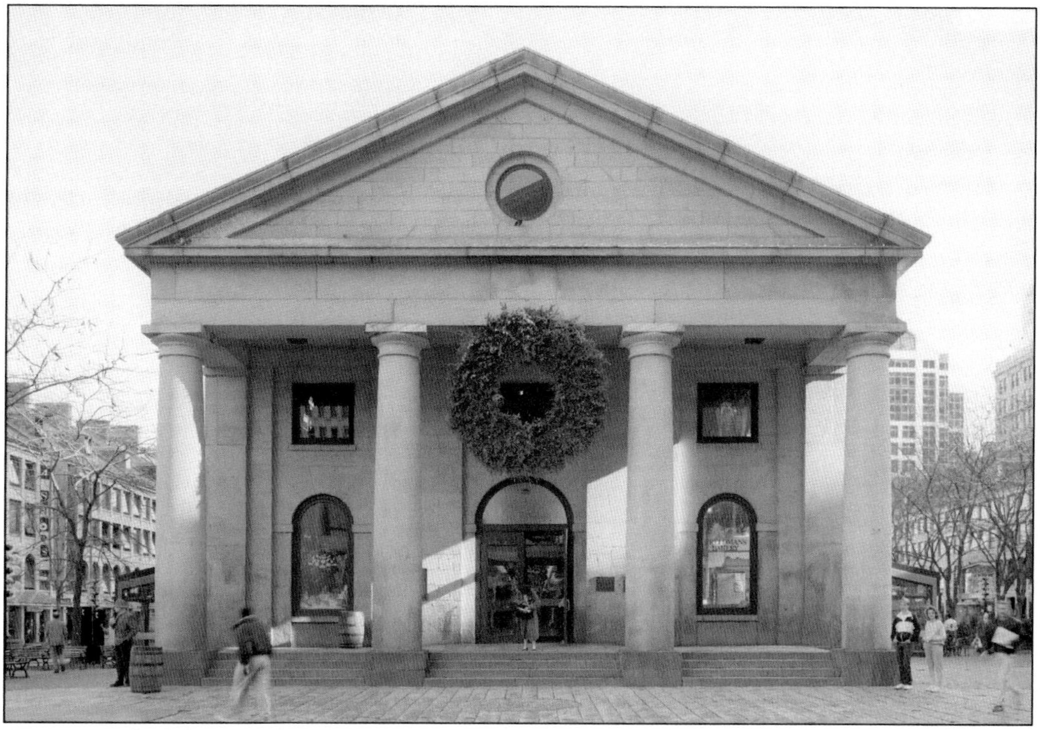

Quincy Market's historical significance extended beyond its engineering innovations. The central market is a prominent example of the Greek Revival style closely associated with Alexander Parris. And taken together, according to a city report, the buildings formed "one of the most impressive and large-scaled urban developments in the United States during the first half of the 19th century." (LOC.)

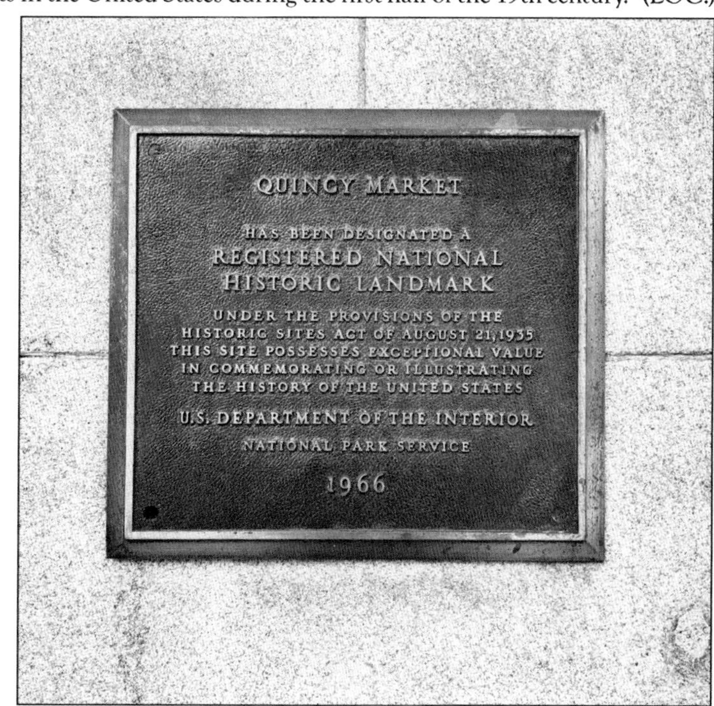

Quincy Market was designated a national historic landmark and added to the National Register of Historic Places in 1966. In 1970, the project boundary was confirmed to include the two flanking buildings, clearing up earlier ambiguity. The Boston Landmarks Commission designated the Quincy Market building a Boston landmark in 1996. The North and South Markets became city landmarks in 2024; the designation covered the exterior only. (Author's collection.)

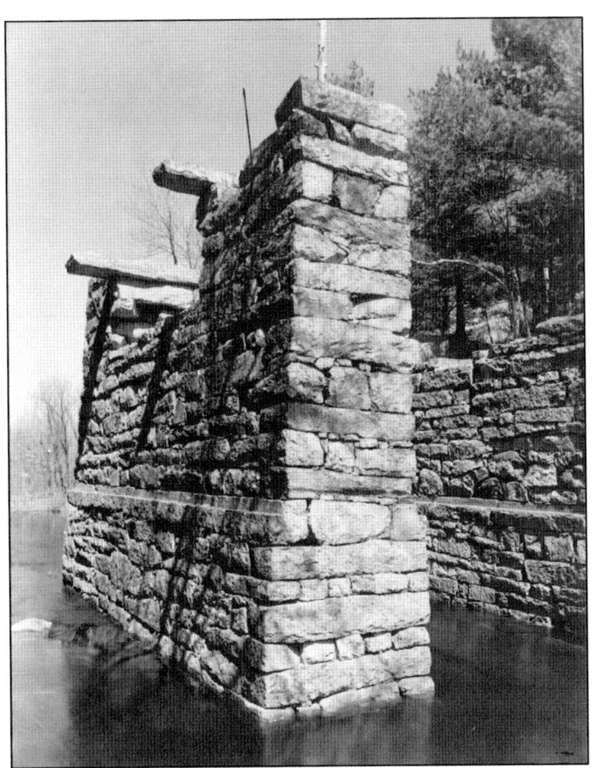

Now largely forgotten and mostly paved over, the Middlesex Canal was once considered an engineering marvel. The 27-mile water highway was built between 1794 and 1803 and connected Lowell, Massachusetts (then called East Chelmsford), with Charlestown. Years later, planners extended the canal through Boston's market district. Shown here is the aqueduct that carried the canal over the Shawsheen River in Wilmington. (LOC.)

The canal made it feasible to transport the granite used for the exterior walls of the main market and the facades of the north and south buildings. Although called Chelmsford granite, the stone was likely quarried in Westford. The granite floated down the Middlesex Canal on barges drawn by horses on each shore. Shown here is a section of the canal in North Billerica. (LOC.)

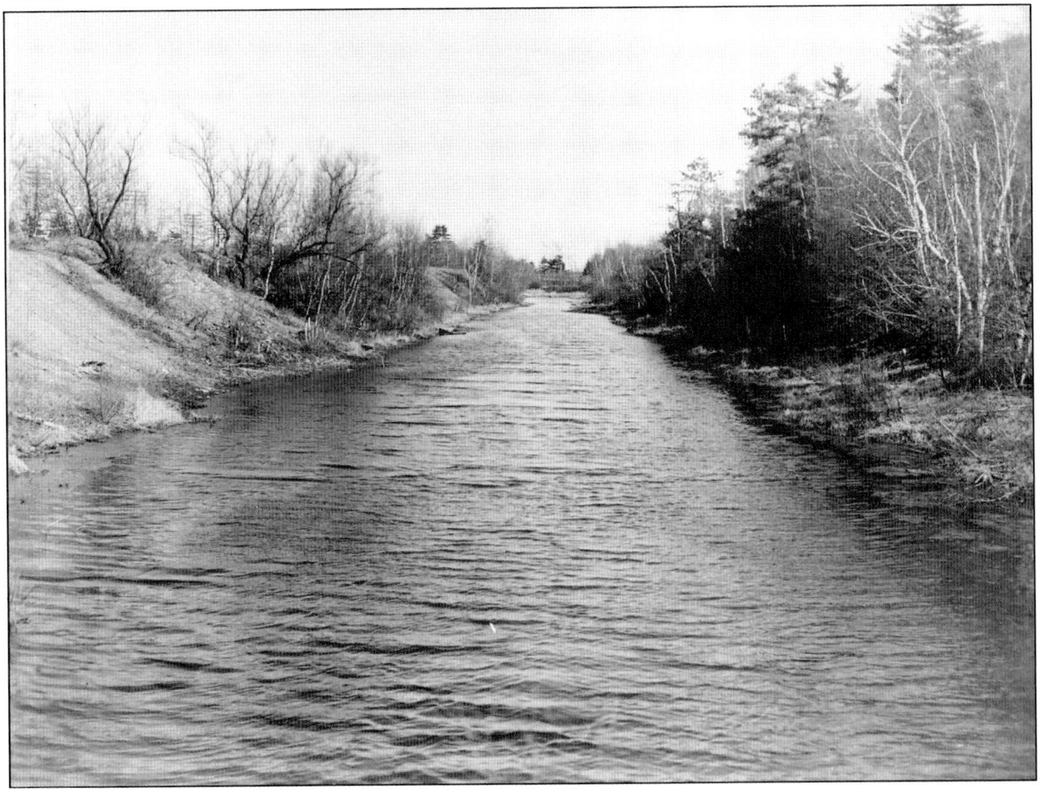

It was widely but inaccurately reported that the city of Quincy provided the granite for the market buildings. Although closer to Boston than Westford, the quarries in Quincy were already supplying granite for the Bunker Hill Monument, also under construction, and could only provide enough material for the Quincy Market foundation. (National Archives.)

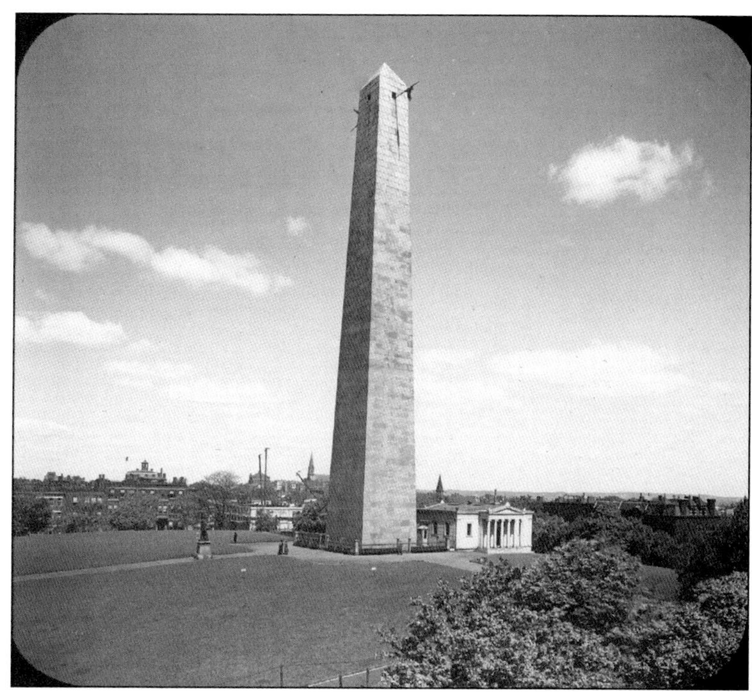

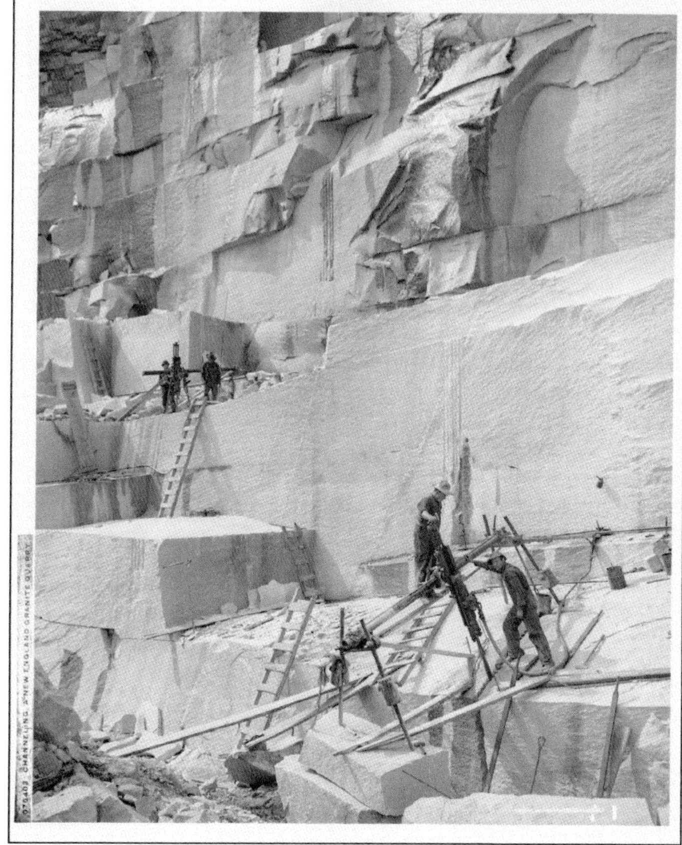

The first four granite columns arrived at the future site of Quincy Market in August 1825, and another four showed up in October. The city engaged convicts participating in the Charlestown State Prison's Stone Works program to help finish the columns. Shown here is a granite quarry in New Hampshire around 1908. (LOC.)

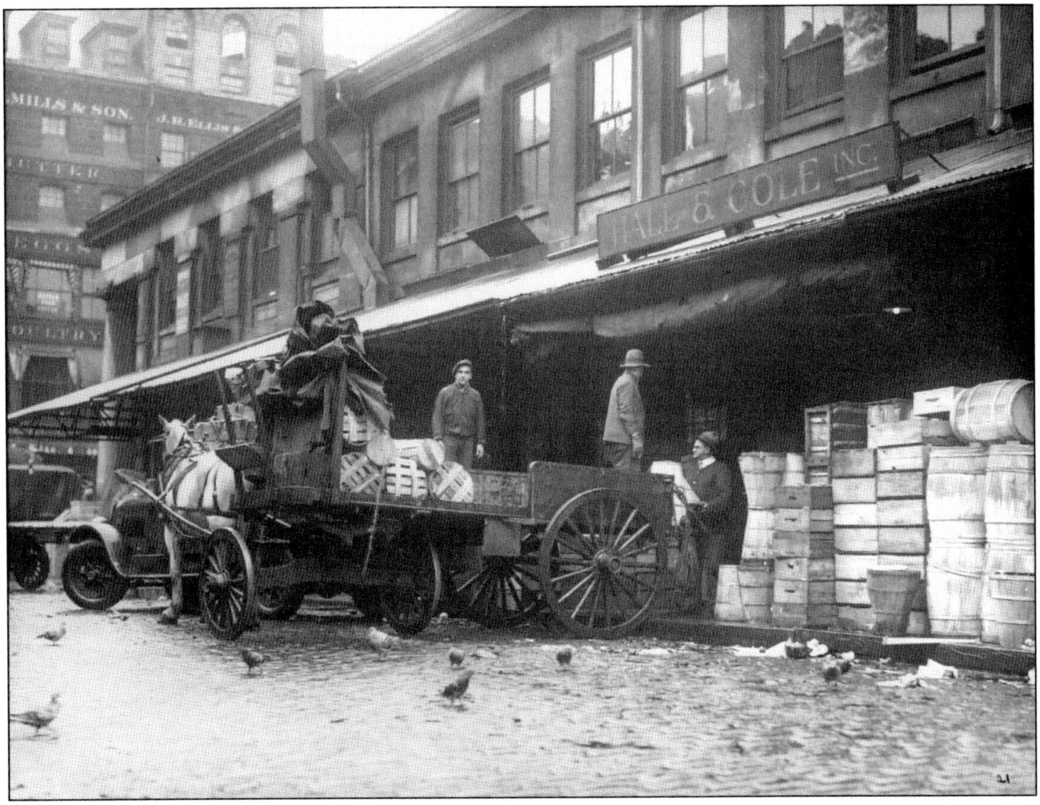

Although not officially completed until November 20, 1826, Quincy Market opened to the public on August 26 of that year. Vendors competed to make the first sale, and Paul Wild was credited with selling a leg of lamb to the market's first customer. The customer's name is not known. (BPL.)

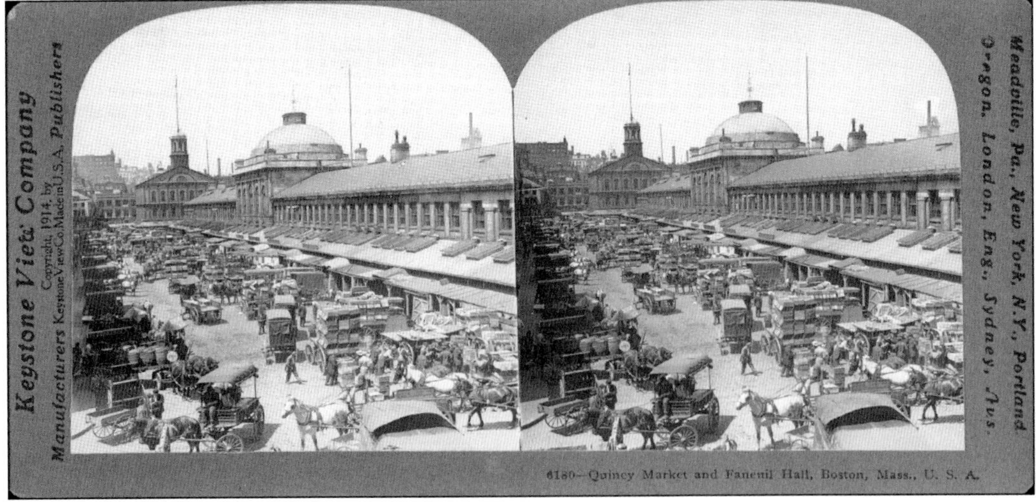

Reports at the time marveled at the marketplace. E.C. Wines was a Philadelphian who penned a series of letters published in 1838 as A *Trip to Boston*. He wrote, "The Bostonians must be huge eaters of cheese, if an inference from the quantities of that article in the market may be trusted." He continued, "The show of fruits, flowers, and vegetables in this market is exceedingly beautiful, and not without a picturesque effect." (LOC.)

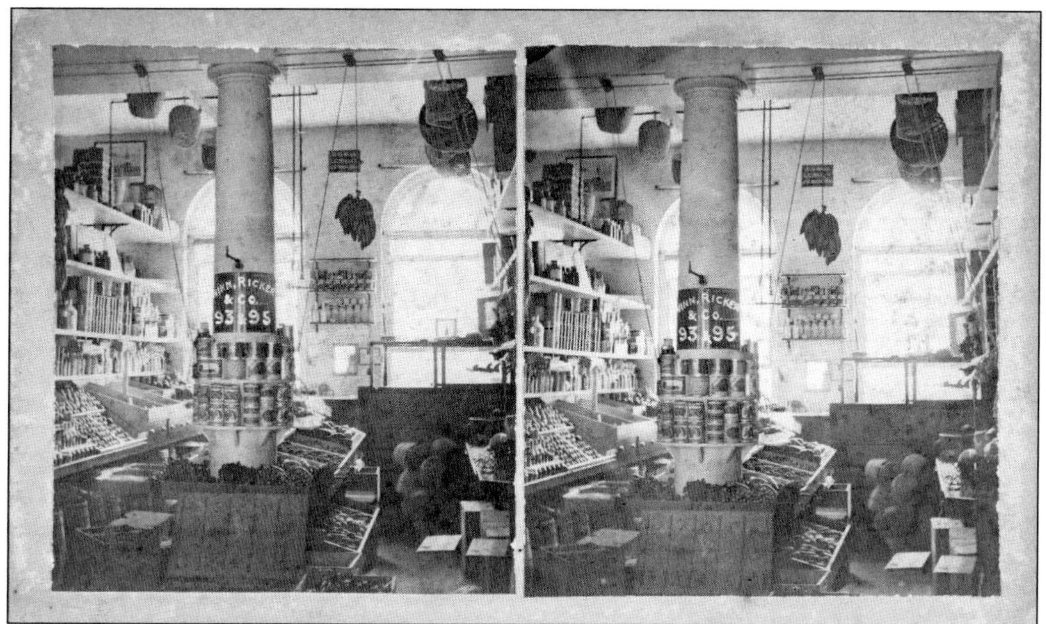

By the 1850s, stalls in Quincy Market were highly coveted. To meet demand, the city's aldermen considered a proposal to expand the market's height and footprint. Although Bulfinch's expansion of Faneuil Hall provided a precedent for such a major change, the city solicitor helped shut down the proposal. Instead, the market stalls in Faneuil Hall—closed for years—were reopened in 1858 to accommodate additional vendors. (LOC.)

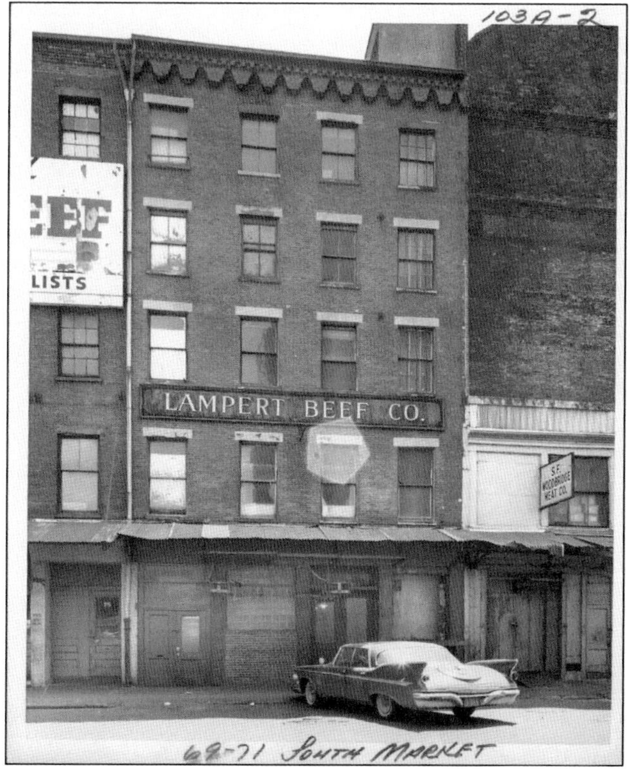

Restoring the vendor spaces in Faneuil Hall helped address the crowding in Quincy Market—although the new space was confusingly renamed New Faneuil Hall Market—but in 1853, Abbott Lawrence and other owners in the North and South Markets wanted to expand and lobbied the city for relief from the deed restrictions that Parris put in place three decades earlier. The city granted the request in 1855. (BOS.)

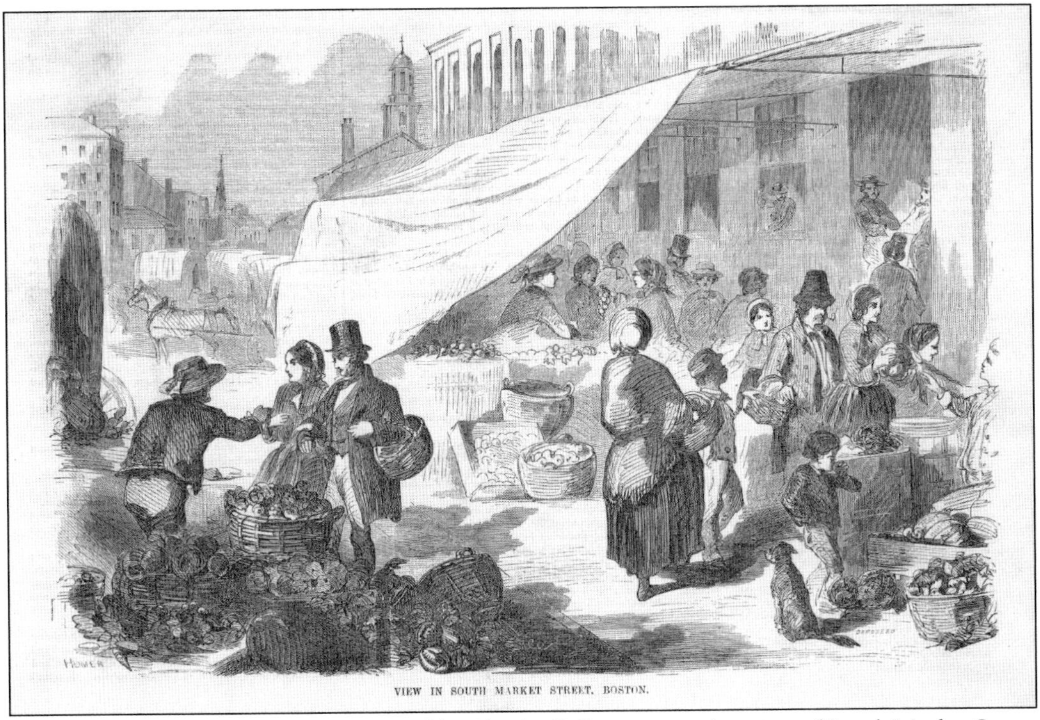

VIEW IN SOUTH MARKET STREET, BOSTON.

Drawn by Winslow Homer and engraved by Charles F. Damoreau, this view of South Market Street was published in *Ballou's Pictorial* on October 3, 1857. A century later, Christopher P. Monkhouse wryly described the scene in a monograph prepared for the 1969 annual meeting of the Bostonian Society and the Society for Architectural Historians. He wrote, "Obviously Homer was more interested in the marketers than the architecture of the Market." (BPL.)

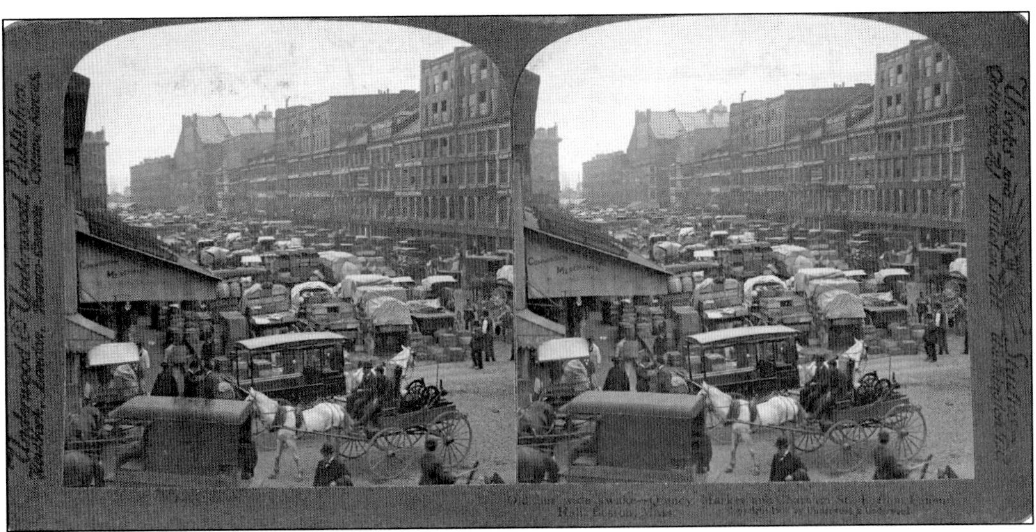

Quincy Market was bustling in the early years of the 20th century. This 1903 photograph depicts a lively marketplace along Chatham Street—described in the caption as "old but wide awake"—chock-full of trucks overflowing with wooden crates and barrels. (LOC.)

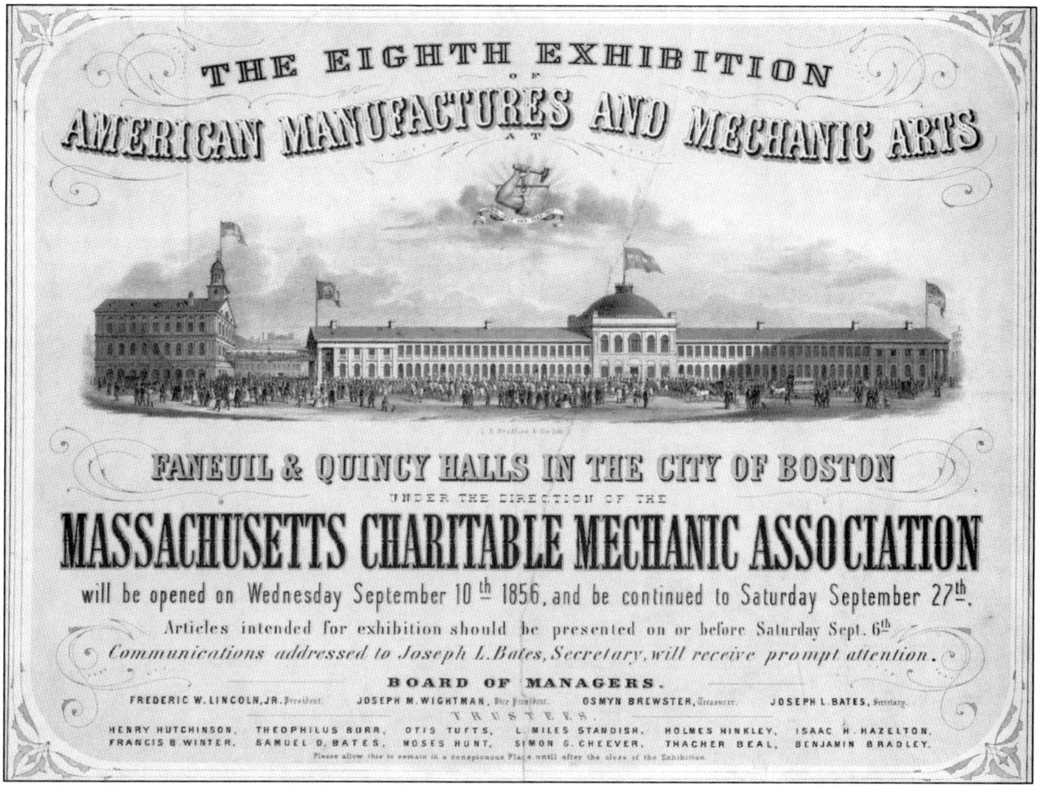

THE EIGHTH EXHIBITION
OF
AMERICAN MANUFACTURES AND MECHANIC ARTS
AT
FANEUIL & QUINCY HALLS IN THE CITY OF BOSTON
UNDER THE DIRECTION OF THE
MASSACHUSETTS CHARITABLE MECHANIC ASSOCIATION
will be opened on Wednesday September 10th 1856, and be continued to Saturday September 27th.
Articles intended for exhibition should be presented on or before Saturday Sept. 6th
Communications addressed to Joseph L. Bates, Secretary, will receive prompt attention.

BOARD OF MANAGERS.

FREDERIC W. LINCOLN, JR. President. JOSEPH M. WIGHTMAN, Vice President. OSMYN BREWSTER, Treasurer. JOSEPH L. BATES, Secretary.

TRUSTEES.

HENRY HUTCHINSON, THEOPHILUS BURR, OTIS TUFTS, L. MILES STANDISH, HOLMES HINKLEY, ISAAC H. HAZELTON, FRANCIS B. WINTER, SAMUEL D. BATES, MOSES HUNT, SIMON G. CHEEVER, THACHER BEAL, BENJAMIN BRADLEY.

Please allow this to remain in a conspicuous Place until after the close of the Exhibition

From 1827 to 1832, the New England Society for the Promotion of Manufacturers and Mechanic Arts mounted semiannual exhibitions on the second story of Quincy Market. Starting again in 1837, and under new sponsorship, the society held showcases in the meeting rooms of Quincy Market and Faneuil Hall. A covered walkway, visible in this engraving, was built to link the buildings through their second floors. (BPL.)

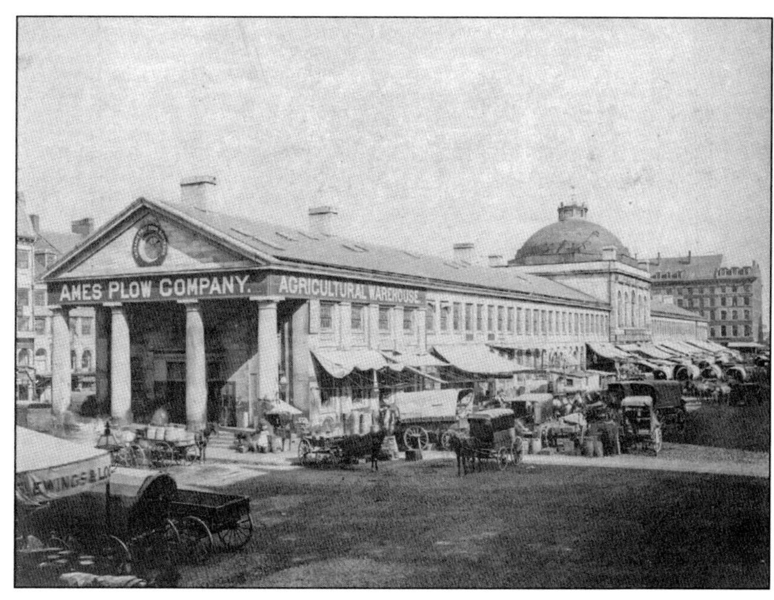

The Ames Plow Company occupied a warehouse in Faneuil Hall Market from 1862 to 1909. The company was established as Ruggles, Nourse & Mason in the 1830s and incorporated as Oliver Ames & Sons in 1864. Ames manufactured agricultural implements and machines, including its line of New England Chilled plows. (BPL.)

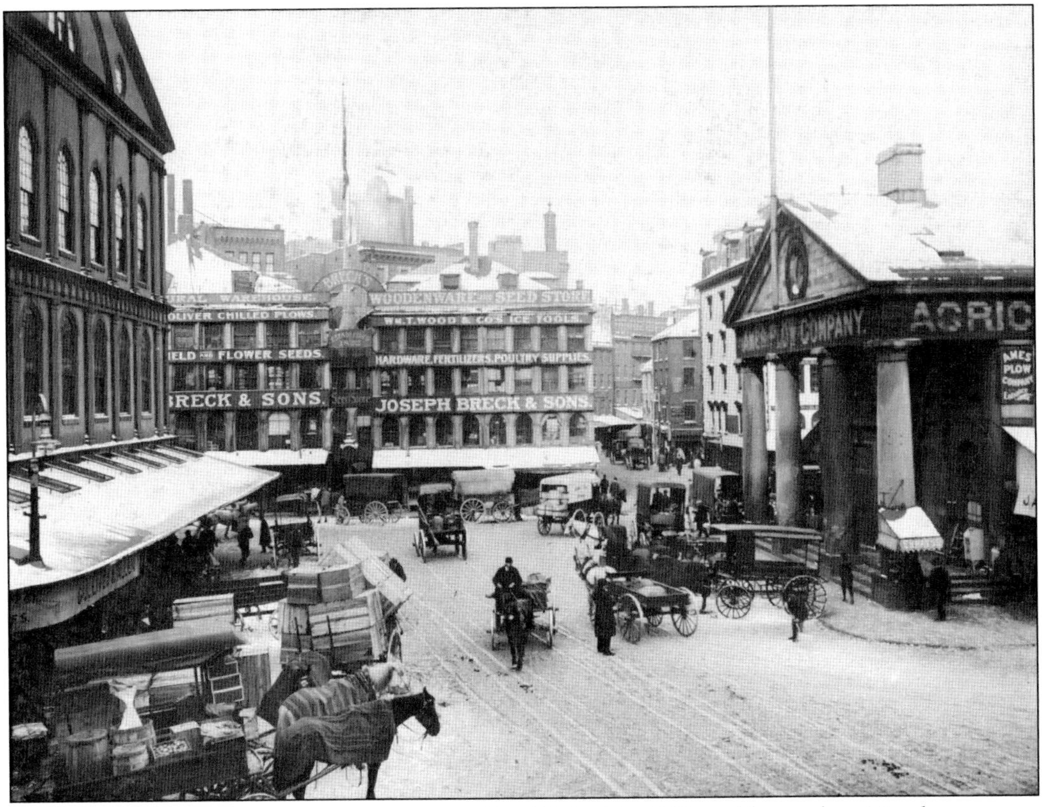

Established in 1822 and located on North Market Street for years, Joseph Breck & Sons sold seeds, flowers, plants, and agricultural equipment. An 1898 catalogue offered seeds for Lazy Wife's stringless beans, Breck's Beats All beets, and Quincy Market corn. Shown here is a view of Breck's from Merchants Row. (BPL.)

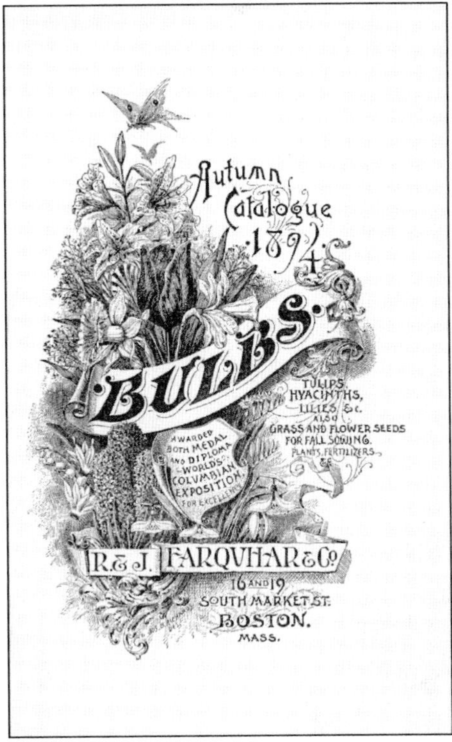

R. & J. Farquhar and Company sold seeds and bulbs from various storefronts on South Market Street in the late 19th and early 20th centuries. The company was founded by Robert Farquhar, a Scottish immigrant who arrived in the United States around 1865. According to an 1897 catalogue, Farquhar's seeds were used at Gray Gables, Pres. Grover Cleveland's summer home in Bourne, Massachusetts, and Queen Victoria's gardens at Balmoral Castle in Scotland. (Biodiversity Heritage Library.)

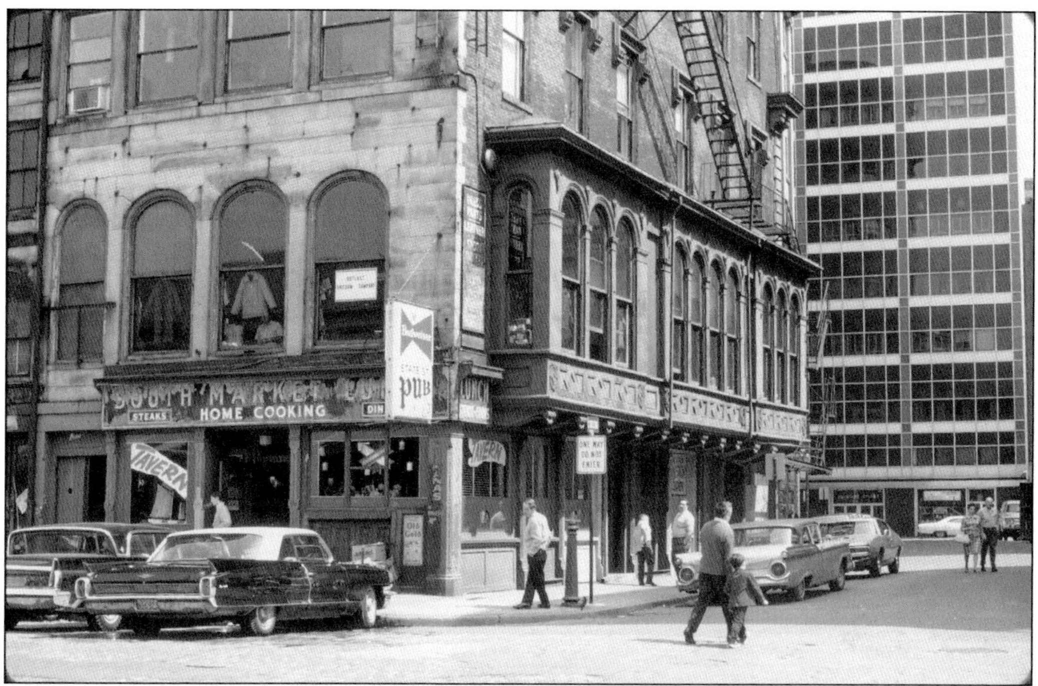

Nathan Robbins, a poultry vendor in Faneuil Hall Market (originally in Stall 33), founded the Faneuil Hall Bank in 1851. Whether from selling chickens or running the bank, Robbins became the wealthiest man in Arlington, Massachusetts, where he lived in a mansion near the center of town. The bank moved into the second floor of 2 South Market Street in 1854. After the bank left in 1900, the space was occupied by a social club, a speakeasy, and, as shown here, the Outlast Uniform Company. (Photograph by Edmund L. Mitchell, BPL.)

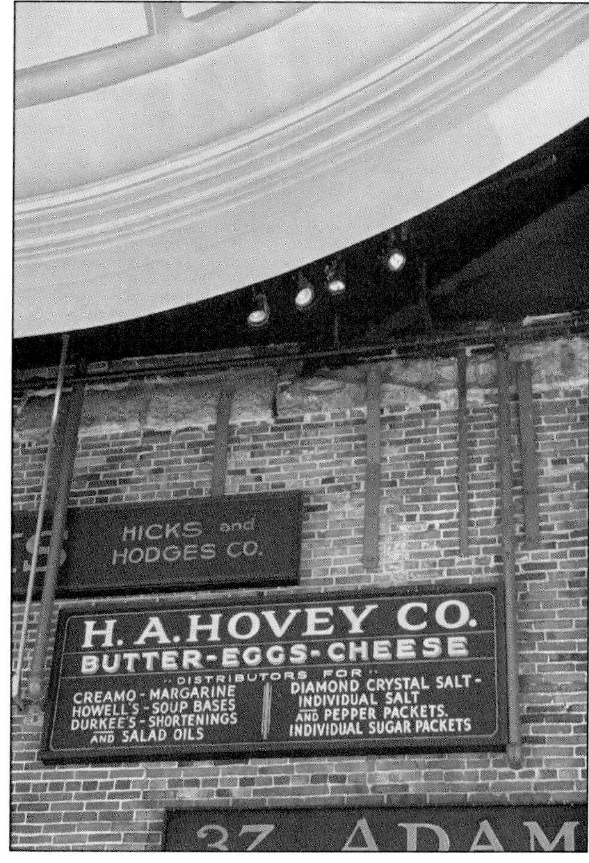

H.A. Hovey and Company occupied Stall 32 in Faneuil Hall Market from 1826 to 1948. The company sold butter, eggs, cheese, and according to the vintage sign now decorating the Quincy Market rotunda, a product called Creamo margarine. (Author's collection.)

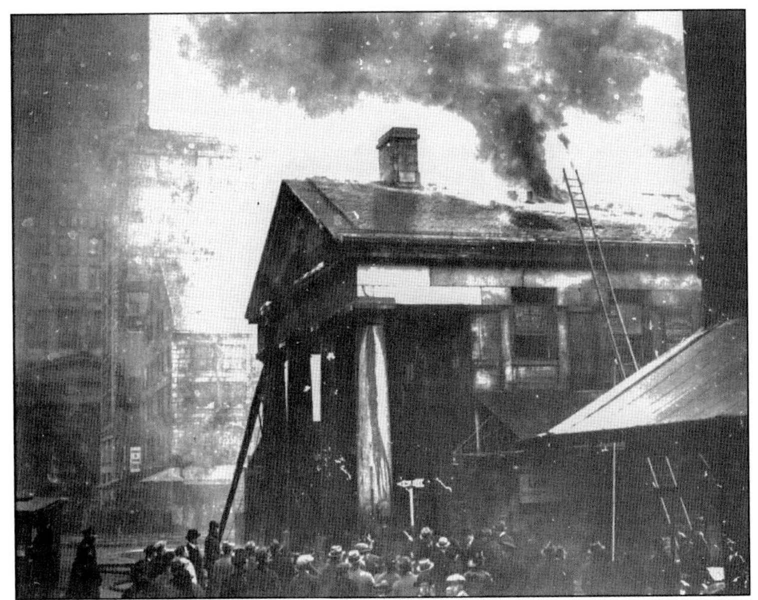

A fire broke out in the central market building on May 8, 1925. The blaze was confined to the upper floors of the east wing, the so-called cock loft. Seventeen firefighters were injured in the four-alarm blaze, and damage was estimated at over $100,000. Thousands of spectators turned out to watch the flames, including Mayor James M. Curley. The roof was replaced the next year. (Revolutionary Spaces.)

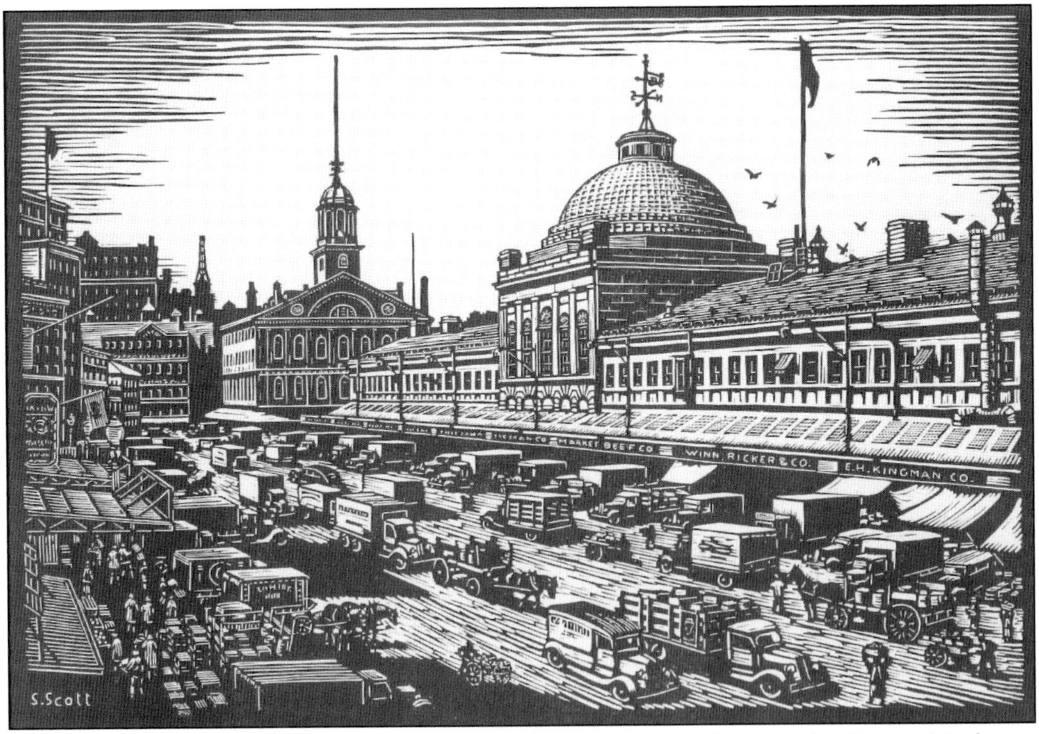

The federal Public Works Administration funded major structural repairs for Quincy Market in 1935 under the oversight of Boston architectural firms McLaughlin & Burr and John M. Gray Co. Work included replacing the floors and support structures and adding canopies on both sides of the building. The dome was reinforced with steel trusses and a ceiling installed to hide the supports (and the dome). (Linocut by Stanley Scott, National Archives.)

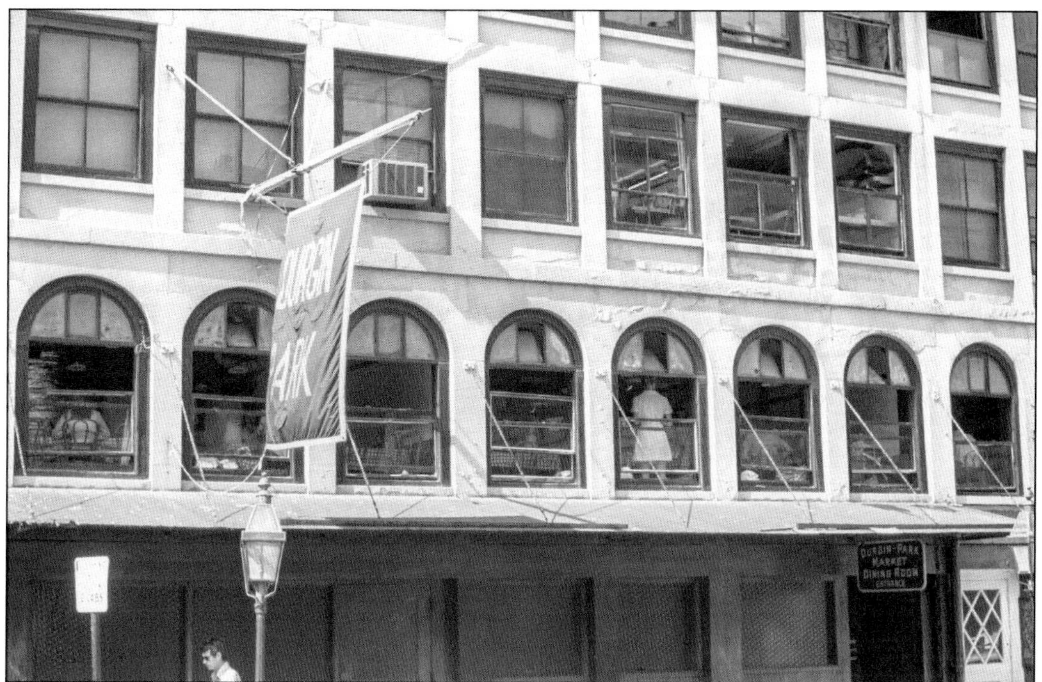

“Your grandfather and perhaps your great-grandfather dined with us.” Not many restaurants could make that claim, but Durgin-Park was one of a kind. The purveyor of hearty Yankee-style food began serving workers and merchants in Faneuil Hall in the 1740s. Eldridge Park and John Durgin bought the place in 1827 and moved it to the North Market building. John Chandler became a partner around 1840. After Park and Durgin passed away, Chandler named the restaurant in their honor, and his family ran the restaurant until 1945. James Hallett bought the venture from the Chandlers, and the Kelley family bought the business in the 1970s. The Kelleys sold Durgin-Park to the Ark Restaurant Group in 2007, and Ark closed the historic eatery in 2019. (Above, photograph by Edmund L. Mitchell, BPL; below, photograph by Ernst Halberstadt, BPL.)

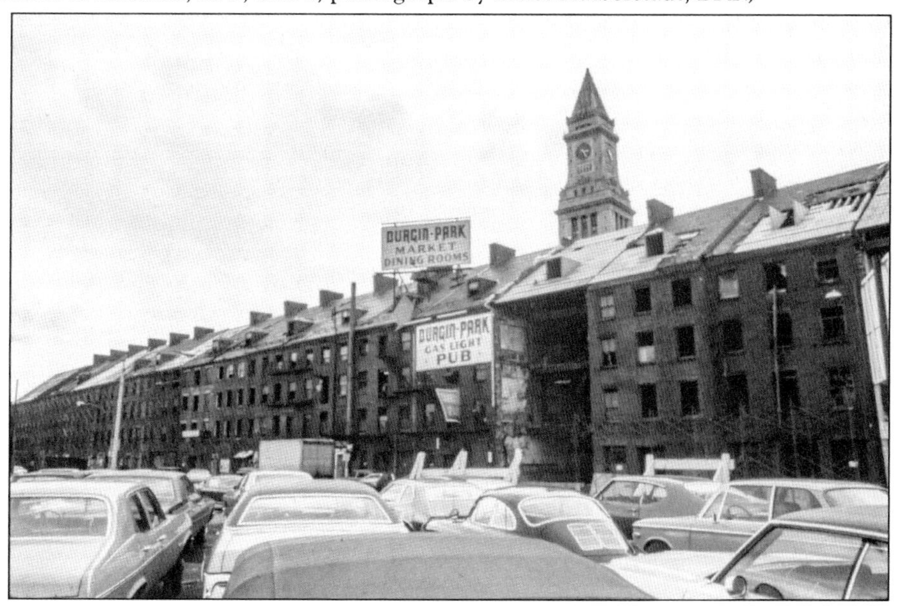

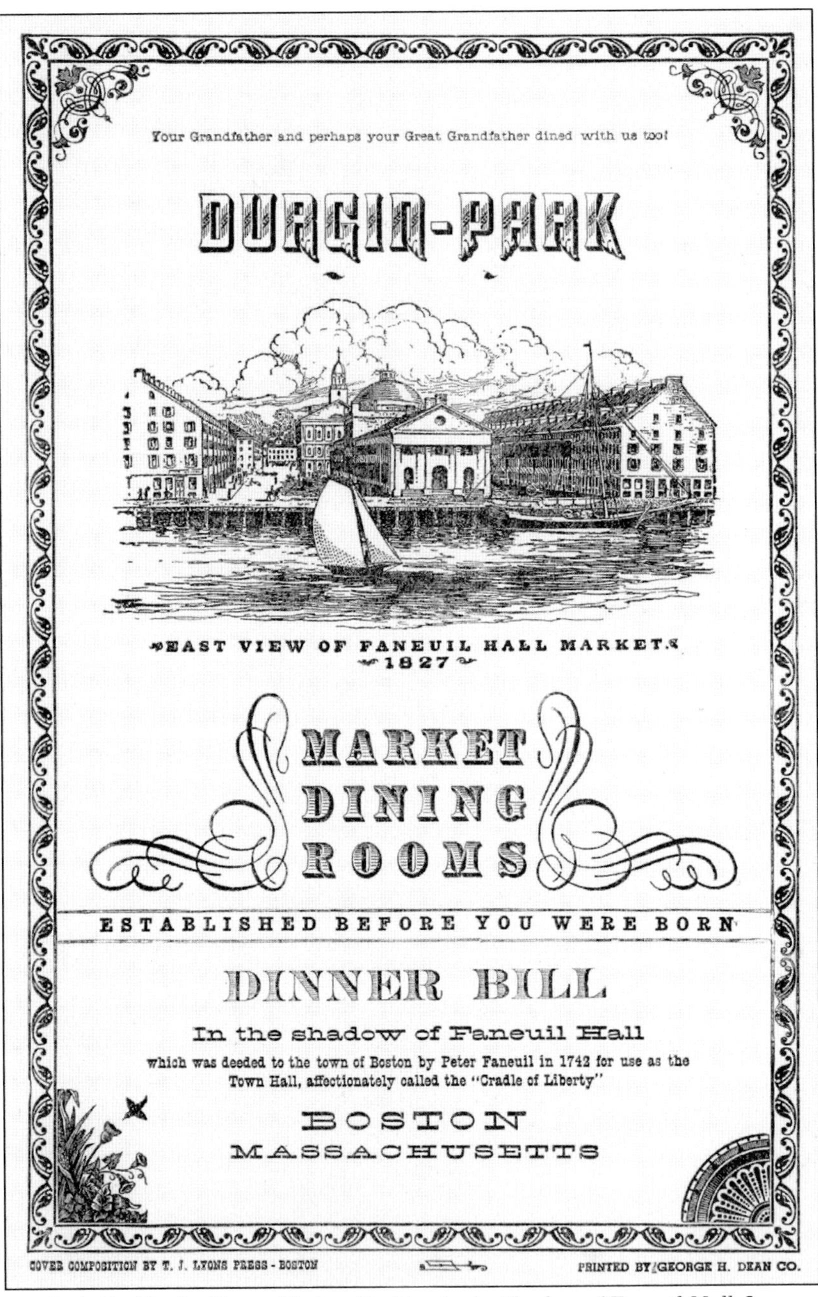

In *The Durgin-Park Cookbook: Classic Yankee Cooking in the Shadow of Faneuil Hall*, Jane and Michael Stern described the restaurant's classic dishes: "Durgin-Park sets the standard for Yankee cookery. Its stone-crock Boston baked beans and Indian pudding are definitive; the balance of its broad menu—Atlantic seafood and mighty cuts of beef—is timeless." But people also came for the experience. Customers were seated elbow-to-elbow with strangers at communal tables, and the servers were sassy. "Brusque service is part of the package," the Sterns wrote. "And while today's waitstaff no longer offers what a headline writer once called 'service with a sneer,' neither do any of the veterans go out of their way to pretend that making and serving these heavy plates of food is anything but hard work." (Author's collection.)

Three

Revolution, Politics, and Social Justice

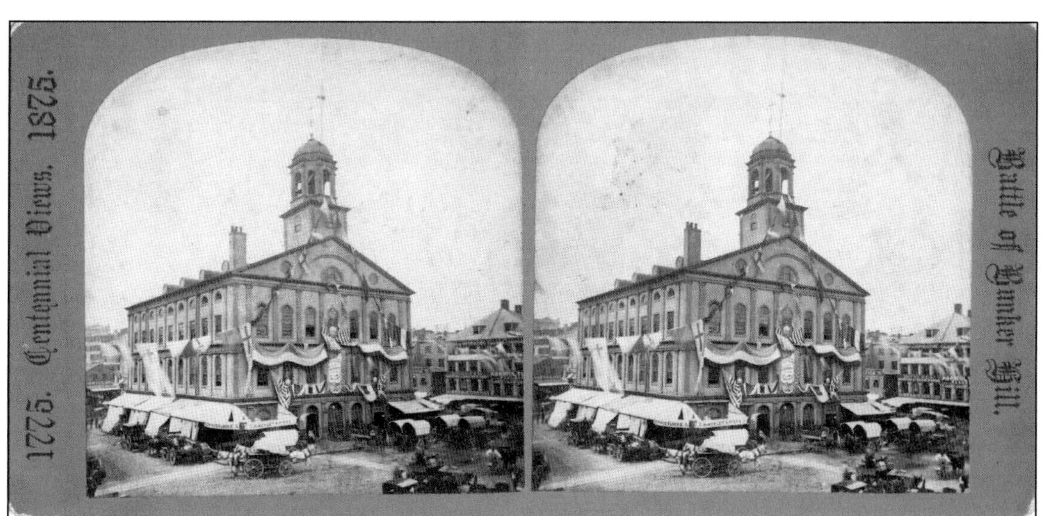

Throughout its history, Faneuil Hall has been a place where people came to demand change—revolutionaries arguing against British rule, abolitionists denouncing slavery, and suffragists rallying for the right to vote. Today, its role is mostly ceremonial, and the Cradle of Liberty is more likely to host celebrations than protests. (Photograph by Thomas R. Lewis, BPL.)

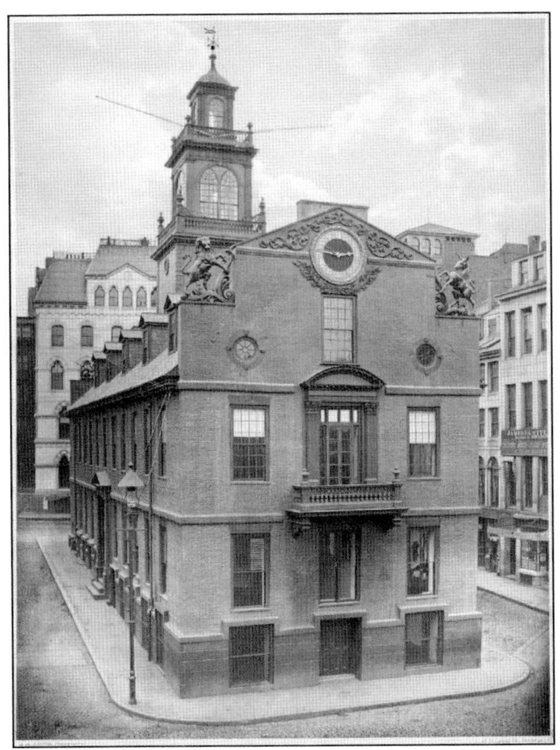

When Faneuil Hall opened, Bostonians finally had a "place all their own," according to historian Jonathan Beagle. Town meetings moved from the Town House—where local governance shared space with the royal governor and the colonial legislature—to the Great Hall. The move created a physical and symbolic separation between local rule and royal affairs and gave patriots a "safe space" to gather in opposition to the crown. "Local control of Faneuil Hall in conjunction with its town meeting tradition provided an autonomous place of protest that reinforced community bonds and gave opposition leaders popular credibility," Beagle wrote in 2003. (Left, photograph by A.H. Folsom, BPL; below, BPL.)

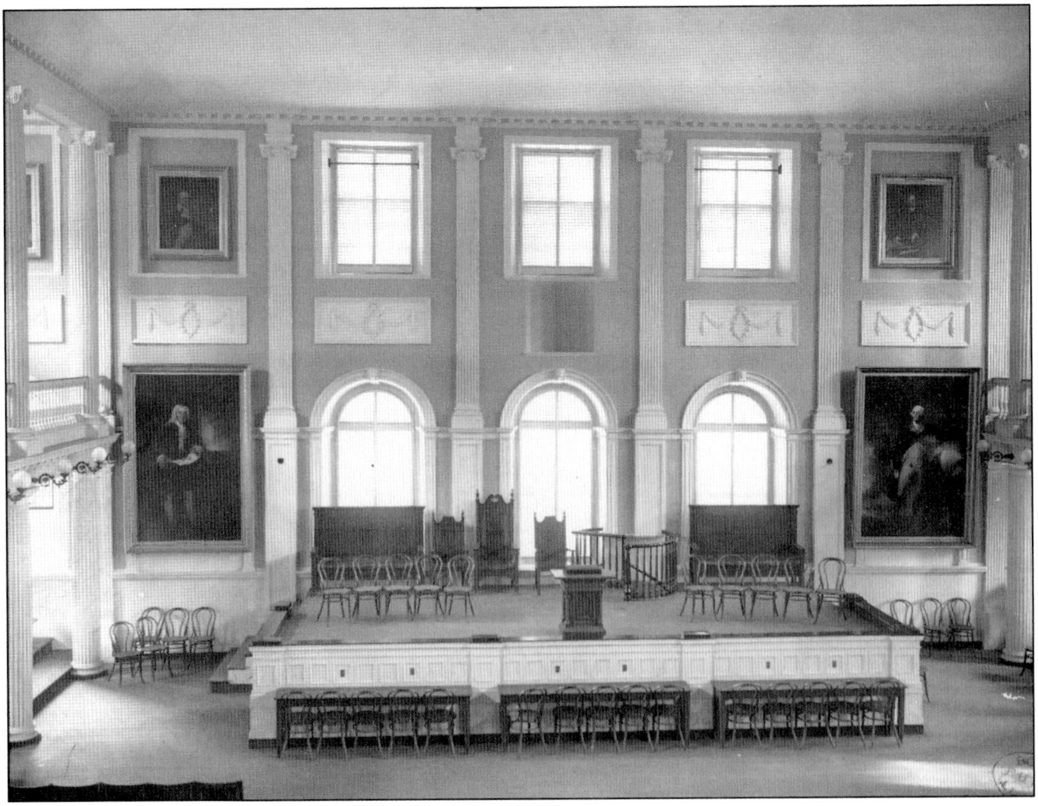

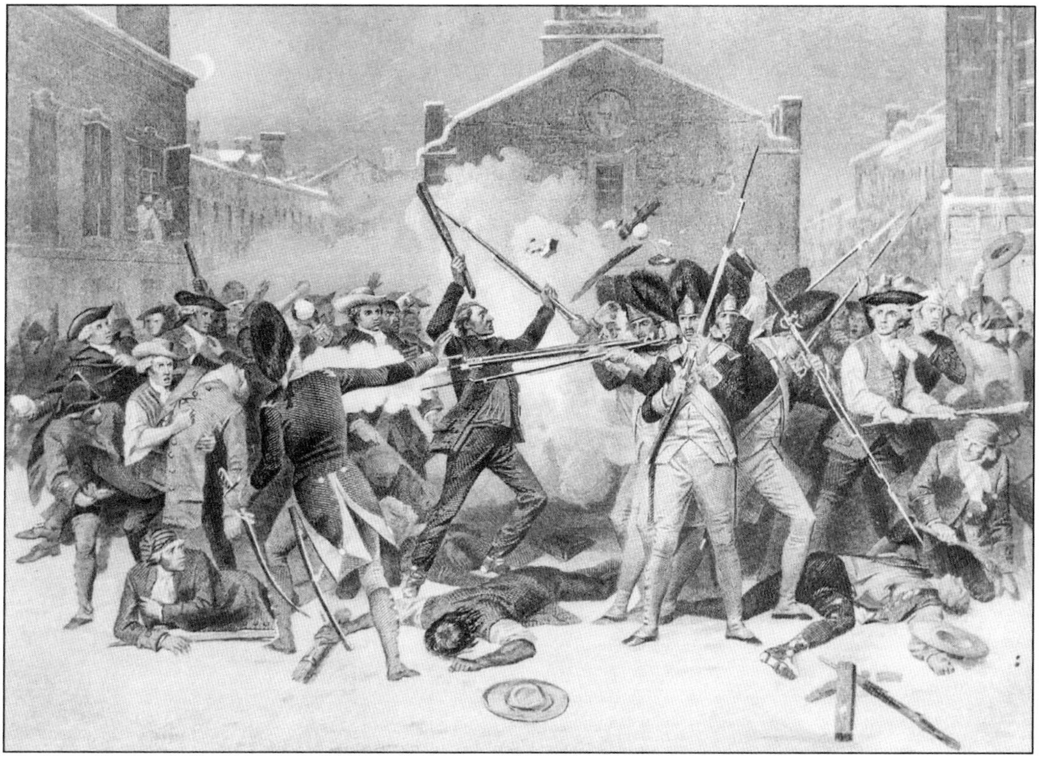

Amid growing tensions between colonists and the crown, British soldiers were dispatched to Boston in 1768. The military presence exacerbated the fraught situation, and violence erupted on the snowy night of March 3, 1770. Colonists taunted a group of British soldiers on King Street (now State Street), and the soldiers fired into the crowd. Five Bostonians were killed—Crispus Attucks, Patrick Carr, Samuel Gray, Samuel Maverick, and James Caldwell—in an altercation known today as the Boston Massacre. (National Archives.)

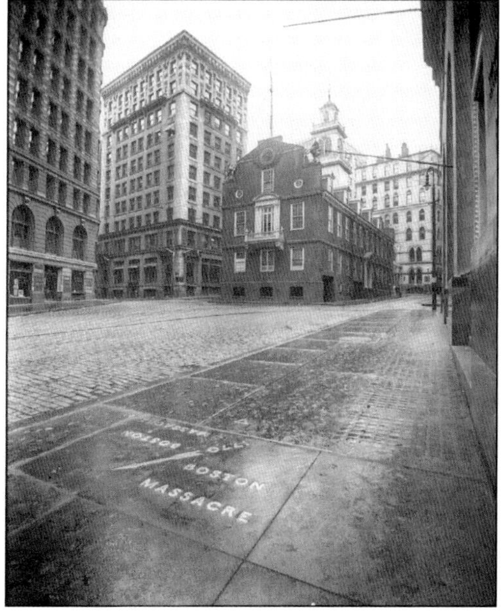

Many consider Attucks the first victim of the American Revolution. As the National Park Service wrote, "Death instantly transformed Attucks from an anonymous sailor into a martyr for a burgeoning revolutionary cause." The 47-year-old was of African and Wampanoag descent and may have escaped enslavement in 1750. Without local relatives, both Attucks and Caldwell lay in state at Faneuil Hall. All five victims were interred at the Granary Burying Ground. (Photograph by Leon H. Abdalian, BPL.)

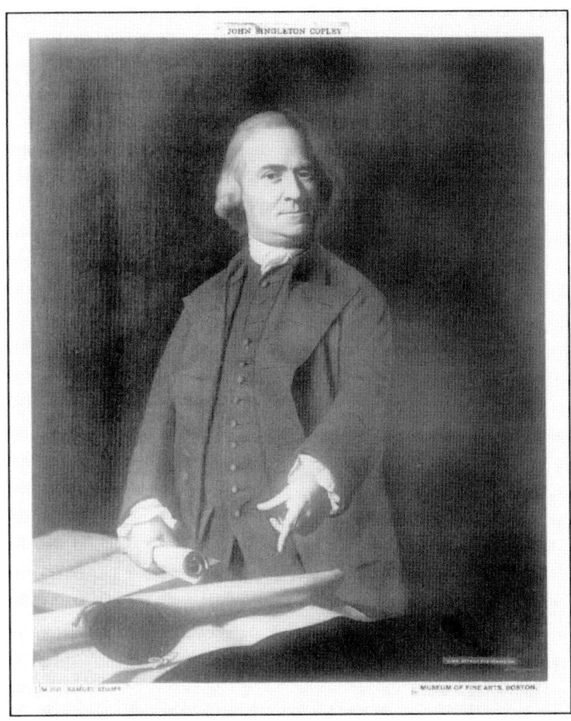

Samuel Adams wore many hats—activist, patriot, rabble-rouser, and (briefly) maltster—and he used his considerable organizing and rhetorical skills to galvanize Bostonians to rebel against oppressive British policies. He articulated his revolutionary philosophy through pamphlets, essays, and newspaper articles and drew upon his political savvy to organize opposition to the crown. He helped found the Sons of Liberty, an underground network of resistance to British rule; members included Paul Revere, Joseph Warren, James Otis Jr., and John Hancock. Adams served in the Massachusetts legislature and the Continental Congress; he was a signatory to the Declaration of Independence and helped draft the Articles of Confederation. After independence, he served as the fourth governor of Massachusetts. (Left, LOC; below, photograph by Leon H. Abdalian, BPL.)

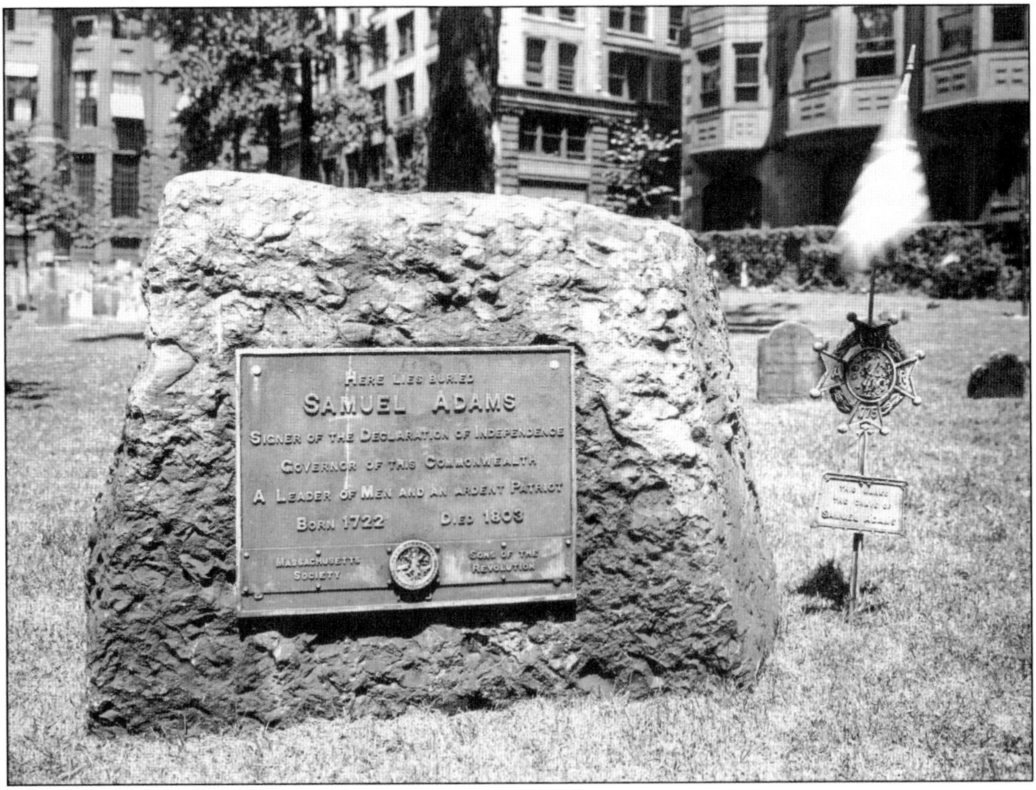

Starting in 1764, Great Britain enacted a series of taxes on the American colonies to help pay off the national debt amassed during the Seven Years' War (also called the French and Indian War). The Sugar Act, Stamp Act, and Townshend Acts were perceived as "taxation without representation," and patriots like Samuel Adams, John Hancock, and James Otis Jr. frequently addressed crowds in the Great Hall to voice their opposition to these actions. (LOC.)

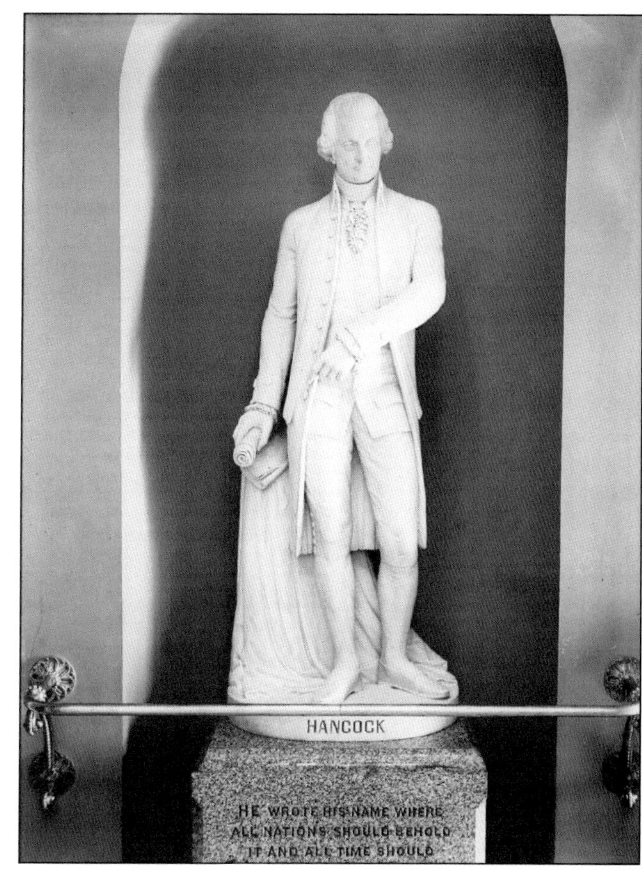

The Townshend Acts imposed duties on multiple imports, including tea, and the tea tax remained even after the acts were repealed in 1770. When Boston's merchants found a way to evade the tax by buying tea from Dutch smugglers, the British crown retaliated with the Tea Act. The 1773 law granted a monopoly to the East India Company. (New York Public Library.)

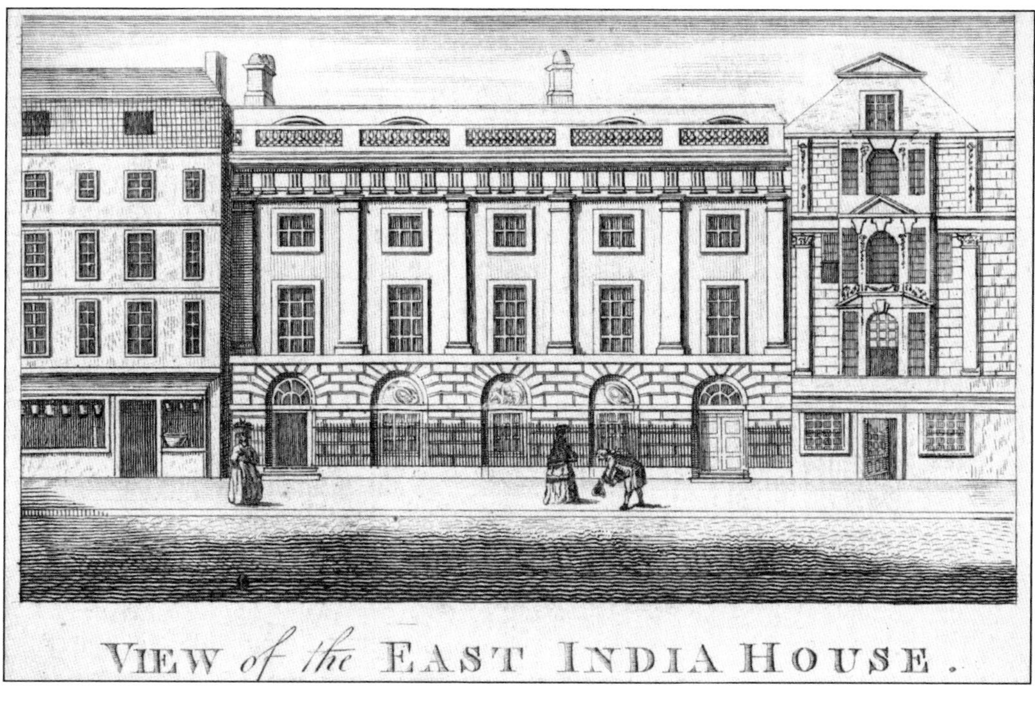

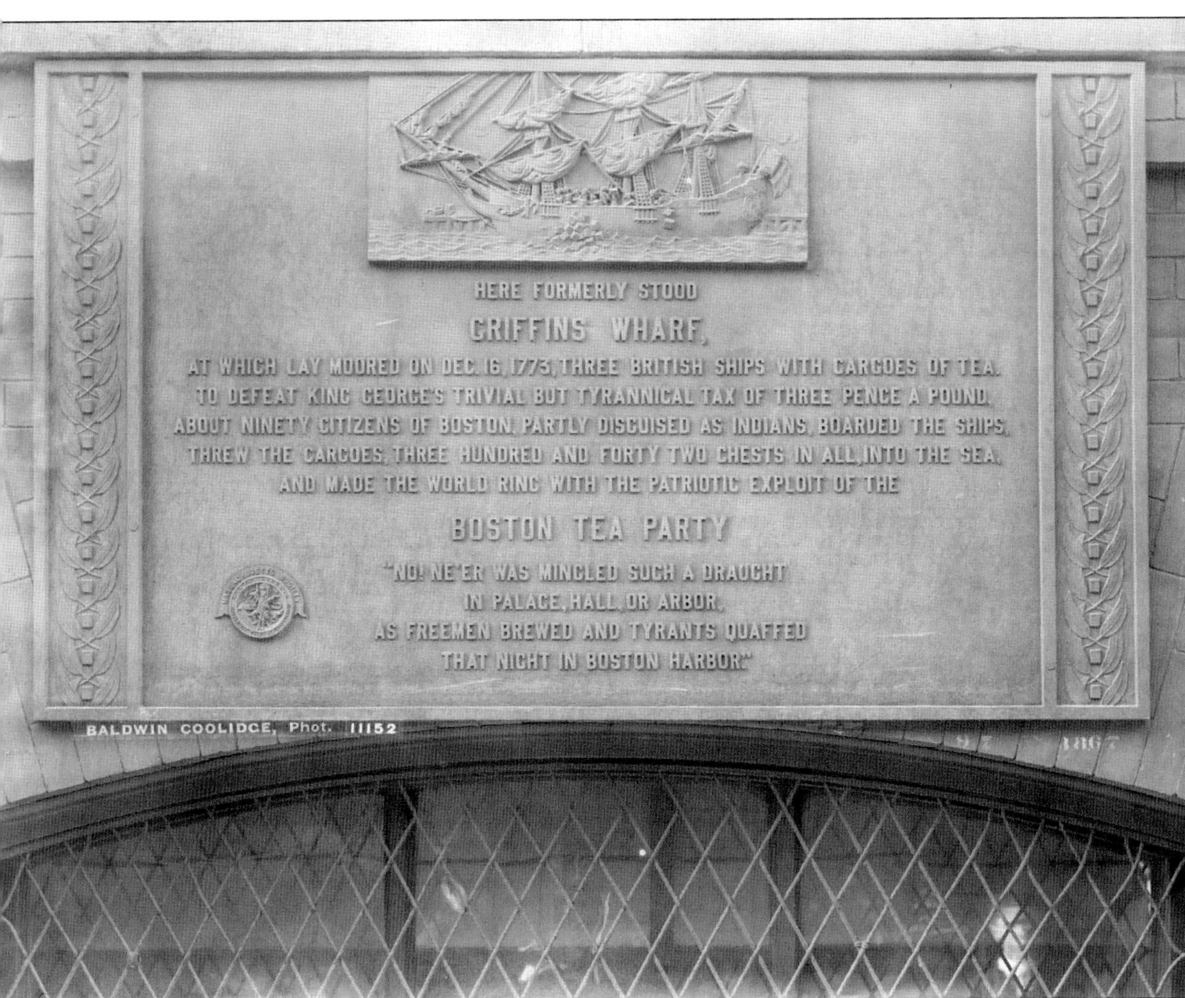

The *Dartmouth* sailed into Boston Harbor on November 28, 1773, loaded with tea. Protesting the imposition of the Tea Act, Bostonians convened in Faneuil Hall to plot a course of action. The overflowing crowd moved to the larger Old South Meeting House, where they demanded that the tea be returned and called upon the tea merchants (known as consignees)—one of whom was Peter Faneuil's nephew Benjamin—to resign. Nothing changed, and the *Eleanor* and the *Beaver* arrived by December 15, also laden with tea. Bostonians gathered again at Old South on December 16. Upon learning that Gov. Thomas Hutchinson would not let the ships leave Boston with the tea onboard, Samuel Adams reportedly told the crowd, "This meeting can do nothing more to save the country." Some say it was a signal to act. After the meeting ended, a party of men disguised themselves as Native Americans, boarded the three ships at Griffin's Wharf, and dumped 342 chests of tea into the harbor. The event became known as the Boston Tea Party. (Photograph by Baldwin Coolidge, BPL.)

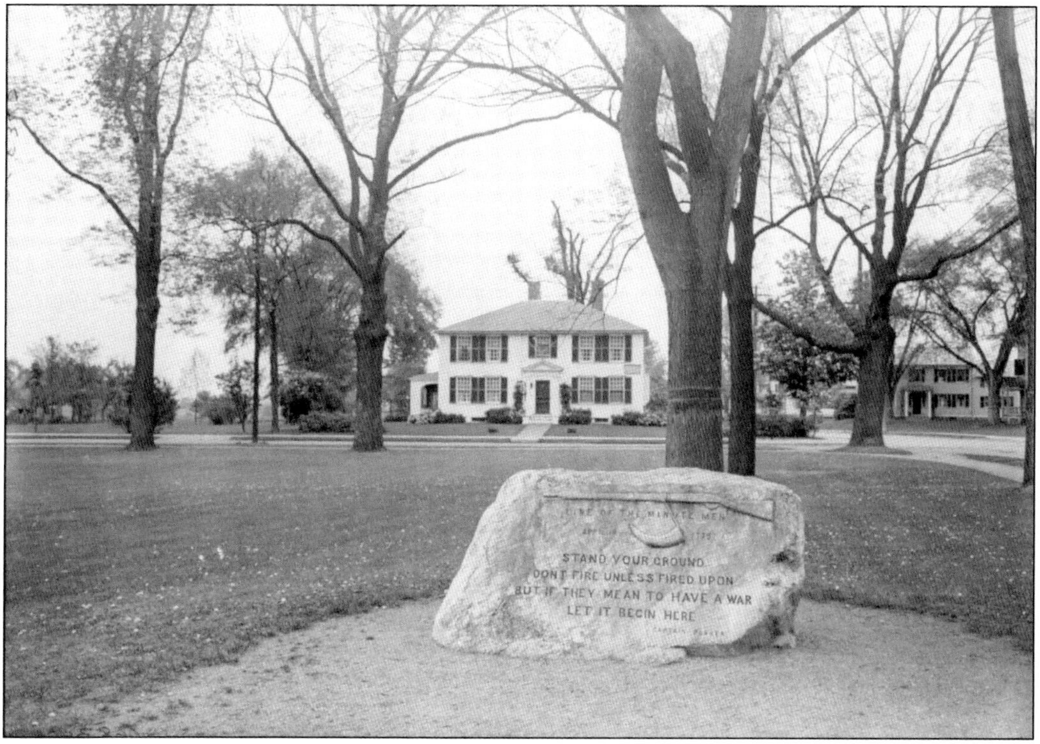

The American Revolution began when hostilities broke out between Massachusetts colonists and the British military in Lexington and Concord on April 19, 1775. When the British troops retreated to Boston, the new Continental Army contained them in the city, marking the beginning of the Siege of Boston. The Redcoats took advantage of their position by commandeering Faneuil Hall. Shown here is a monument to Capt. John Parker, who led the American militia at the Battle of Lexington. (LOC.)

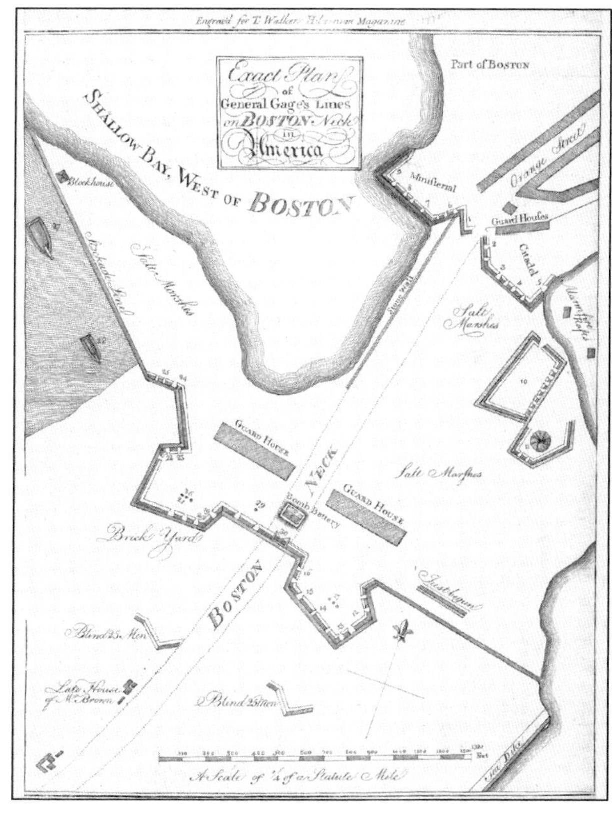

A few days after the siege began, British commander-in-chief Gen. Thomas Gage ordered Bostonians to turn in their firearms to be stored in Faneuil Hall. Gage collected the following according to a published account: "1778 fire-arms, 634 pistols, 973 bayonets, and 38 blunder-busses." This map shows British blockades during the siege. (BPL/Leventhal.)

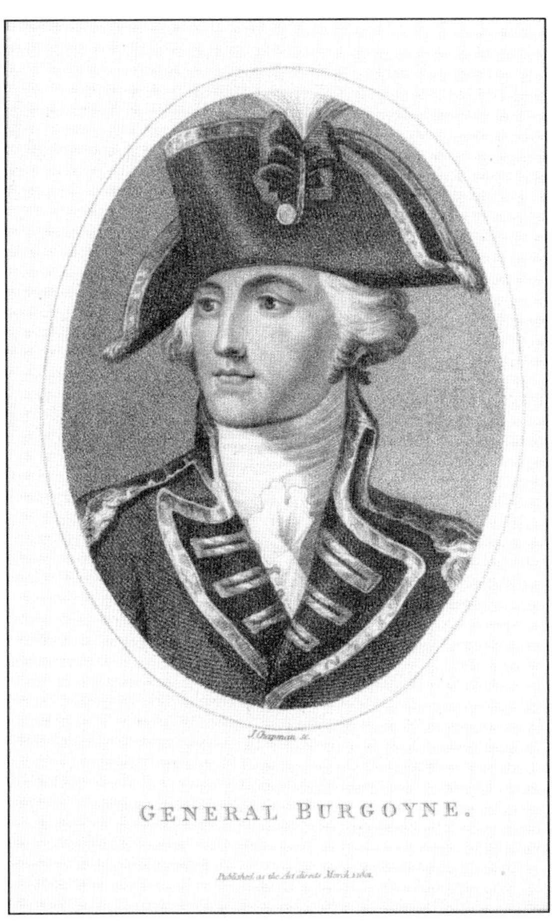

With nowhere to go, the British forces staged theatrical productions in Faneuil Hall during the siege. Plays included the *Tragedy of Zara* and a farce called the *Blockade of Boston*. The latter was the work of Gen. John Burgoyne, nicknamed "Gentleman Johnny." The satire ridiculed the colonists for their provincialism and military shortcomings. (New York Public Library.)

The Siege of Boston lasted almost a year, until Gen. George Washington fortified Dorchester Heights using artillery retrieved from Fort Ticonderoga by Gen. Henry Knox. By then, some 10,000 British troops were trapped in Boston. The British army, under the leadership of Gen. William Howe (who replaced Gage), evacuated the city on March 17, 1776, a date still known as Evacuation Day. This monument in Watertown, Massachusetts, is one of many markers that line Knox's arduous route from New York State to Boston. (Watertown Free Library.)

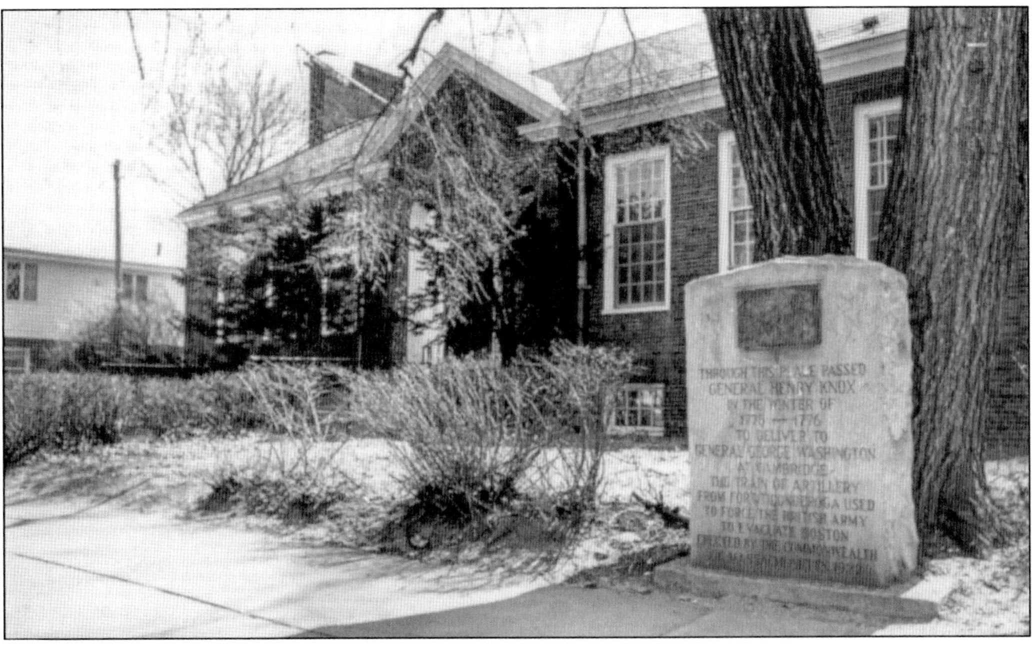

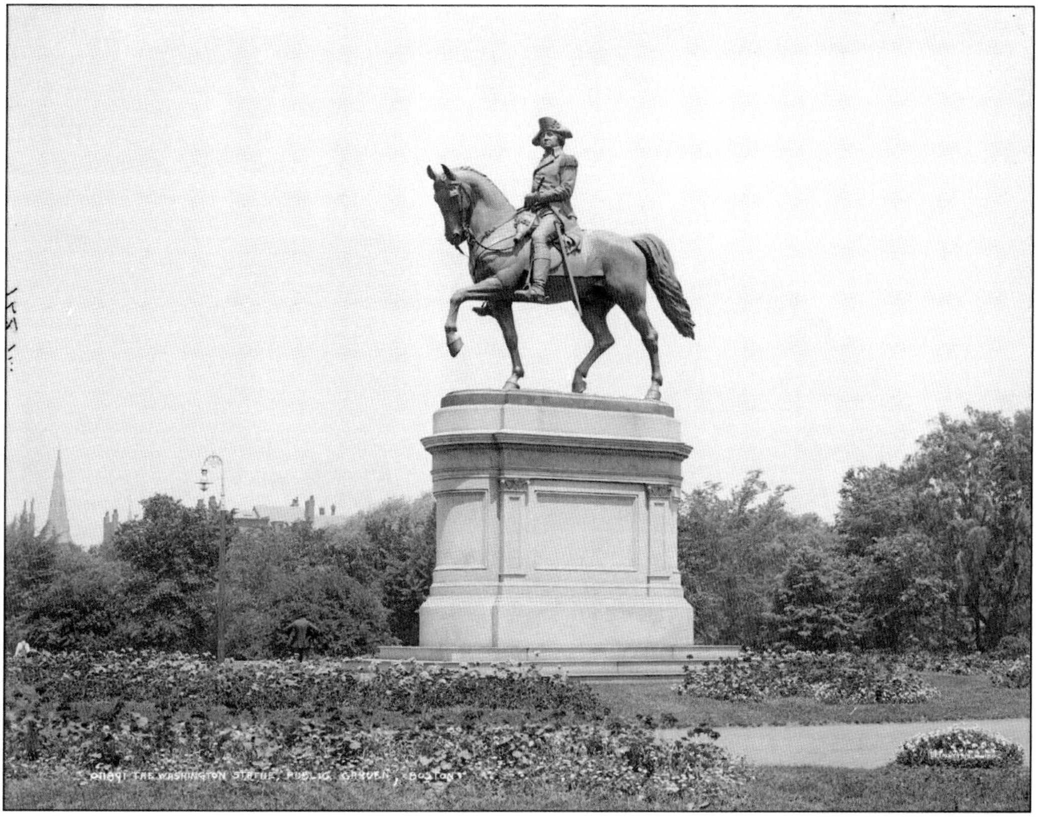

Pres. George Washington made a triumphant return to Boston in 1789—his first visit since his troops ended the Siege of Boston. As part of his New England tour, Washington visited nearly 60 towns in Connecticut, Massachusetts, and New Hampshire. He spent five days in Boston and was feted with fireworks and a banquet at Faneuil Hall on October 27. (LOC.)

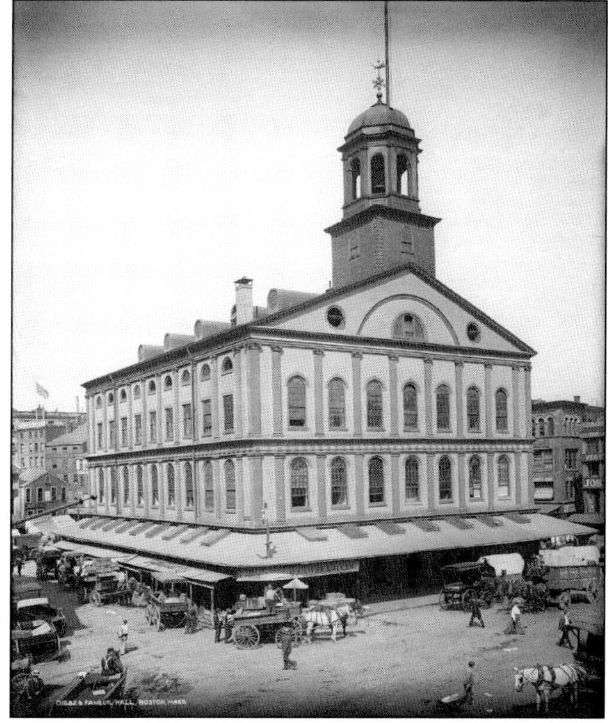

Besides presidential galas, the Great Hall was the site of lottery drawings, business negotiations, worship services, conventions, and countless celebrations. By the 1800s, Faneuil Hall had also become a meeting place for rallies in support of (and opposition to) most of the social issues of the day, and Bostonians filled Faneuil Hall to debate abolition, states' rights, suffrage, fair wages, and freedom of the press. (LOC.)

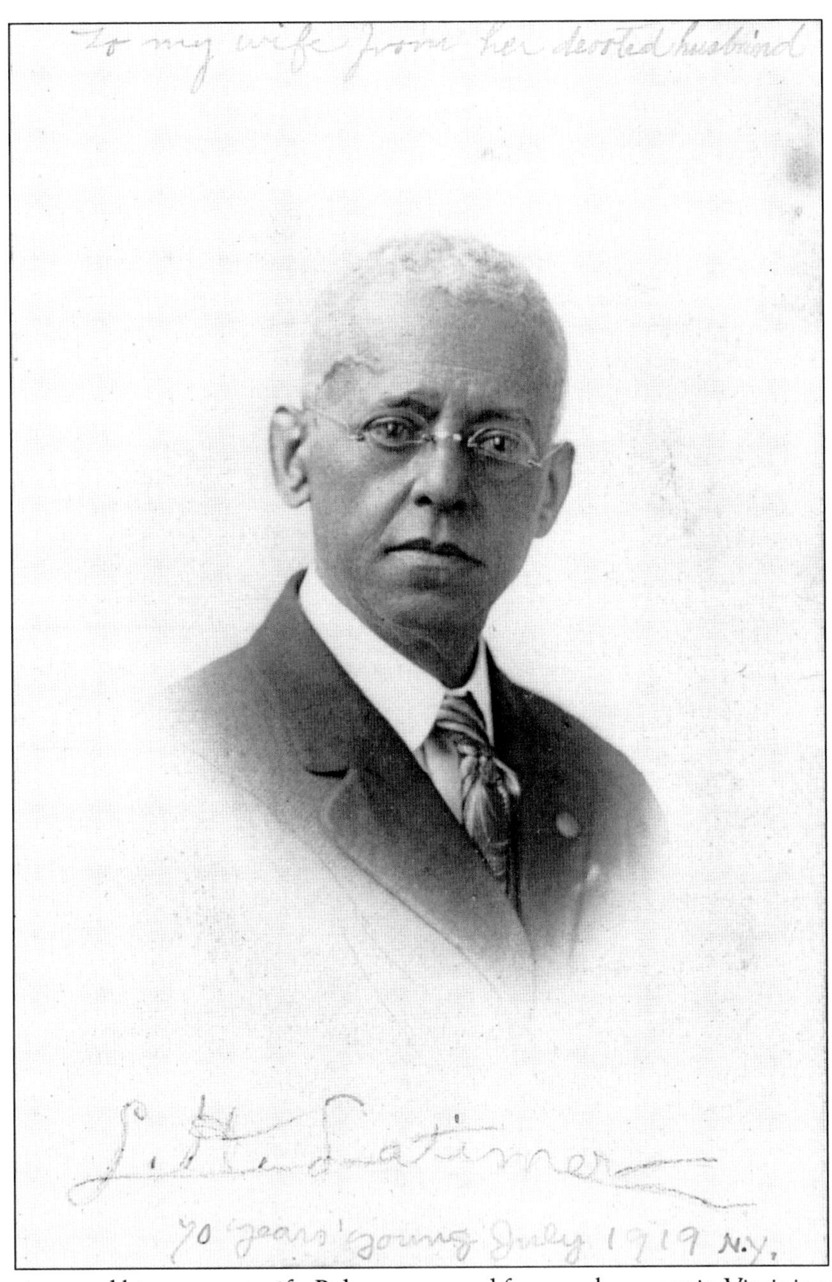

George Latimer and his pregnant wife, Rebecca, escaped from enslavement in Virginia and arrived in Boston in 1842. Someone tipped off George's enslaver, James Gray, who traveled to Boston and had him arrested on October 18. (Rebecca was safe in hiding.) Boston abolitionists rallied to George's defense and held "Latimer meetings" at Faneuil Hall, among other locations, and Rev. Nathaniel Colver secured his freedom for $400. Rebecca's enslaver dropped the charges against her. The public uproar around Latimer's case encouraged Massachusetts to adopt the Personal Liberty Act in 1843. The so-called "Latimer Law" prohibited the state from apprehending fugitive slaves and was the model for legislation in other states. The Latimers remained in the Boston area; their son Lewis Howard Latimer (shown here "at 70 years young") was an inventor who worked with Thomas Edison and Alexander Graham Bell. (Thomas Edison National Historical Park.)

The passage of the federal Fugitive Slave Act of 1850 sparked protests at Faneuil Hall. Abolitionist Frederick Douglass addressed a crowd of thousands in October 1850. "If you are prepared to see the streets of Boston flowing with innocent blood," he said, "if you are prepared to see sufferings such as perhaps no country ever before witnessed, just give in your adhesion to the fugitive slave bill." (Photograph by C.F. Conly, LOC.)

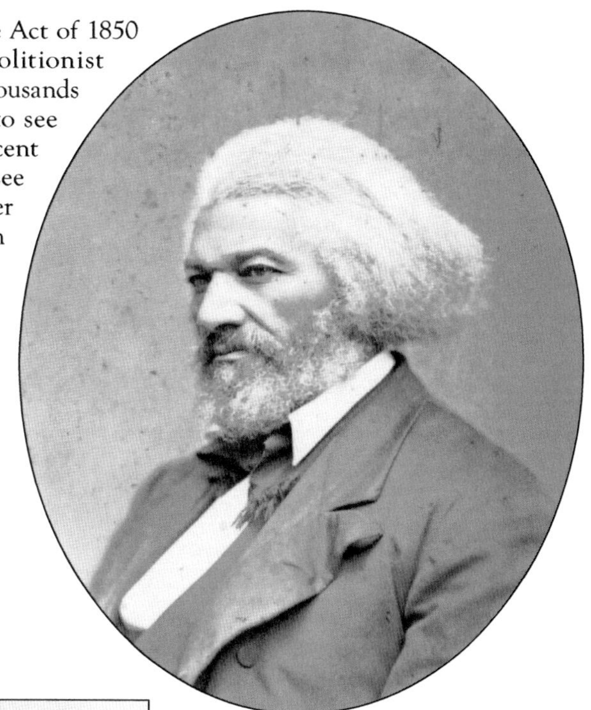

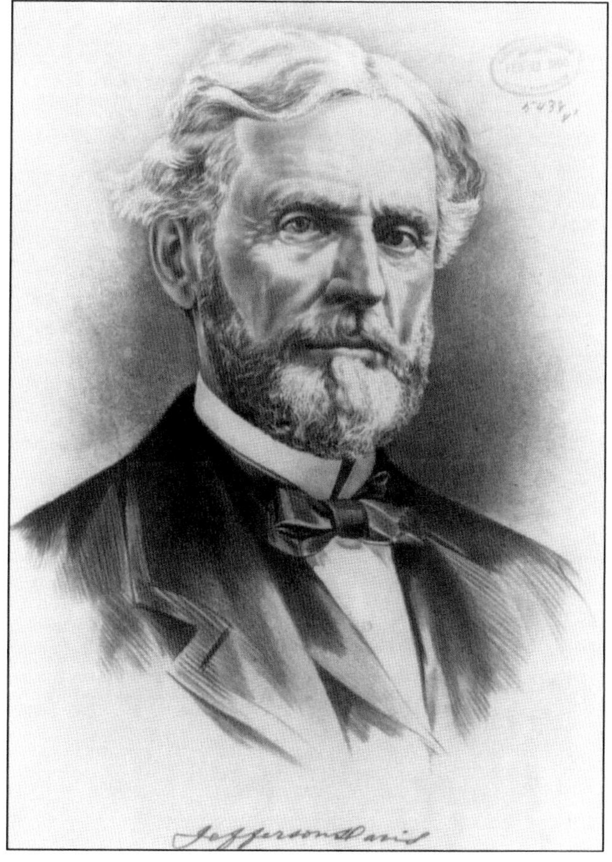

Not everyone who spoke about slavery at Faneuil Hall was an abolitionist. Mississippi Sen. Jefferson Davis addressed an audience on the topic of states' rights in October 1858. He argued that the federal government had no jurisdiction over slavery and that abolitionists were tearing the country apart. Less than three years later, Davis was elected president of the Confederate States. (Lithograph by I.S. Johnson & Co., LOC.)

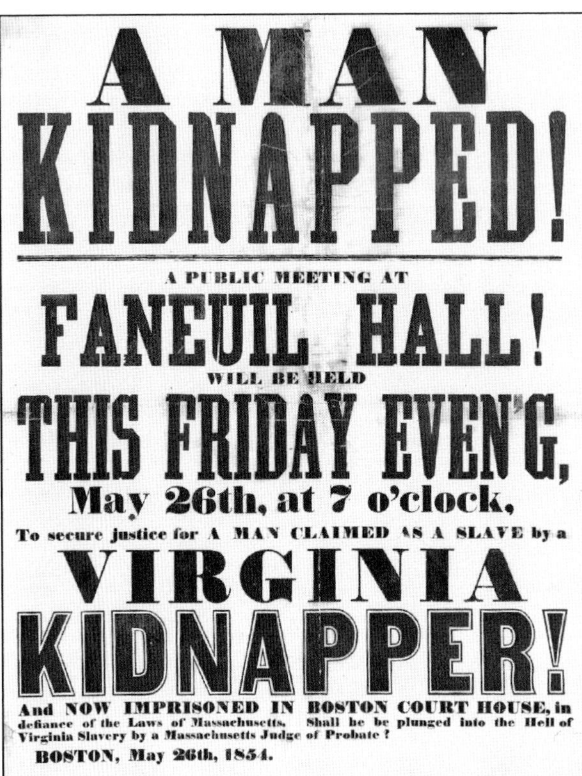

Anthony Burns was born into slavery in Virginia in 1834. He escaped to Massachusetts in 1854 and found work in Boston, but he was arrested on May 24 and tried under the Fugitive Slave Act of 1850. The trial attracted widespread attention from abolitionists, some of whom met in Faneuil Hall to devise a plan to free Burns. (BPL.)

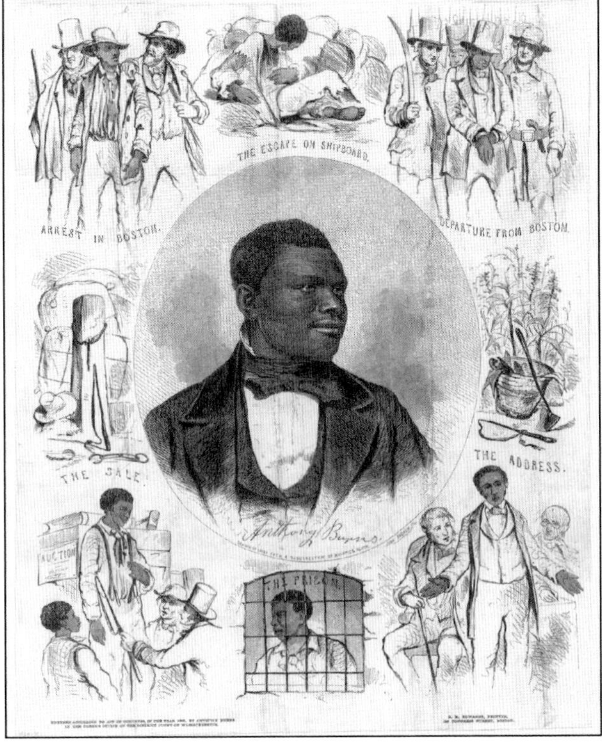

On the evening of May 26, a group of Bostonians broke into the courthouse where Burns was held. A riot ensued, and a US marshal was killed; Burns remained in custody. He was convicted and sent back to Virginia on June 2, only to return north after a church group purchased his freedom. Burns went on to attend Oberlin College and become a minister, but he died of tuberculosis at the age of 28. (LOC.)

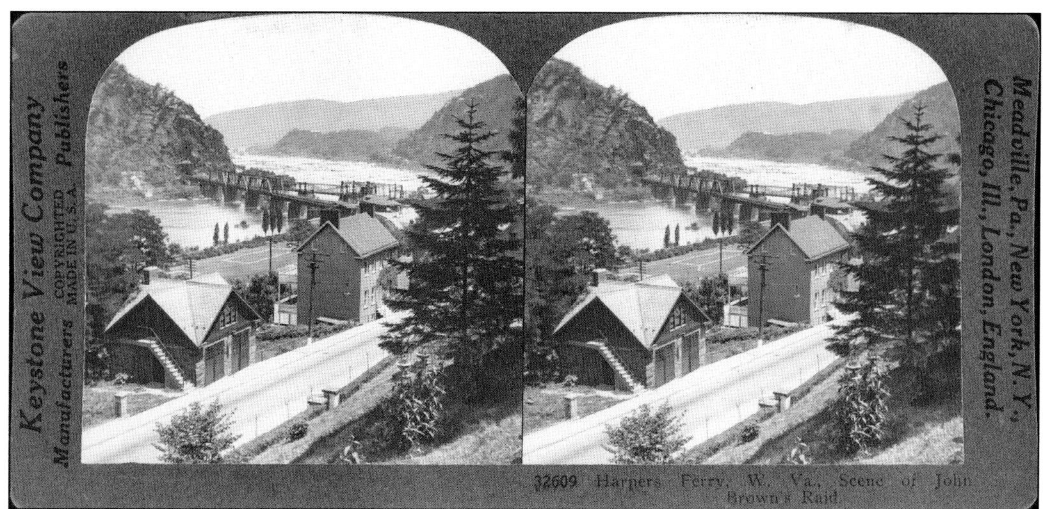

Bostonians crowded into Faneuil Hall on December 2, 1909, to memorialize John Brown on the 50th anniversary of his execution. Brown was an abolitionist who led a raid on a federal arsenal in Harpers Ferry, West Virginia, in October 1859 with a goal of encouraging a slave rebellion. The plan failed, and Brown was captured, tried, and hanged. (LOC.)

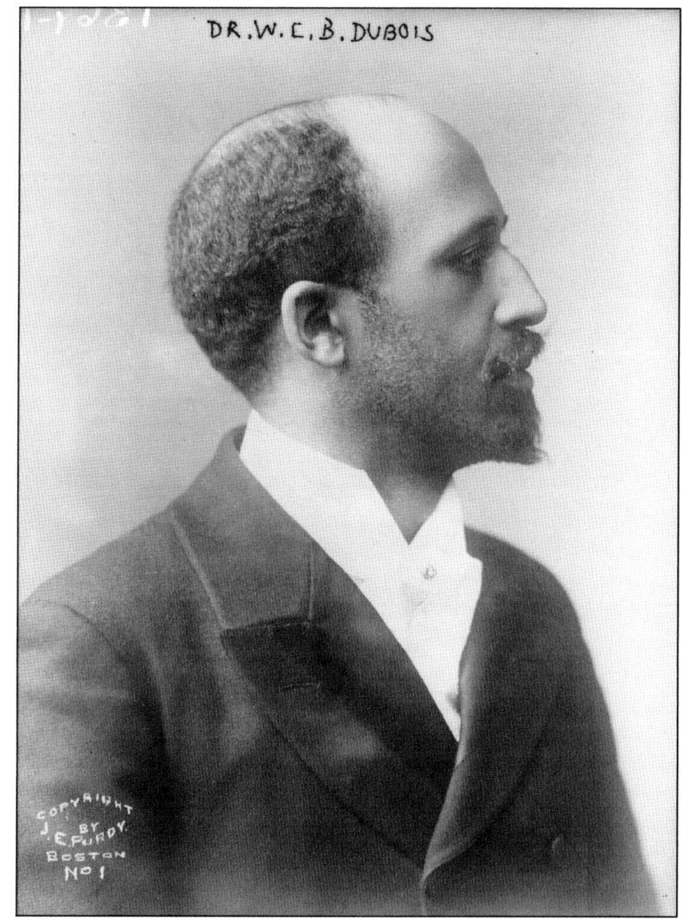

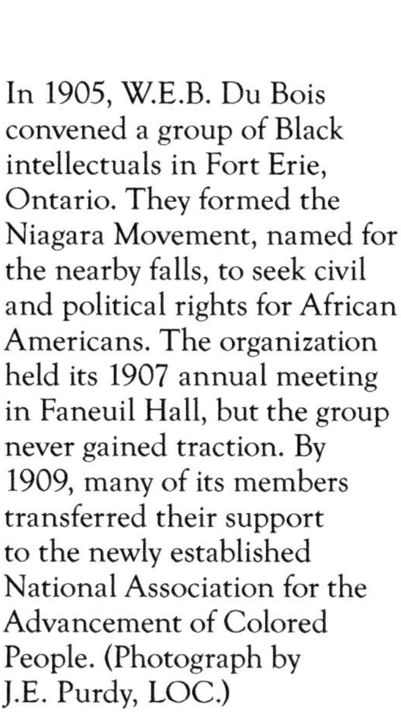

In 1905, W.E.B. Du Bois convened a group of Black intellectuals in Fort Erie, Ontario. They formed the Niagara Movement, named for the nearby falls, to seek civil and political rights for African Americans. The organization held its 1907 annual meeting in Faneuil Hall, but the group never gained traction. By 1909, many of its members transferred their support to the newly established National Association for the Advancement of Colored People. (Photograph by J.E. Purdy, LOC.)

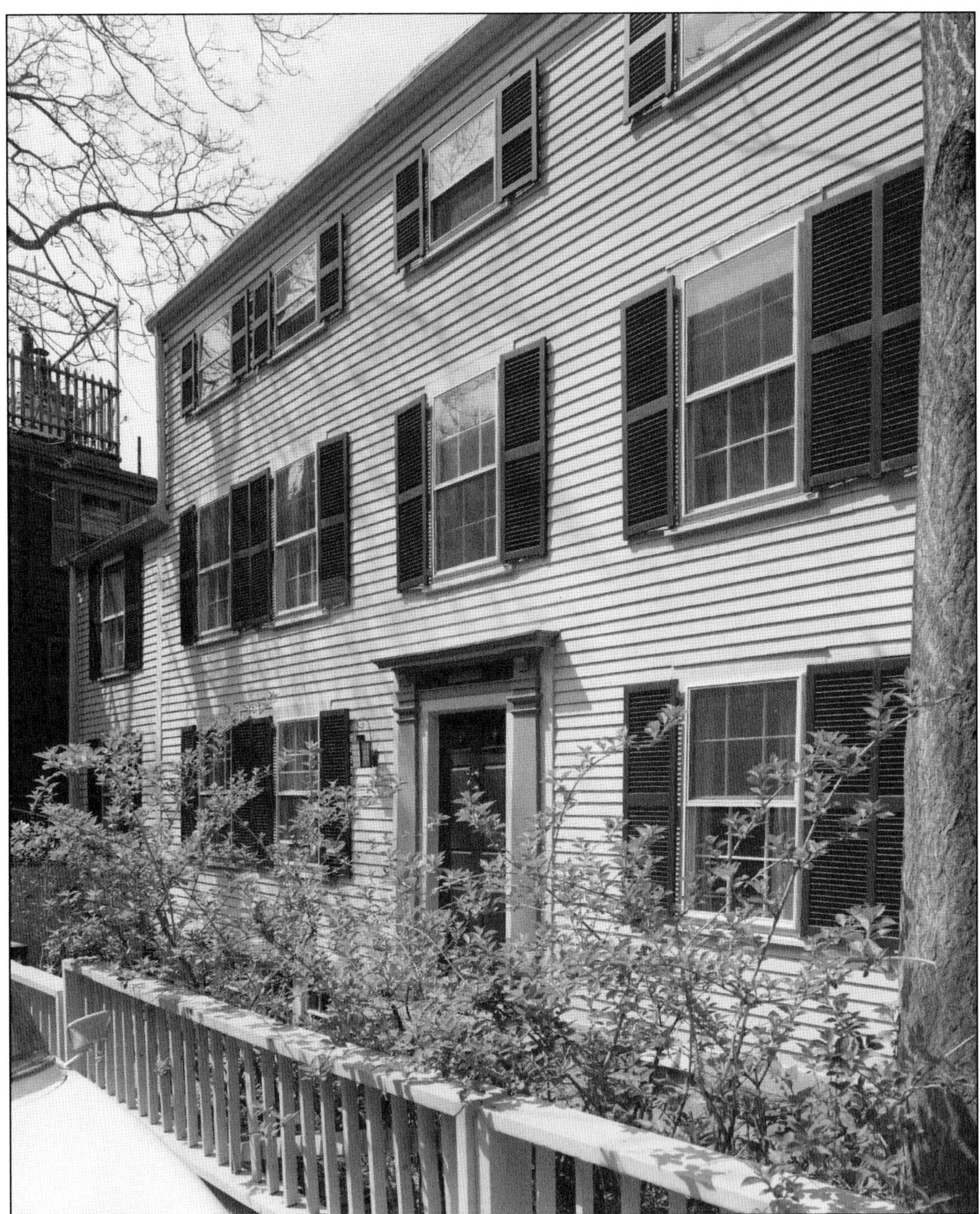

Born in 1816, William Cooper Nell was an abolitionist and historian who grew up in Boston's free Black community centered on Beacon Hill. When he was a 13-year-old student at the segregated Abiel Smith School, he and two of his classmates were honored for excellence in scholarship. White students attended an awards dinner at Faneuil Hall, but the Black students were barred from the event. Nell got inside anyway by switching places with one of the servers and confronted an official about his exclusion from the ceremony. He reportedly vowed, "God willing, I will do my best to hasten the day when the color of the skin will be no barrier to equal school rights." And thanks to his leadership, the state desegregated public schools in 1855. From 1850 to 1857, Nell lived on Smith Court (shown here), where he sheltered freedom seekers. (LOC.)

When the African Meeting House opened on Smith Court on Beacon Hill in 1806, the new church was called the "Black Faneuil Hall" because it served as the religious, cultural, and political center for Boston's Black community. The meetinghouse is shown here around 1933, after the building was sold to a Jewish congregation. (LOC.)

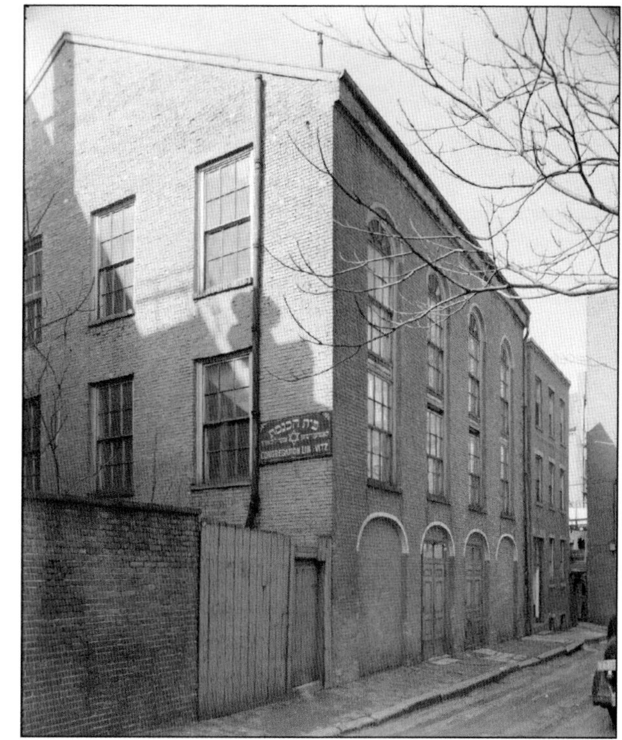

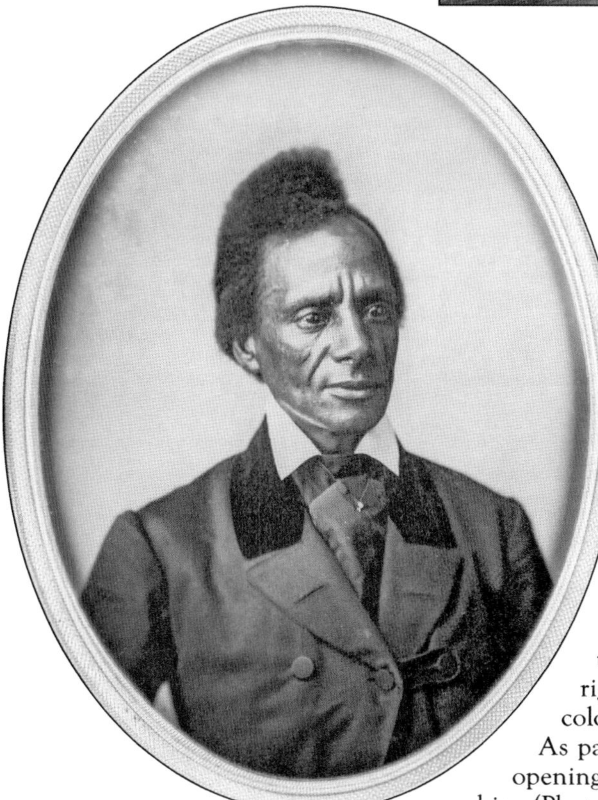

Abolitionist Charles Lenox Remond was booed off the stage when he tried to address a crowd at Faneuil Hall in 1842. Years later, in 1870, thousands of Bostonians celebrated the passage of the 15th Amendment, which granted the right to vote to all men, regardless of "race, color, or previous condition of servitude." As part of the festivities, Remond delivered opening remarks in the hall that once rejected him. (Photograph by S. Broadbent, BPL.)

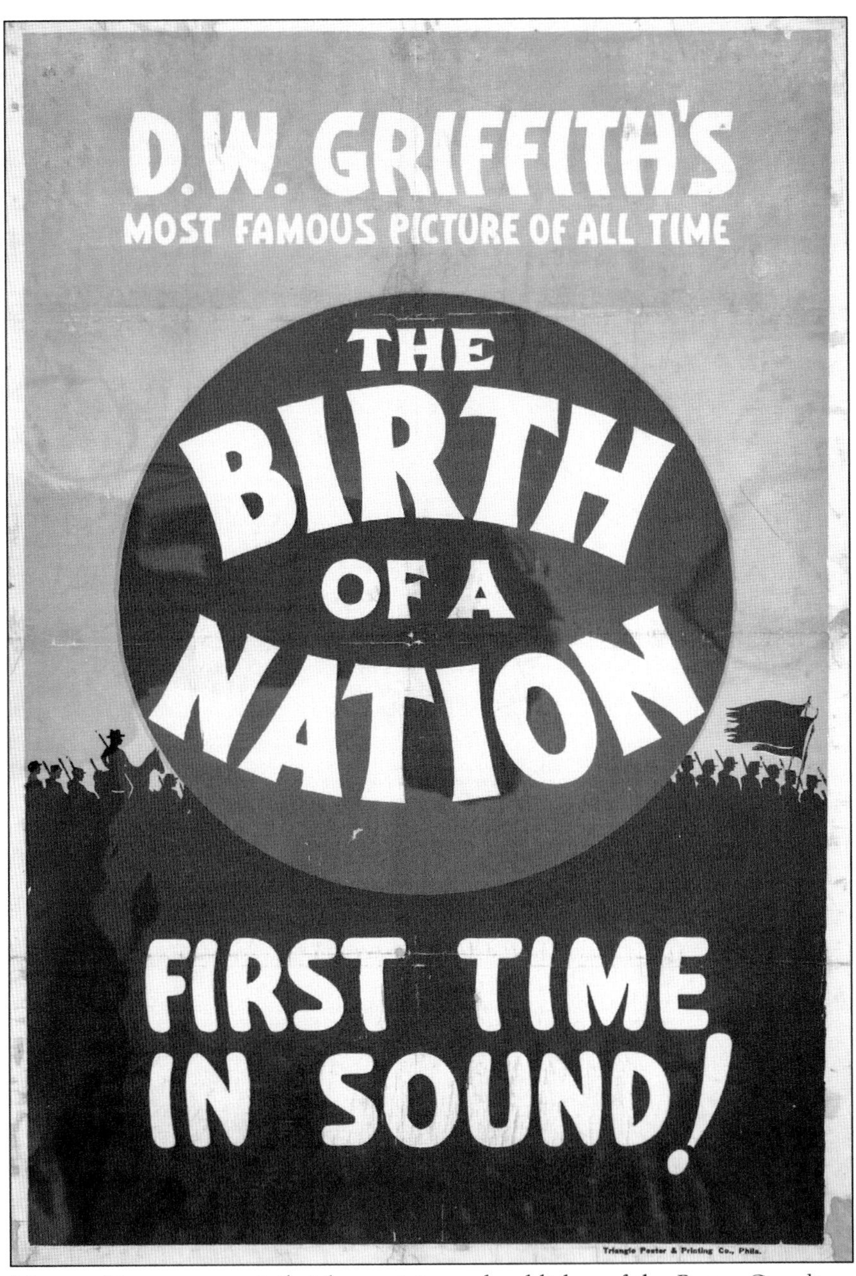

William Monroe Trotter was a civil rights activist and publisher of the *Boston Guardian*, a weekly newspaper for Boston's African American community. He made headlines himself in 1915 at a screening of *The Birth of a Nation*, D.W. Griffith's film that glorified the Ku Klux Klan. Trotter was arrested at a protest at the theater and charged with disorderly conduct. Speaking before a multiracial crowd of 1,500 people at Faneuil Hall the next day, he called the movie "an incentive to great racial hatred here in Boston." Despite marches and meetings over the next few weeks, the theater continued to screen the film. But Trotter's actions are considered the first Black mass protest movement of the new century. Some 20 years later, Trotter helped establish Crispus Attucks Day—first celebrated on March 5, 1934—to commemorate the contributions of Black and Indigenous people in the American Revolution. (LOC.)

The SS *Atlantic* was sailing from Liverpool to New York City with about 975 people onboard when it sank off the coast of Nova Scotia early in the morning of April 1, 1873. At least 535 people died in the accident. Survivors were brought to Faneuil Hall, where they received aid—and breakfast—before continuing to New York via rail. A monument marks the mass grave for the *Atlantic*'s victims in Prospect, Nova Scotia. (Photograph by Allen Fraser.)

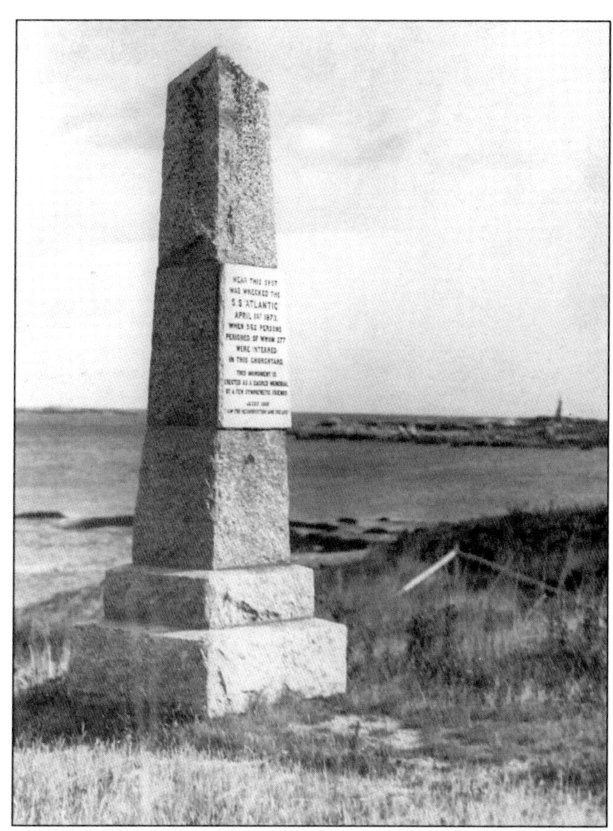

George W. Parker hosted an annual Christmas dinner for indigent men in Faneuil Hall in the 1880s. A reformed gambler, Parker established the Helping Hand Mission after renouncing his "30 heedless years of dishonesty and vice," according to an 1889 story in the *Boston Globe*. As part of the mission's outreach, Parker invited as many as 500 men for a turkey dinner, followed by religious services and a temperance pledge. (LOC.)

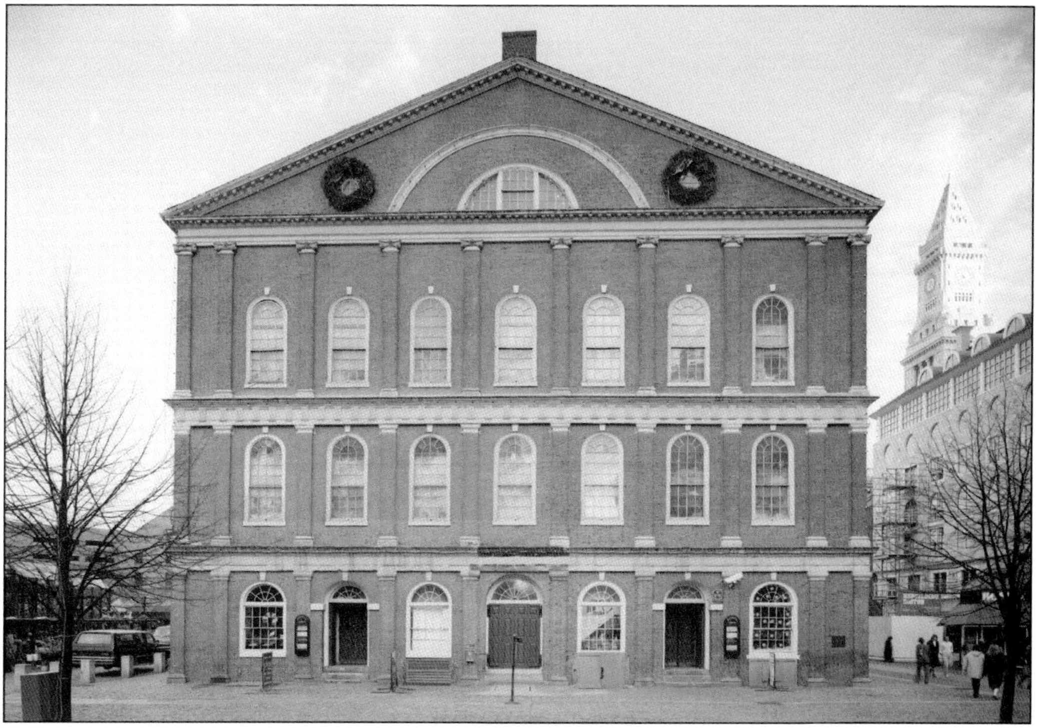

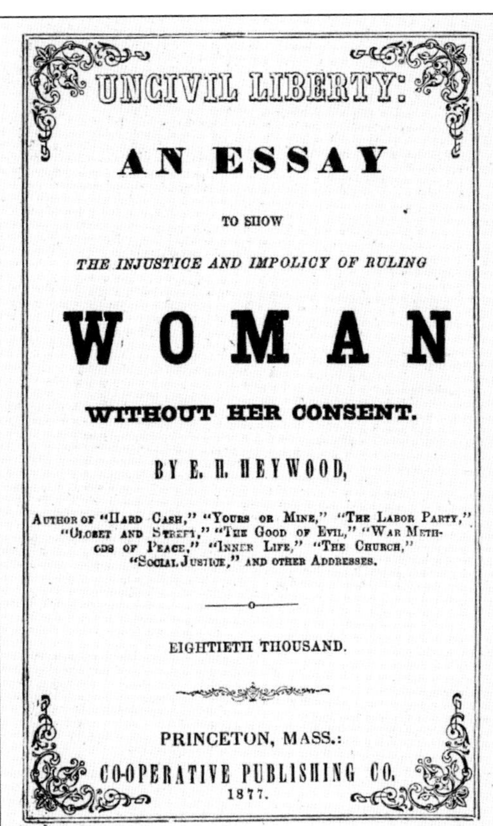

UNCIVIL LIBERTY:

AN ESSAY

TO SHOW

THE INJUSTICE AND IMPOLICY OF RULING

WOMAN

WITHOUT HER CONSENT.

BY E. H. HEYWOOD,

AUTHOR OF "HARD CASH," "YOURS OR MINE," "THE LABOR PARTY," "CLOSET AND STREET," "THE GOOD OF EVIL," "WAR METHODS OF PEACE," "INNER LIFE," "THE CHURCH," "SOCIAL JUSTICE," AND OTHER ADDRESSES.

EIGHTIETH THOUSAND.

PRINCETON, MASS.:
CO-OPERATIVE PUBLISHING CO.
1877.

Ezra Heywood and his wife, Angela Tilton, were activists who published pamphlets supporting a woman's freedom to choose in matters of love and marriage. Circulating these publications by mail put Heywood in violation of the Comstock Act, an 1873 anti-obscenity law, and he was arrested in November 1877. After he was sentenced to two years in prison, some 5,000 supporters showed up at Faneuil Hall at a so-called Indignation Meeting in August 1878. Heywood received a presidential pardon that year. (Harvard University.)

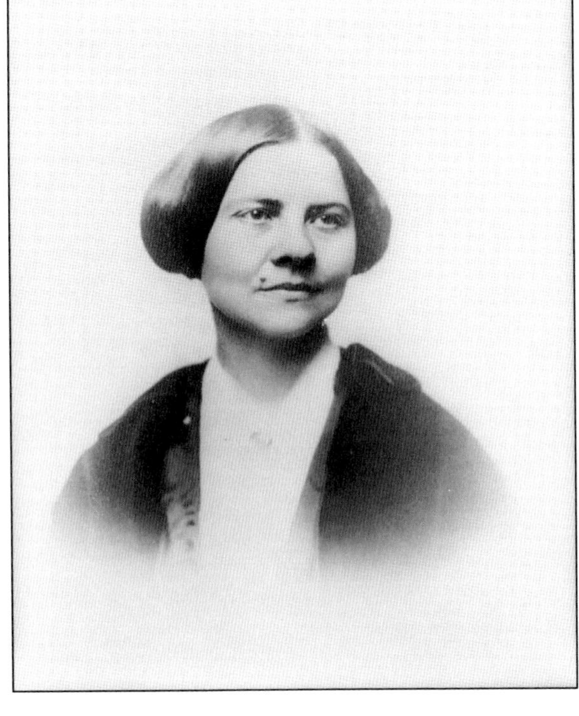

Lucy Stone was a suffragist and abolitionist born near West Brookfield, Massachusetts, in 1818. She attended Oberlin College and became the first woman in her home state to earn a bachelor's degree. Stone and her husband, Henry Blackwell (Stone defied gender norms of the day by not taking Blackwell's name), founded a newspaper called the *Women's Journal* in 1870 to spread the word about the women's vote. (LOC.)

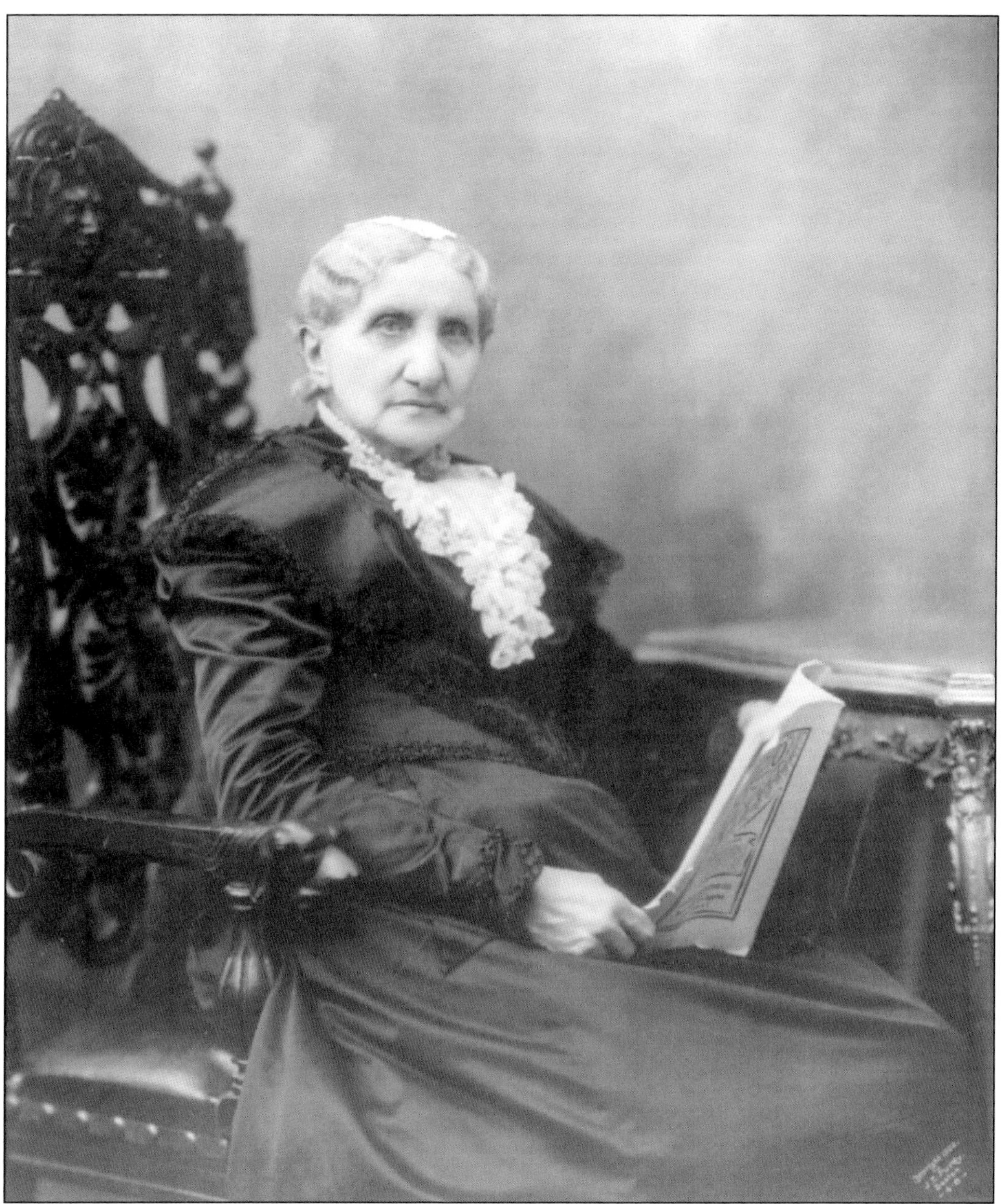

One hundred years after the Boston Tea Party, thousands of men and women streamed into Faneuil Hall on December 15, 1873, to support the right of women to vote. Speakers at the New England Women's Tea Party were a who's-who of social reformers, including Mary A. Livermore (pictured here), Lucy Stone, Wendell Phillips, Bronson Alcott, and Julia Ward Howe. Livermore was an editor of the *Woman's Journal* and a cofounder of the Massachusetts Woman Suffrage Association. She compared the suffragists to the revolutionaries who spoke in the Great Hall a century earlier: "The Woman Suffrage movement has been often spoken of as a new movement. It is, but it is based on old principles—the principles that were fought for and maintained on the field of battle nearly a hundred years ago." (Photograph by J.E. Purdy, LOC.)

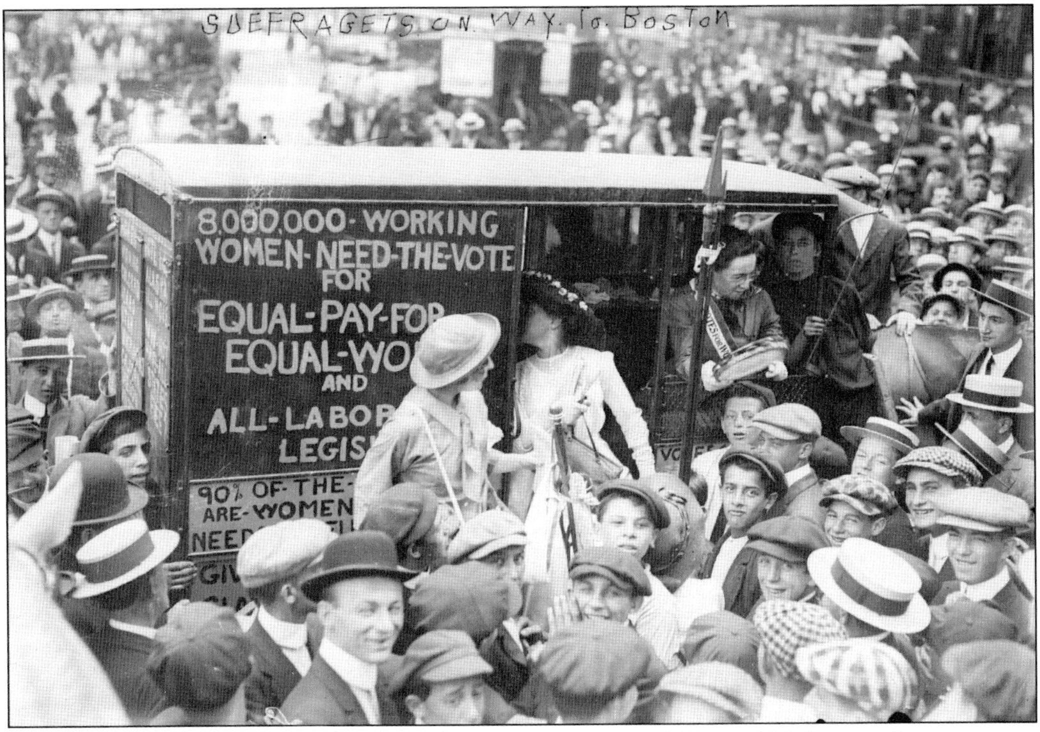

As the debate over women's right to vote became more spirited, Faneuil Hall was a frequent stage for those supporting women's suffrage—and those opposed. In March 1912, suffragists representing Boston and surrounding communities convened at Faneuil Hall to establish the Woman Suffrage Party of Massachusetts. But just two years later, in April 1914, an overflow crowd came to hear leaders of the anti-suffrage movement from New York and Massachusetts claim that women, in fact, did not want a voice at the ballot box. (Both, LOC.)

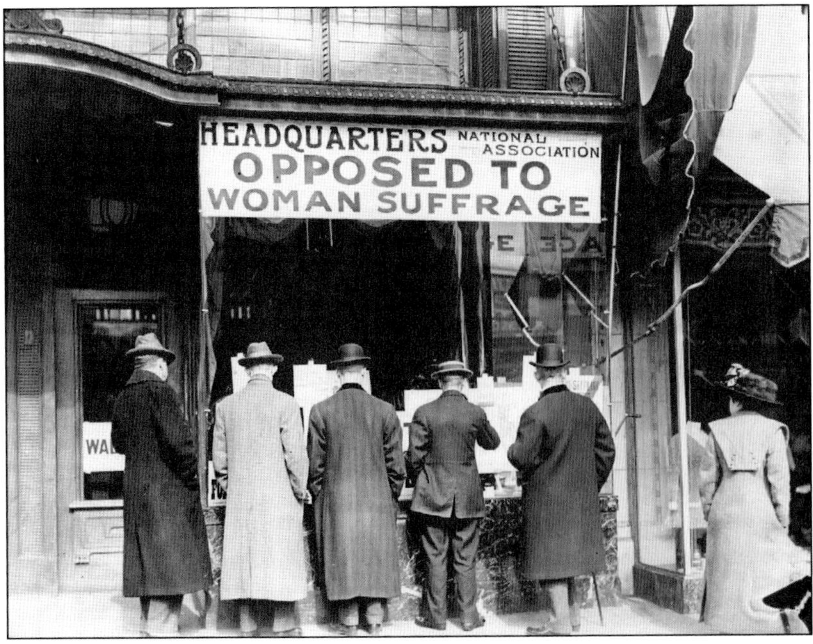

In 1834, workers came to Faneuil Hall to celebrate the formation of the Boston General Trades' Union (GTU). The GTU was founded a year earlier in New York City, where it organized one of the first labor strikes in the nation and introduced the concept of collective bargaining. Shown here is Ely Moore, the first president of GTU. (LOC.)

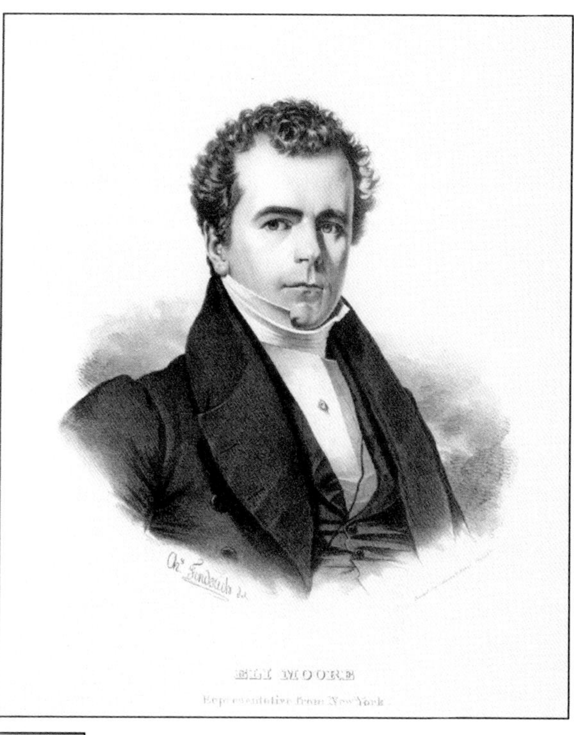

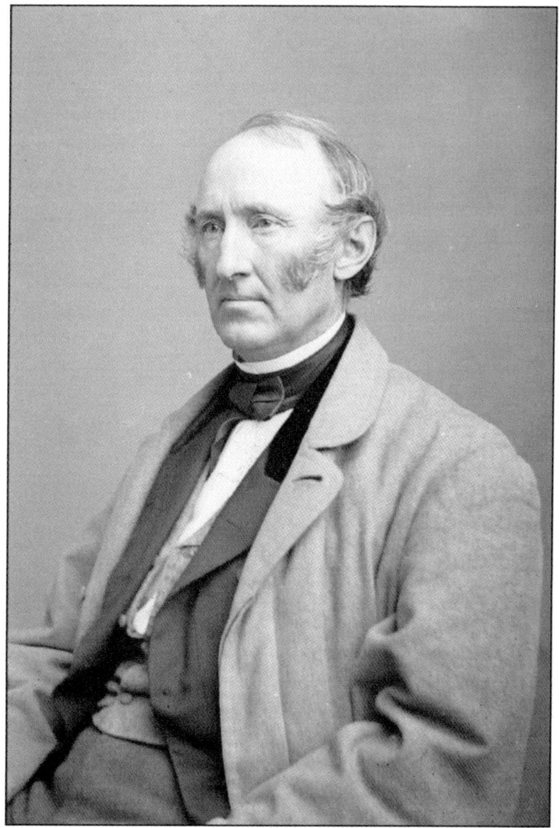

In November 1865, workers attended a rally in Faneuil Hall in support of the eight-hour workday. Abolitionist and labor rights advocate Wendell Phillips (shown here) addressed the crowd. He advised the audience to "go into the political field, and by the voice of 40,000 workmen say, 'We mean that eight hours shall be a day's work, and no man shall go into office who opposes it.'" (LOC.)

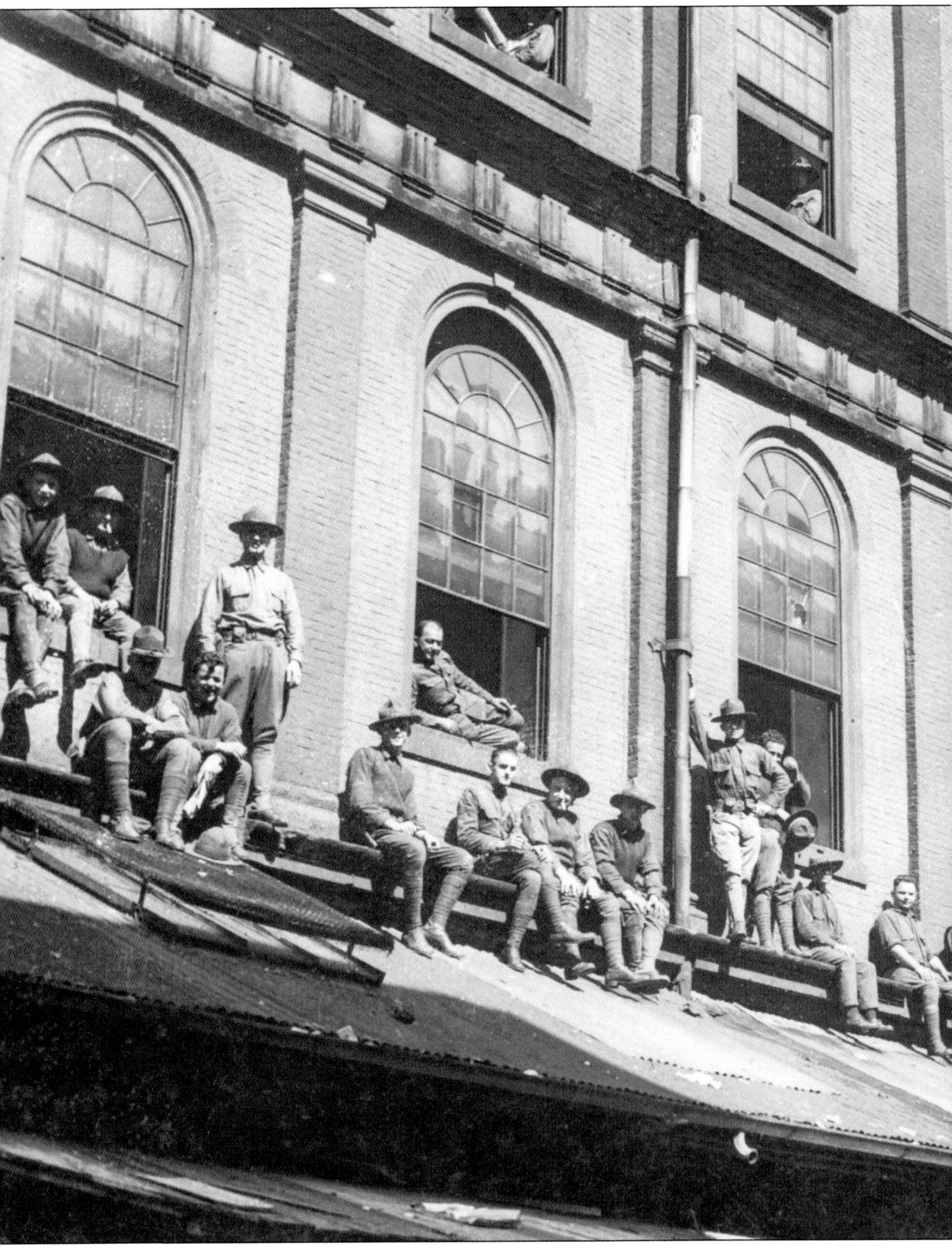

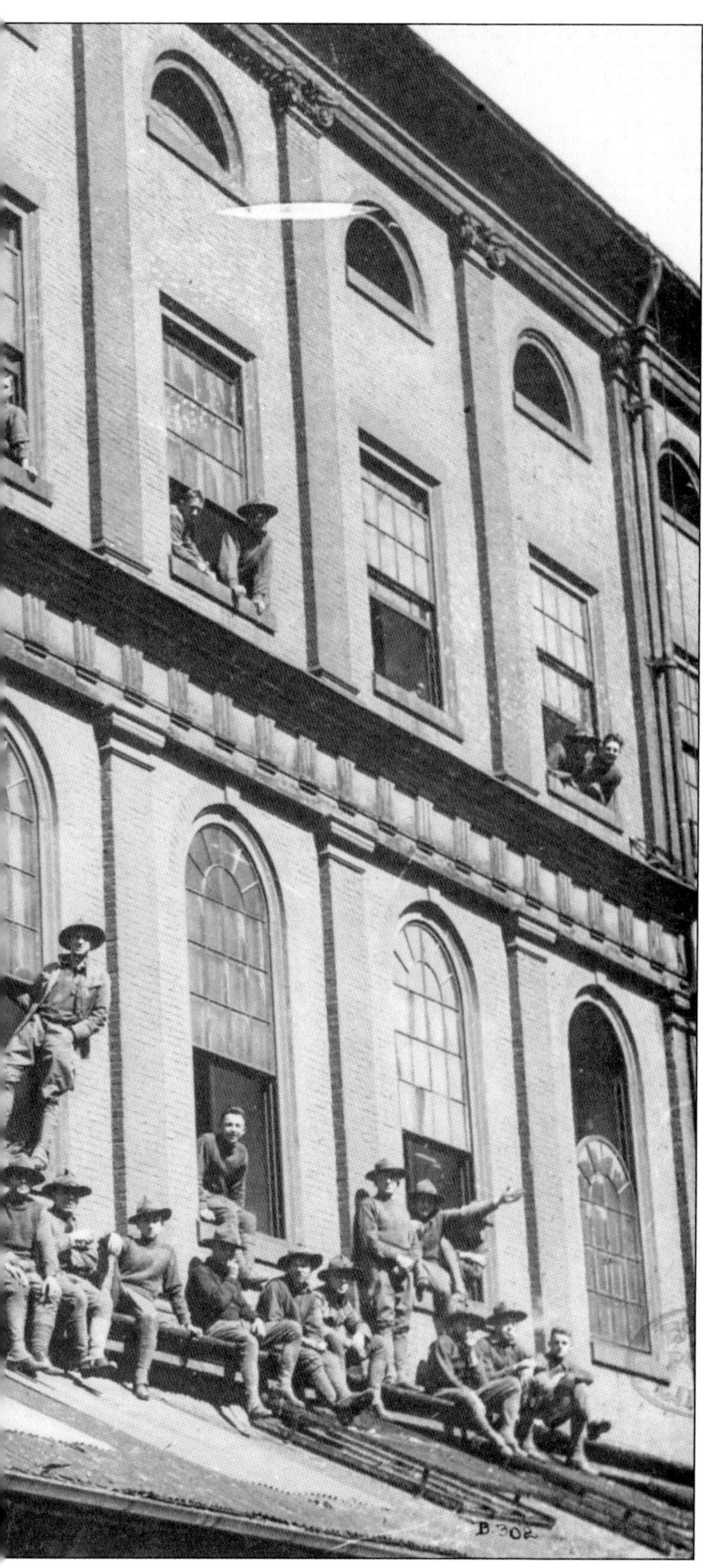

Seeking better pay and improved working conditions, Boston's newly unionized police officers voted to strike on September 9, 1919. Disorder quickly followed the walkout: Shops were looted, property was destroyed, and illegal dice games popped up. Police commissioner Edwin Curtis recruited civilian volunteers to keep the peace, and Mayor Andrew Peters called in the state guard. On Day 3 of the strike, when order had mostly been restored, Gov. Calvin Coolidge called out the full state guard and took control of the police department. "There is no right to strike against the public safety by anybody, anywhere, any time," the governor declared. The striking officers lost their jobs, their replacements got raises, and publicity from the strike propelled Coolidge from the state house to the White House. Shown here are some of the guards who set up barracks in Faneuil Hall. (BPL.)

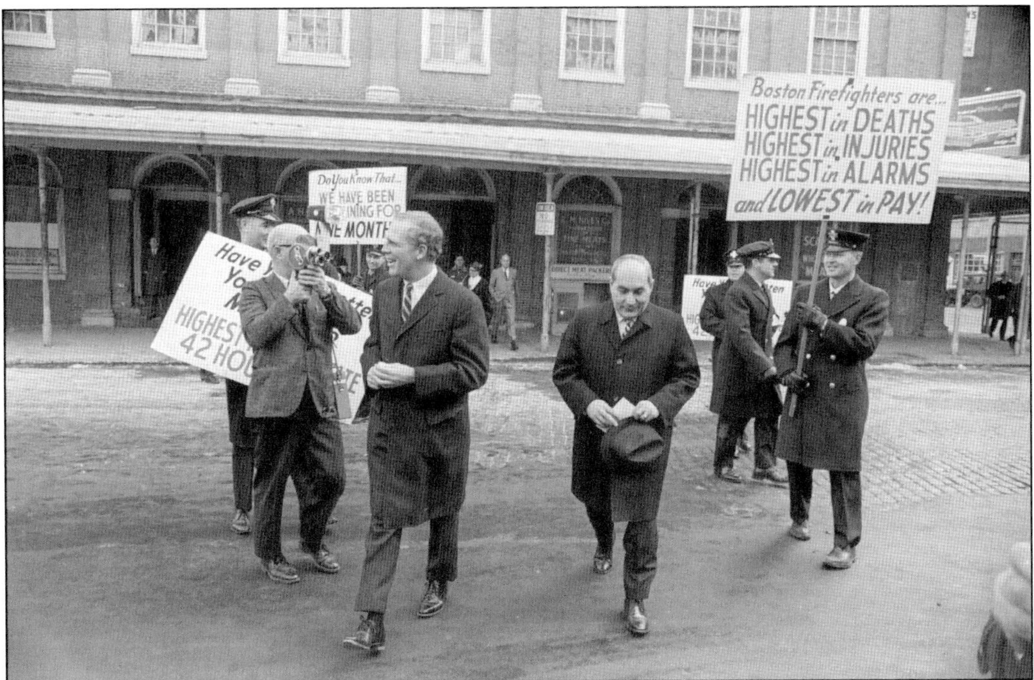

Faneuil Hall was often the go-to spot for mayoral inaugurations and state-of-the-city addresses, but things did not always go as planned. Mayor Kevin H. White and City Councilor Frederick Langone had to dodge picketing firefighters after White's state-of-the-city speech on January 6, 1969 (above). And three years later, on January 3, 1972, Boston police officers picketed outside Faneuil Hall during the inauguration ceremony for White's second term (below). About 1,000 officers formed a double ring around the building and booed White. "The mayor was tight-lipped and seemed disturbed by the demonstration," according to the *Boston Globe*. (Both, BPL.)

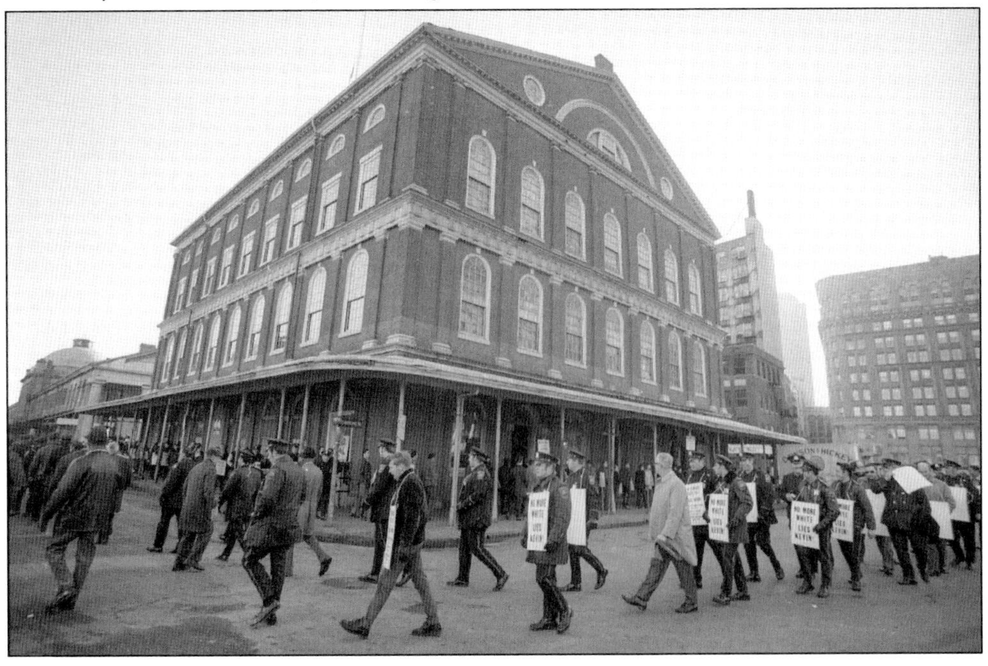

Starting with the memorial for its benefactor, Faneuil Hall has been the site for funerals, wakes, and eulogies for prominent Americans. In 1826, Daniel Webster eulogized John Adams and Thomas Jefferson, who both died on July 4 of that year. Boston Massacre victims Crispus Attucks and James Caldwell lay in state in the hall in 1770. So did diplomat Anson Burlingame (1820–1870), orator Wendell Phillips (1811–1884), and Boston mayor Thomas M. Menino (1942–2014), shown here. (BOS.)

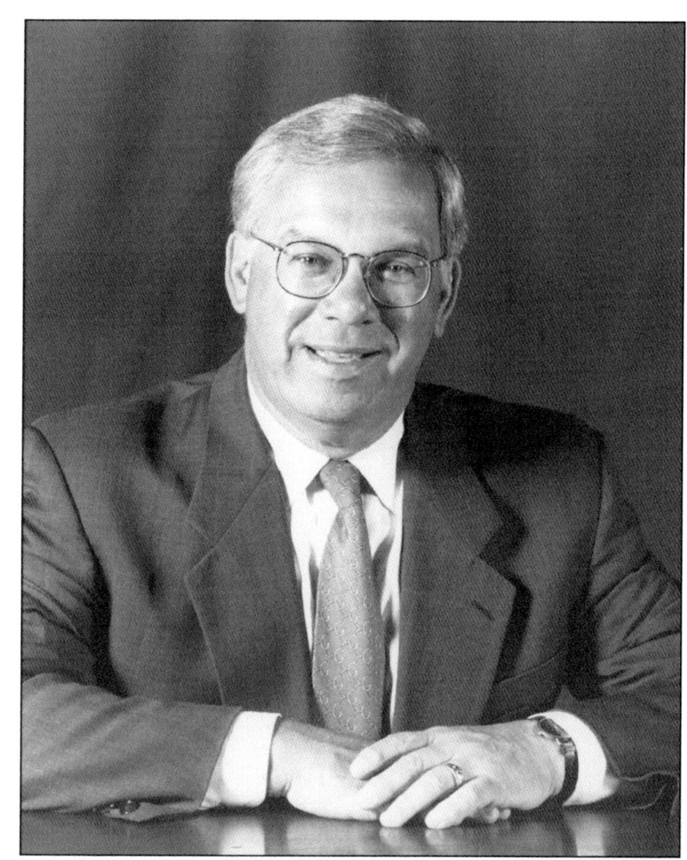

Some 200 guests attended a dinner at Faneuil Hall in honor of the Philippines president Corazon Aquino, who was visiting Boston. The September 1986 event was reportedly the first public dinner in the venue since 1852. Shown here are Aquino (left) and Boston mayor Raymond L. Flynn. (BOS.)

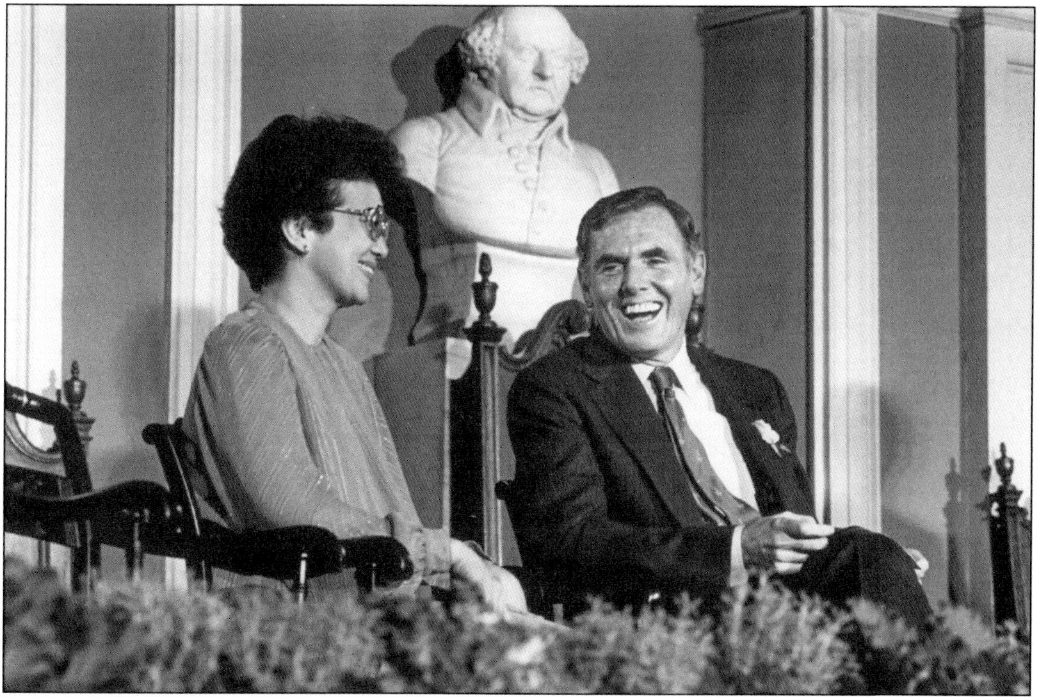

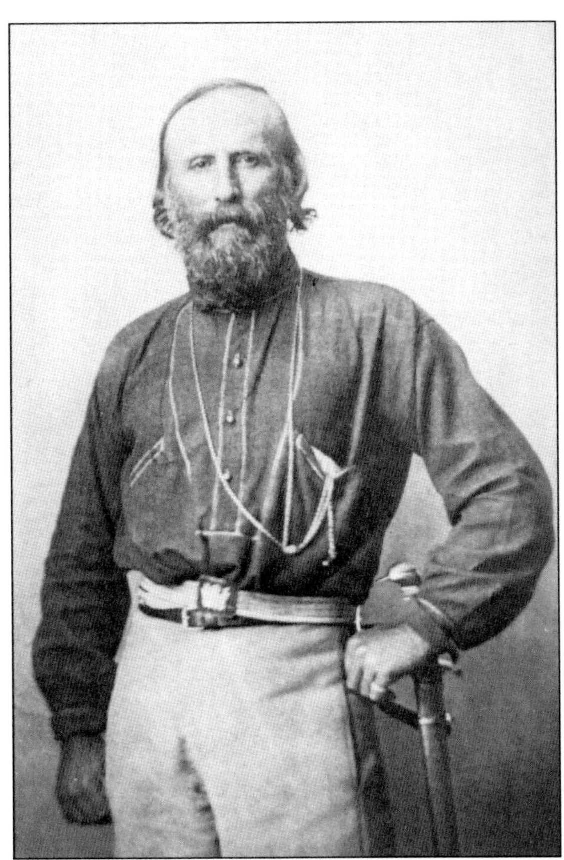

Members of Boston's Italian community gathered in the Great Hall in 1878 to mourn the death of Victor Emmanuel II, who was the first king of unified Italy. They came together again to honor revolutionary Giuseppe Garibaldi (pictured here), who died in 1882. More than 100 years later, Thomas M. Menino was elected as Boston's first Italian American mayor and delivered his inaugural address at Faneuil Hall in 1994. (LOC.)

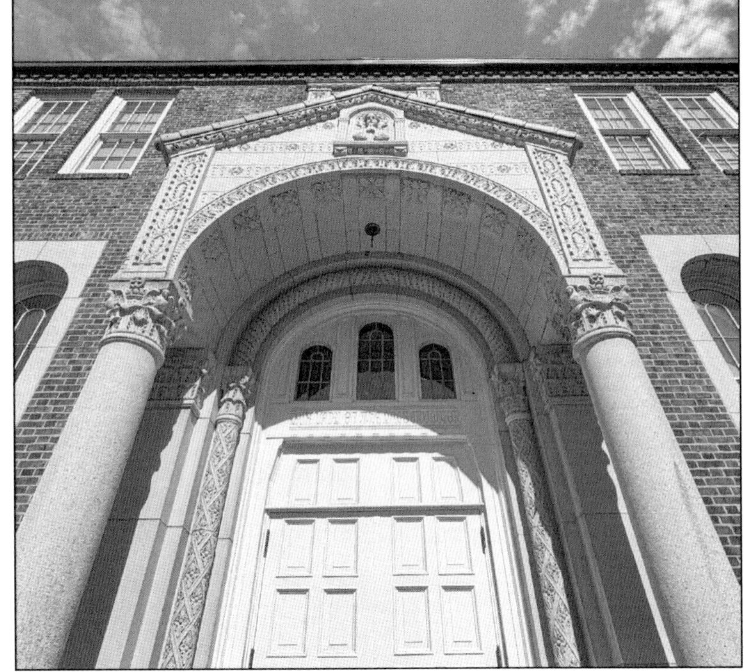

In 2005, the Archdiocese of Boston abruptly shut down Our Lady of the Presentation School in Brighton, locking out students and teachers days before graduation. City officials stepped in and moved the ceremony to Faneuil Hall. "The kids had a traumatic experience," Mayor Thomas M. Menino said. "What we're doing today is just showing those kids there are some people in our community who want to honor them for the great work they did." (Author's collection.)

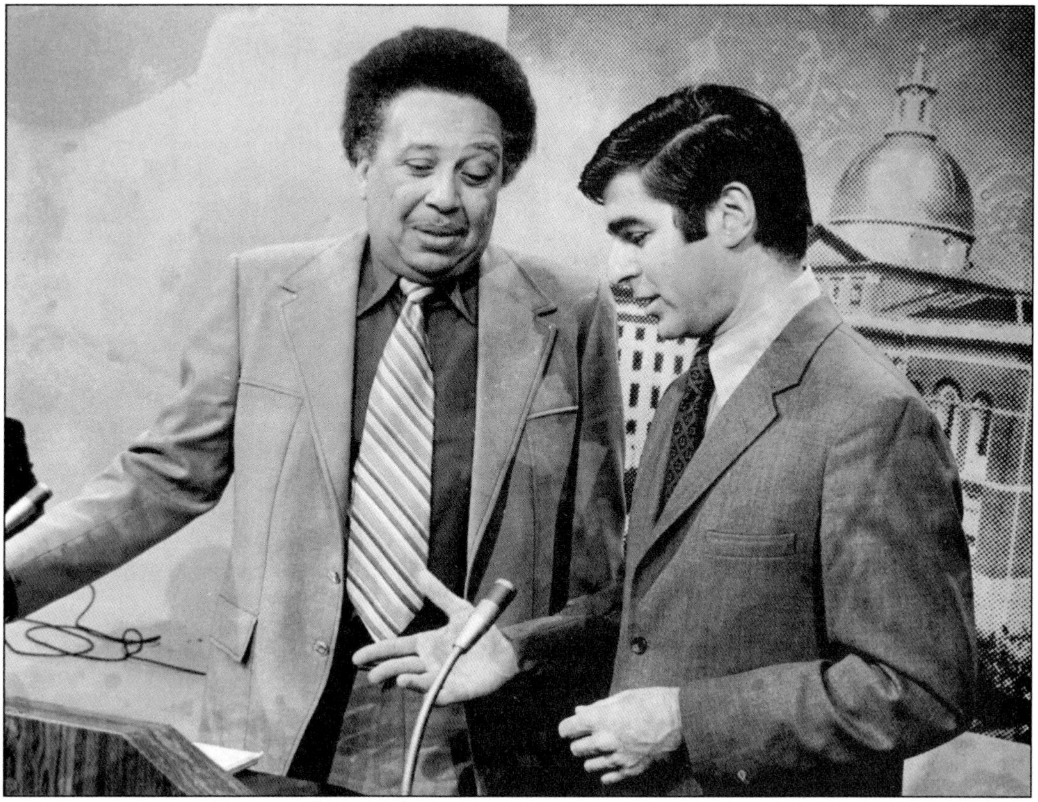

The US Commission on Civil Rights held hearings at Faneuil Hall in October 1966 to investigate inequities in the Boston Public Schools. Paul Parks, who later became the state's education secretary, acknowledged the disconnect of hosting the meeting in a hall dedicated to freedom. "It is ironic," he said, "that these freedoms cannot be obtained by our children who happen to be Negro." Parks (left) is shown here with Gov. Michael S. Dukakis around 1971. (Northeastern University.)

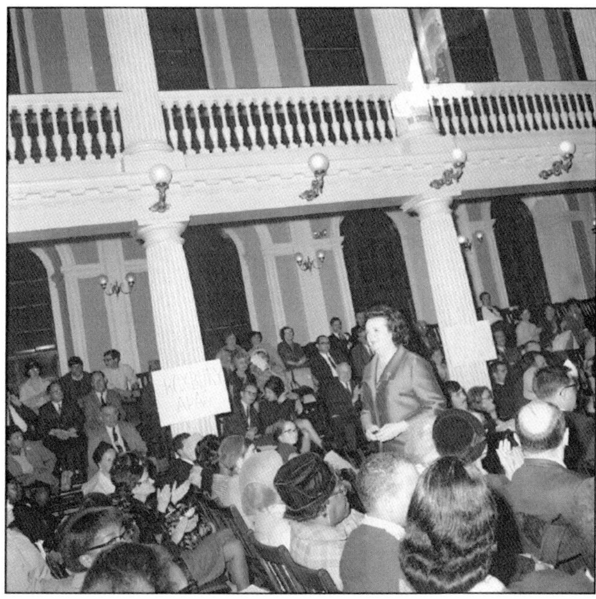

Louise Day Hicks was a Boston politician who was best known for her opposition to the desegregation of the city's public schools through busing. She ran for mayor in 1967 against Kevin White and is shown here in Faneuil Hall during her campaign. White defeated Hicks to win his first of four terms as mayor, but she remained on the political scene. (BPL.)

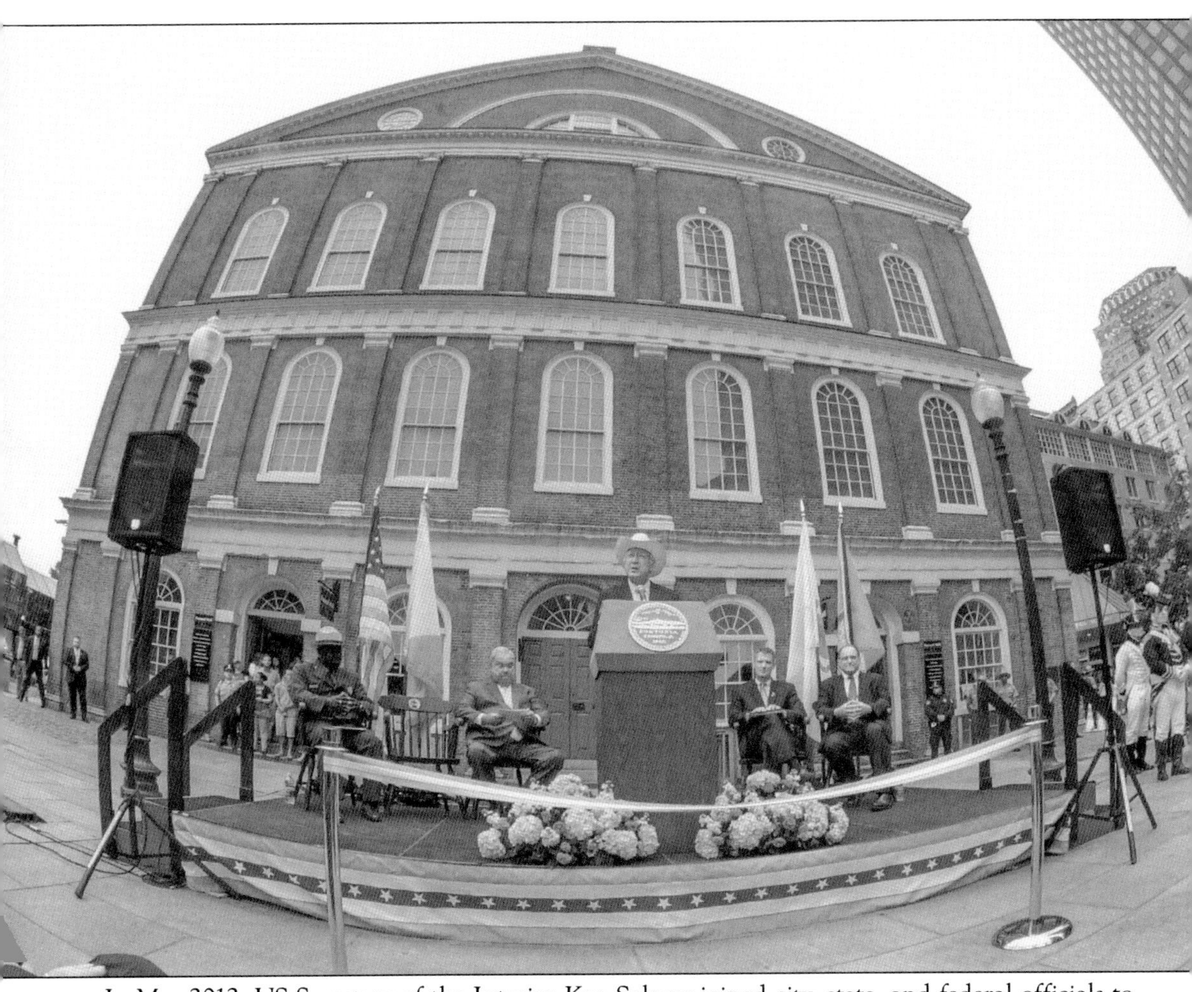

In May 2012, US Secretary of the Interior Ken Salazar joined city, state, and federal officials to dedicate Faneuil Hall's new visitors center. Shown here (left to right) are Boston National Historical Park superintendent Cassius Cash, Boston Mayor Thomas M. Menino, Salazar, Sen. Scott Brown, and Rep. Michael Capuano. Some 10 years later, US Secretary of Homeland Security Alejandro Mayorkas attended a naturalization ceremony in the Great Hall when more than 350 men and women became new US citizens. He said, in part, "This is indeed a place of history, Faneuil Hall. You are now a part of that history, and you will add to that history through your actions as United States citizens." (Photograph by Tami Heilemann, National Archives.)

Four

Artwork, Monuments, and Mementos

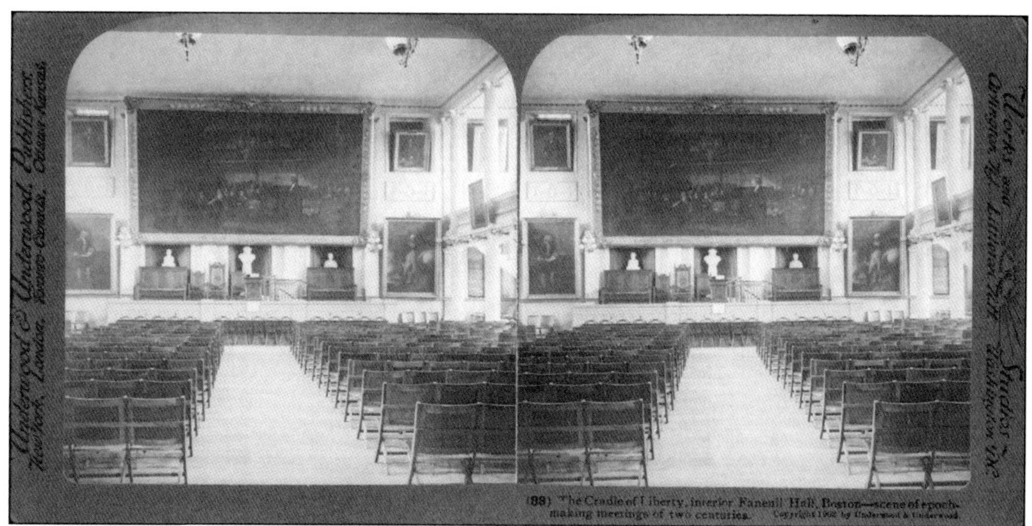

Starting with the portrait of its benefactor in the 1700s, Faneuil Hall has amassed a collection of artwork, ranging from a humble clock to a monumental painting. A few steps outside, sculptures honor mayors, a patriot, and even a celebrated basketball duo. (New York Public Library.)

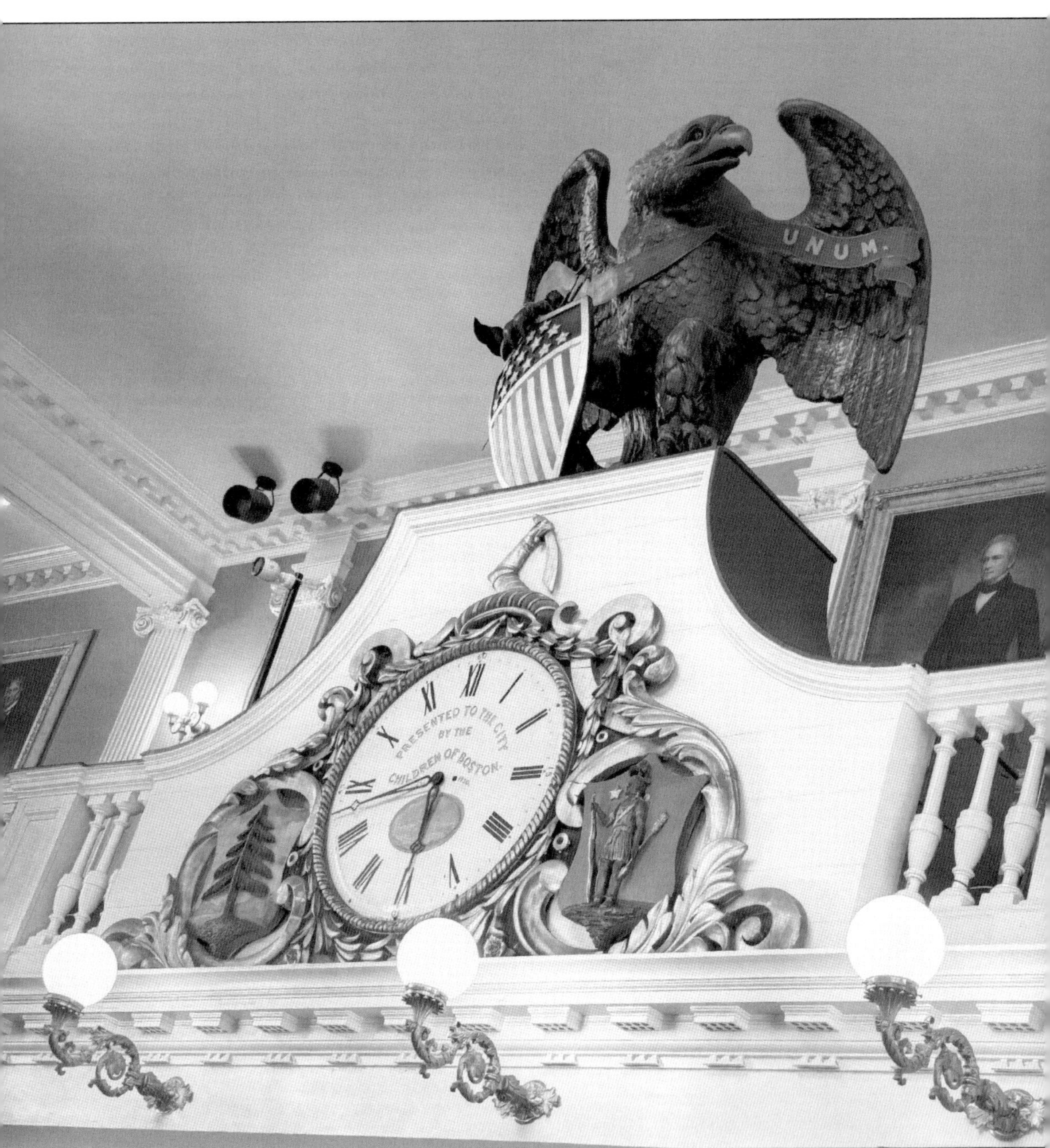

On January 14, 1850, the children of Boston presented a clock to the city for display in Faneuil Hall. Some 600 youngsters pooled their pennies to purchase the clock, dubbed the Children's Clock, which is still on display in the Great Hall. Sadly, their names are lost to history; a time capsule containing the children's names disappeared without a trace. Roxbury clock makers Howard and Davis manufactured the timepiece. An eagle perches above the clock, holding a shield and a set of arrows; a banner reading "E Pluribus Unum" is draped across its chest. The statue originally sat atop the First United States Branch Bank of Boston (designed by Charles Bulfinch) but was moved to the Great Hall in 1824 when the bank was torn down. The eagle is likely the work of Daniel Raynerd and dates from around 1798. (Author's collection.)

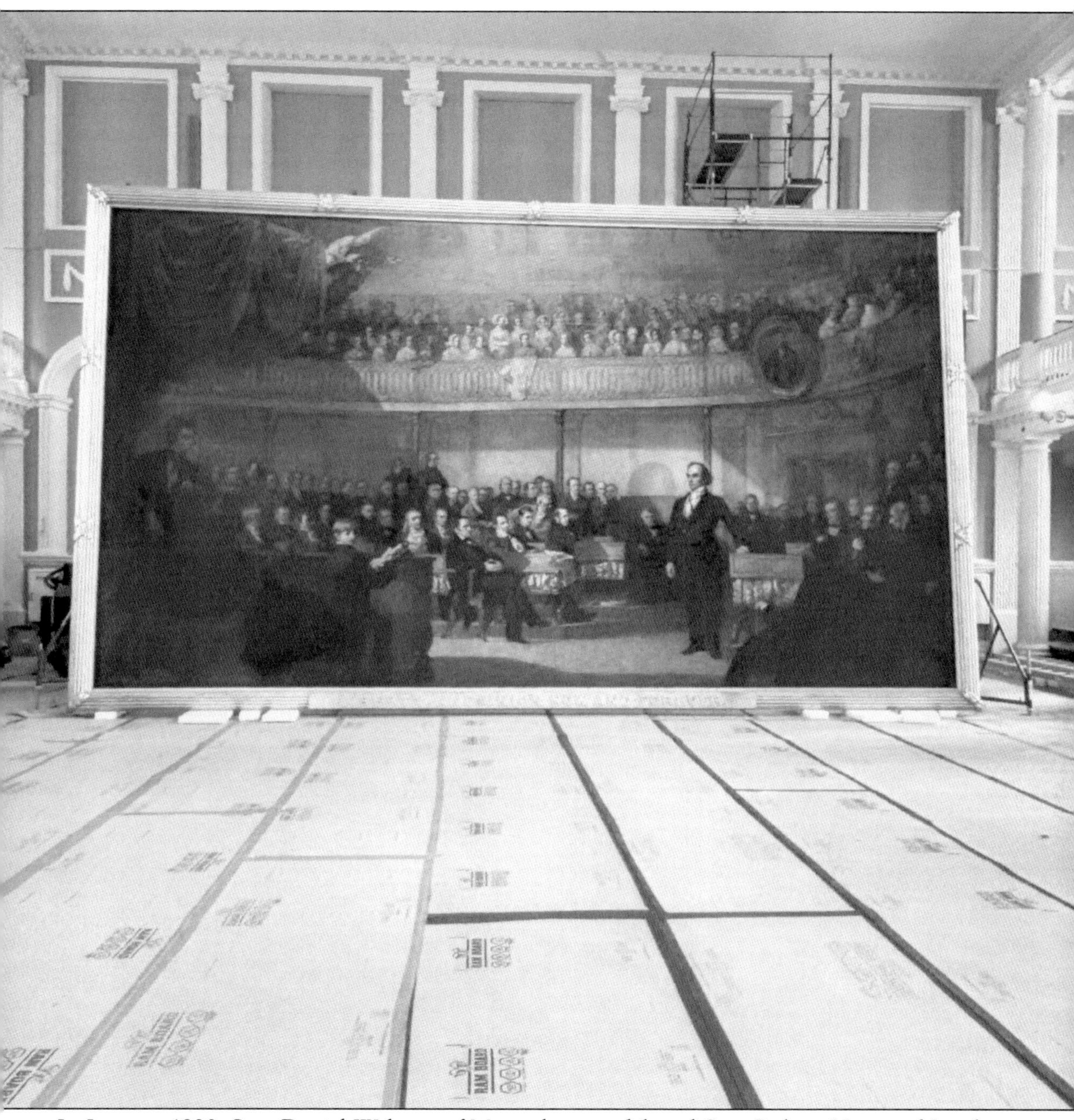

In January 1830, Sen. Daniel Webster of Massachusetts debated Sen. Robert Hayne of South Carolina in the US Senate. In an address celebrated for its eloquence, Webster dismantled the policy of nullification—a state's right to ignore federal law—supported by Southern senators at the time. Webster's speech described the US government as "made for the people, made by the people, and answerable to the people" (a description later paraphrased by Abraham Lincoln). George Healy memorialized the oratory in a massive 1851 painting called *Webster Replying to Hayne*. Healy first displayed the painting at the Boston Athenaeum, which he hoped would be the first stop on a national tour. But the painting received mixed reviews, and the 30-by-16-foot work was too big to transport easily. Enter the City of Boston, which purchased the painting in 1852 to honor Webster, who was in poor health at the time. It has hung in Faneuil Hall ever since. Shown here is the painting removed from the wall for restoration in 2025. (Author's collection.)

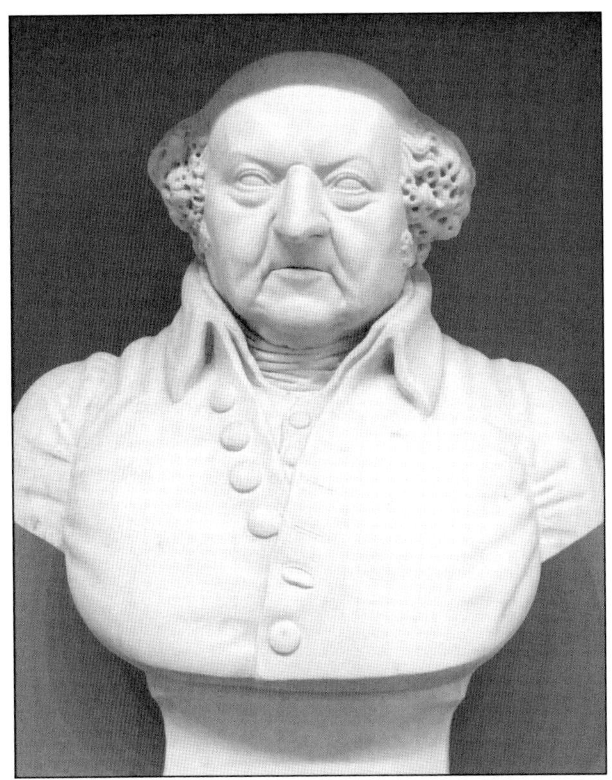

Three white marble busts sit on the rostrum of the Great Hall. French sculptor John-Baptiste Binon carved a likeness of Pres. John Adams, which was completed in 1818 (left). Accepting the honor, Adams said, "As I owe to the town of Boston all the opportunities I ever had of performing any public service, this mark of the benevolence of her Citizens, excites all my sensibility." Scotland-born sculptor John Crookshanks King created statues of Pres. John Quincy Adams in 1845 (below) and Sen. Daniel Webster in 1850. Although he described the process of sitting for the bust as "inconceivably slow," Quincy Adams indicated that "every person who had seen it pronounced it an excellent likeness." Webster was depicted wearing a toga, suggesting a connection between the American lawmaker and ancient Roman senators. (Both, National Park Service.)

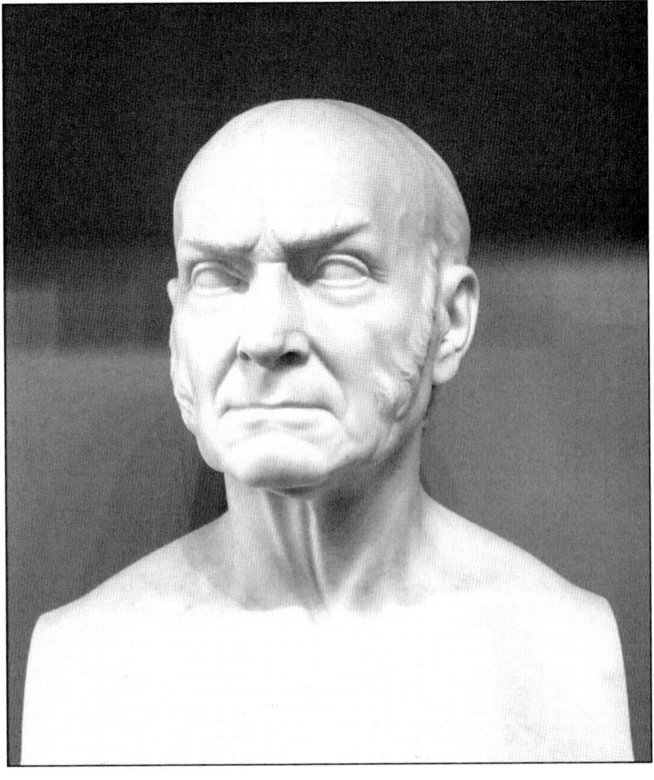

Boston town meeting members commissioned John Smibert to paint a portrait of Peter Faneuil to hang in the hall he built. The full-length oil painting depicted its subject holding the plans for Faneuil Hall. After the painting was damaged (either in the 1761 fire or during the Siege of Boston), the town hired Henry Sargent to create a copy in 1807. Sargent's painting still hangs in the Great Hall. (Author's collection.)

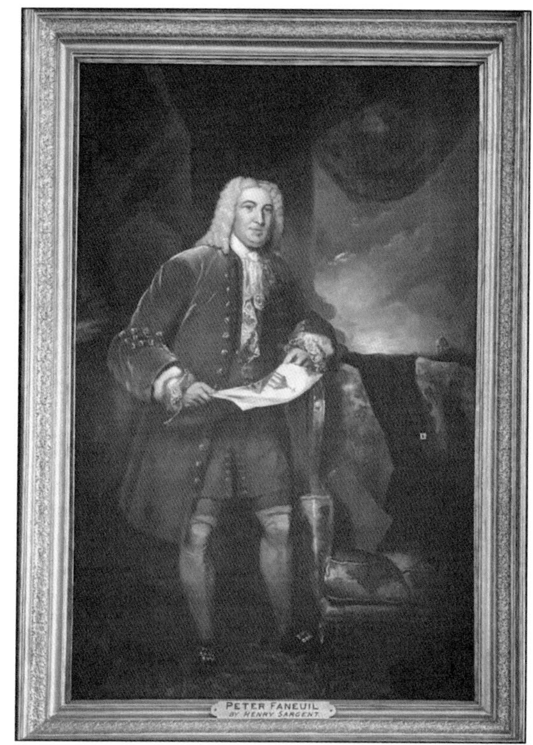

In 1876, the Boston City Council voted to move two paintings from Faneuil Hall to the newly opened Museum of Fine Arts—a painting of George Washington by Gilbert Stuart and a portrait of Joseph Warren by John Singleton Copley. The move was said to protect the paintings from the risk of fire, and the council authorized $2,000 to replace the originals with copies. Jane Stuart copied her father's painting, and an unknown artist reproduced the Copley work. (Photograph by Baldwin Coolidge, BPL.)

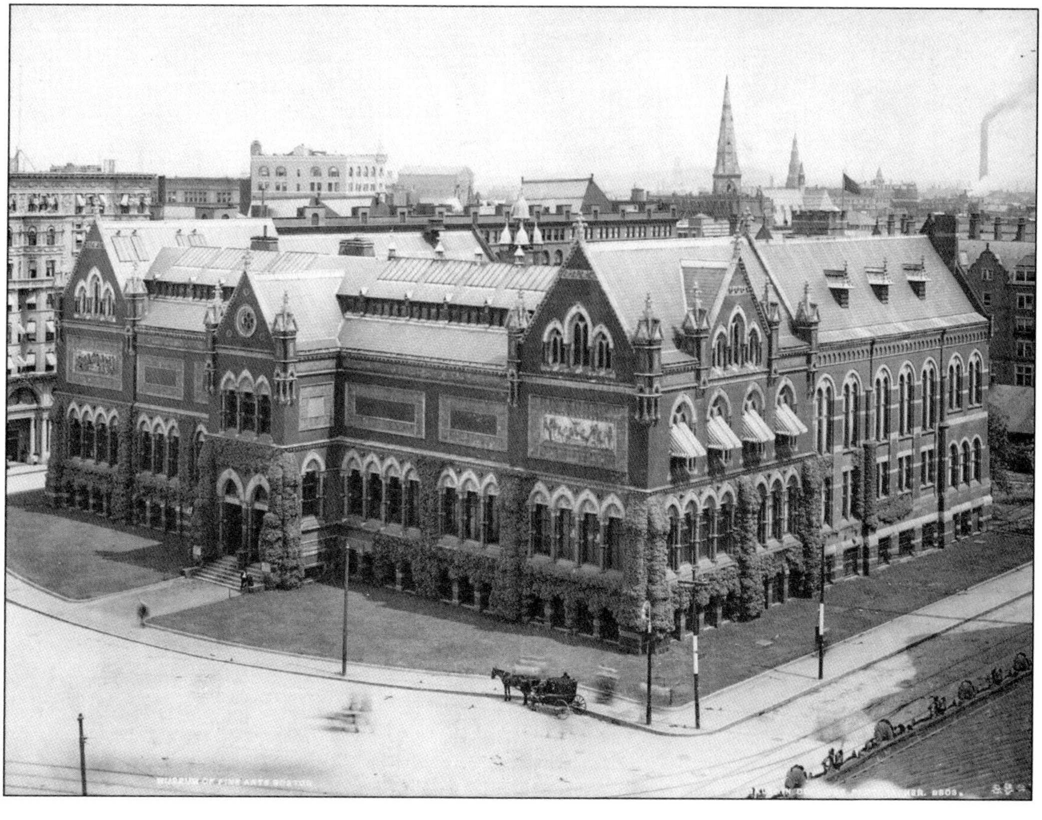

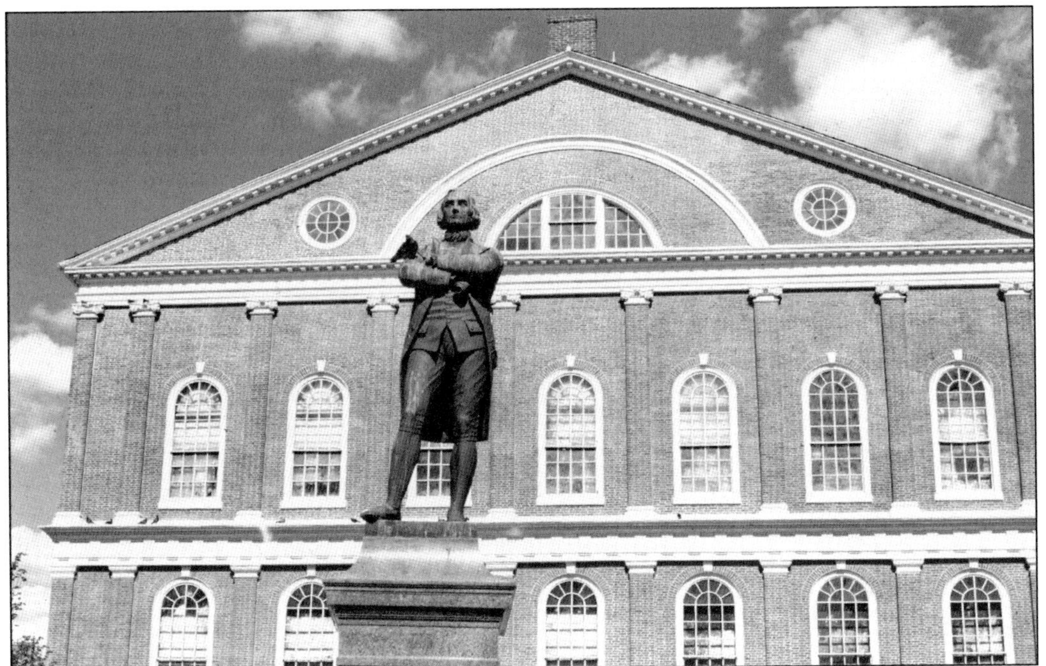

Massachusetts-born sculptor Anne Whitney created two statues of colonial leader Samuel Adams. The first version, made of marble, was presented to the US Capitol in 1876 for display in Statuary Hall. The City of Boston then commissioned Whitney to create a second likeness. (Photograph by Edmund L. Mitchell, BPL.)

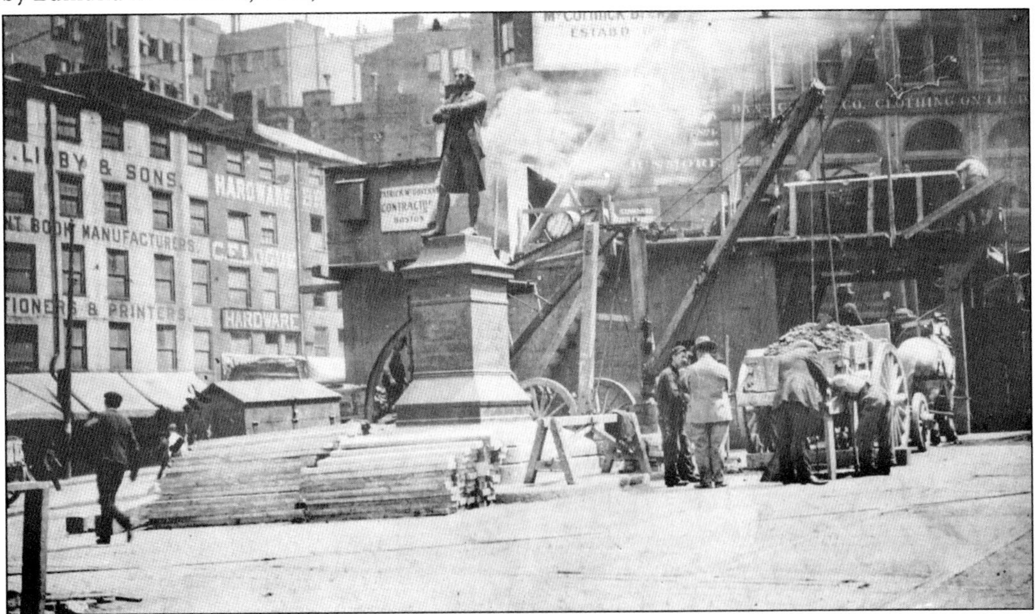

Whitney's second Adams statue, cast in bronze, was installed in Adams Square in 1880. The city named the bustling commercial district at the intersection of Brattle, Cornhill, Devonshire, and Washington Streets in 1879 to honor the revolutionary. The city moved the statue to nearby Dock Square in 1928 to improve traffic flow and moved it closer to Faneuil Hall in the 1960s to make way for Government Center. The scene here dates from the late 1800s. (BPL.)

A larger-than-life bronze statue captures former Boston mayor Kevin H. White striding toward Faneuil Hall with his coat slung over one shoulder. Created by Bolivian sculptor Pablo Eduardo, the 10-foot likeness was installed in 2006 and is shown here with Boston City Hall in the background. (Author's collection.)

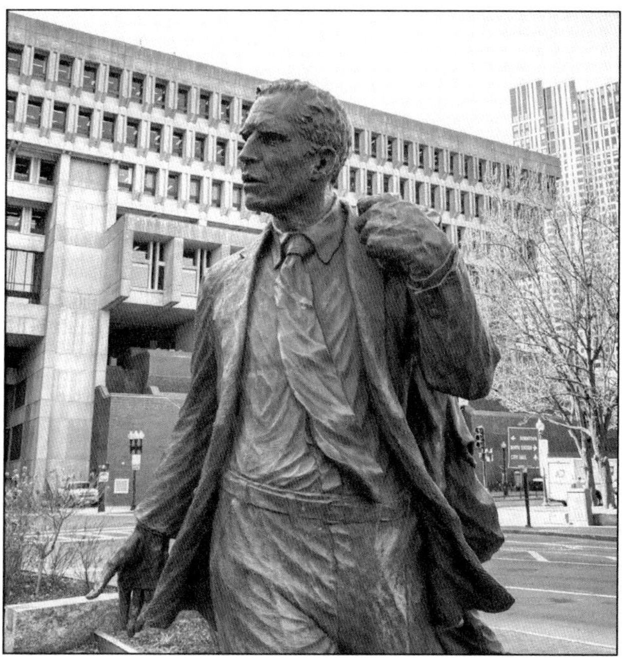

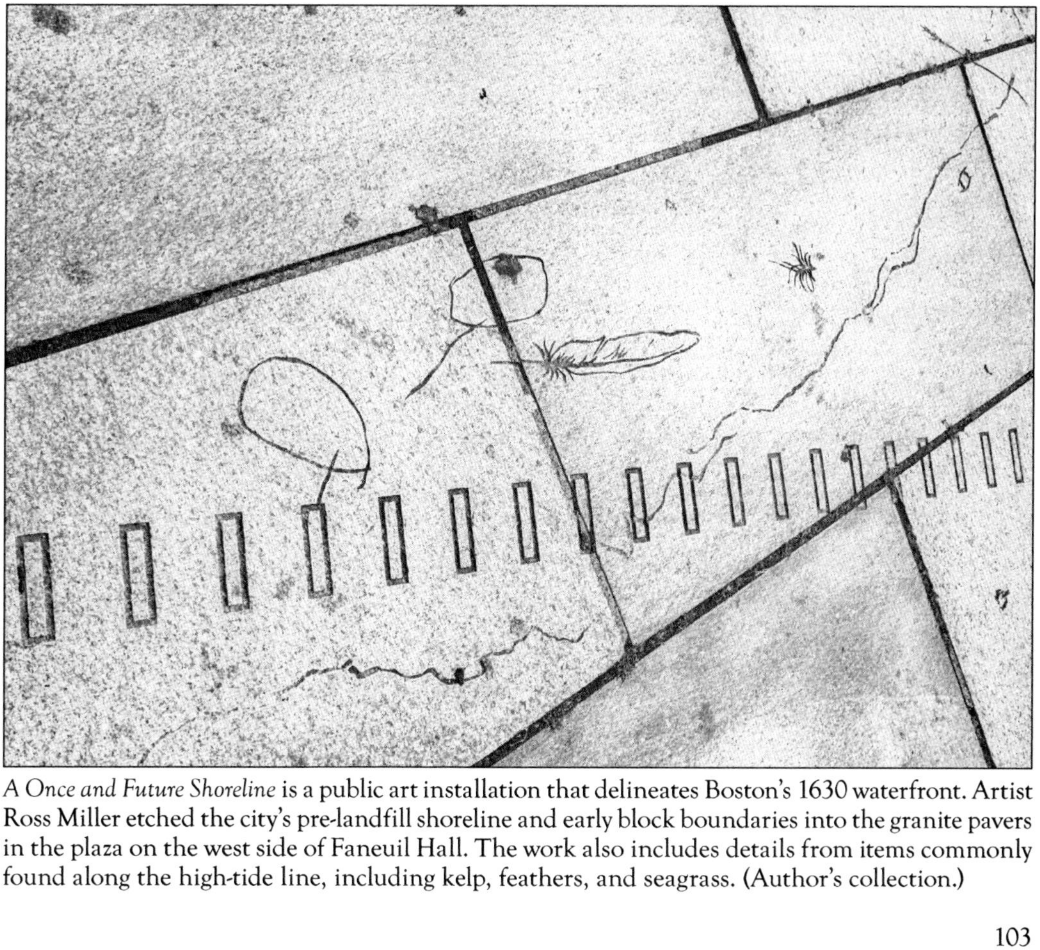

A Once and Future Shoreline is a public art installation that delineates Boston's 1630 waterfront. Artist Ross Miller etched the city's pre-landfill shoreline and early block boundaries into the granite pavers in the plaza on the west side of Faneuil Hall. The work also includes details from items commonly found along the high-tide line, including kelp, feathers, and seagrass. (Author's collection.)

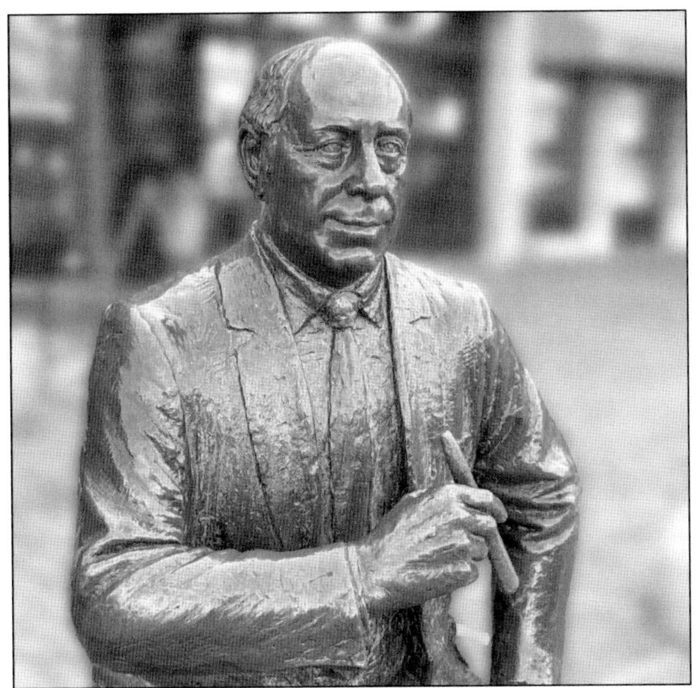

A bronze statue of Arnold "Red" Auerbach, legendary coach of the Boston Celtics, was installed on South Market Street in 1985. Created by Lloyd Lillie, the sculpture depicts Auerbach sitting on a bench and holding one of his signature cigars. A plaque honoring Boston Celtics player Larry Bird—and featuring a pair of bronzed sneakers—is nearby. (Author's collection.)

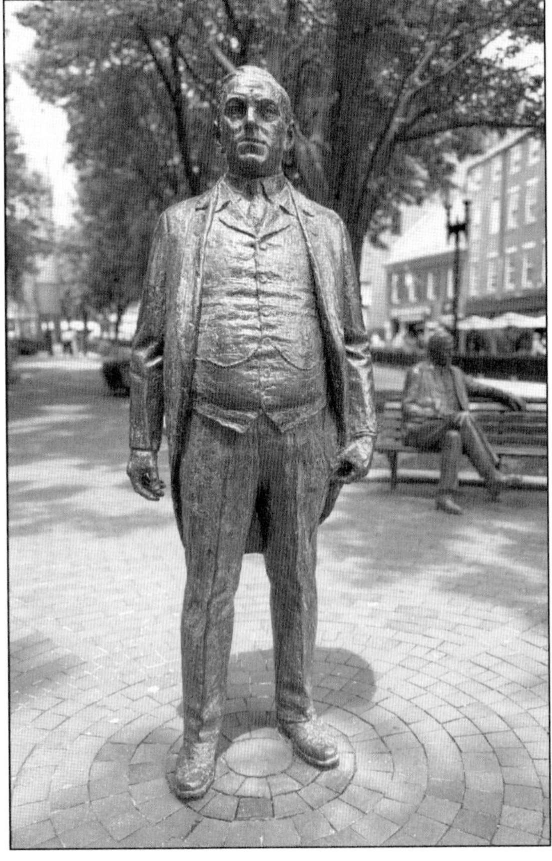

Lillie also created a double portrait of Boston Mayor James Michael Curley, which was dedicated in 1980. Located across North Street from Faneuil Hall, the two bronze sculptures represent both sides of the mayor. "One image, a standing figure, is the James Michael Curley known to other politicians, city and state officials, bankers, contractors, and businessmen," Lillie told the *Boston Globe*. "The opposing image is the Curley known to his constituents and supporters, the mostly poor working class for whom Curley always has time, a sympathetic ear, and an open wallet." (Author's collection.)

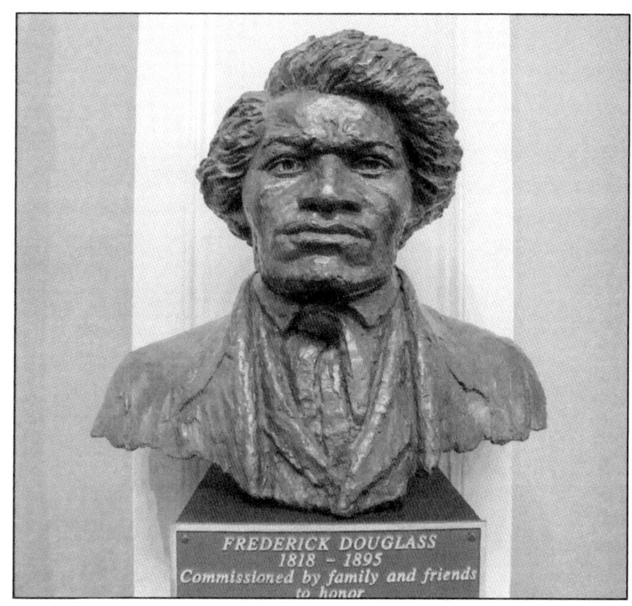

Former Boston Art Commission director Mary O'Donnell Shannon saw Lloyd Lillie's bronze bust of Frederick Douglass in an exhibit and tried to secure the piece for Faneuil Hall. When she passed away before the city could acquire the sculpture, her family raised the necessary funds to purchase the piece and placed it in the Great Hall in 1995. (National Park Service.)

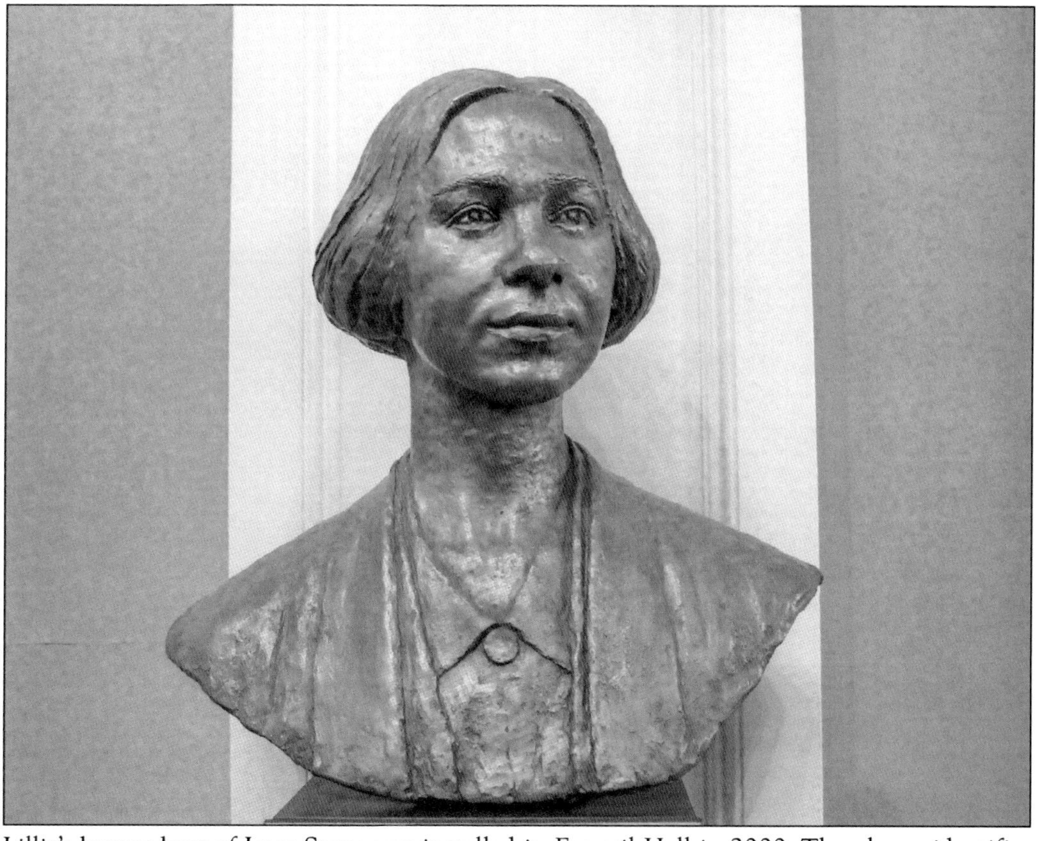

Lillie's bronze bust of Lucy Stone was installed in Faneuil Hall in 2000. The plaque identifies Stone as a "suffragette," often considered a derogatory term in the United States, rather than the usually preferred "suffragist." The Faneuil Hall Preservation and Restoration Trust commissioned the statue. (National Park Service.)

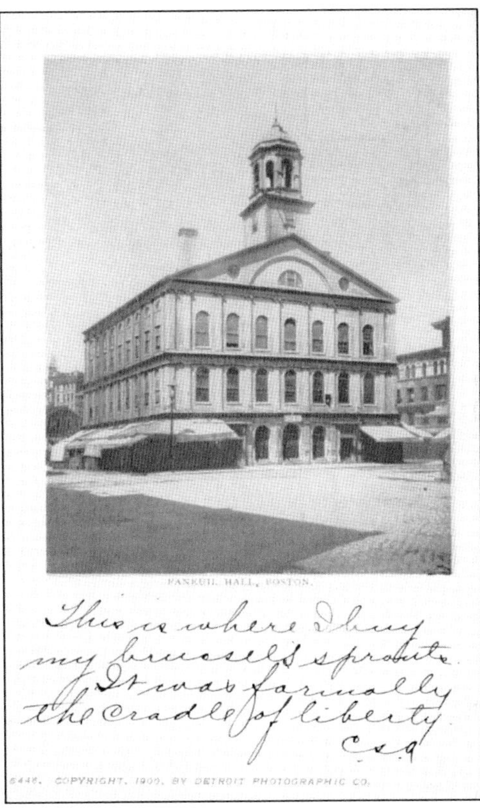

Picture postcards showing Faneuil Hall and Quincy Market were (and still are) widely available. In this vintage view of Faneuil Hall, the writer tried to capture the disconnect between the produce vendors on the ground floor and the Great Hall above. "This is where I buy my brussels sprouts," the sender wrote. "It was formally the Cradle of Liberty." (New York Public Library.)

Aside from Faneuil Hall, only a few reminders of the Faneuil family name remain in Boston. Near Benjamin Faneuil's property in Brighton, Old Indian Lane was renamed Faneuil Street in the 1840s. The Faneuil Branch of the Boston Public Library (shown here) opened on Faneuil Street in 1931 and is Boston's only library building in the Art Deco style. And the Peter Faneuil School on Boston's Beacon Hill, which dates from 1910, now provides affordable housing for people affected by HIV/AIDS. (BPL.)

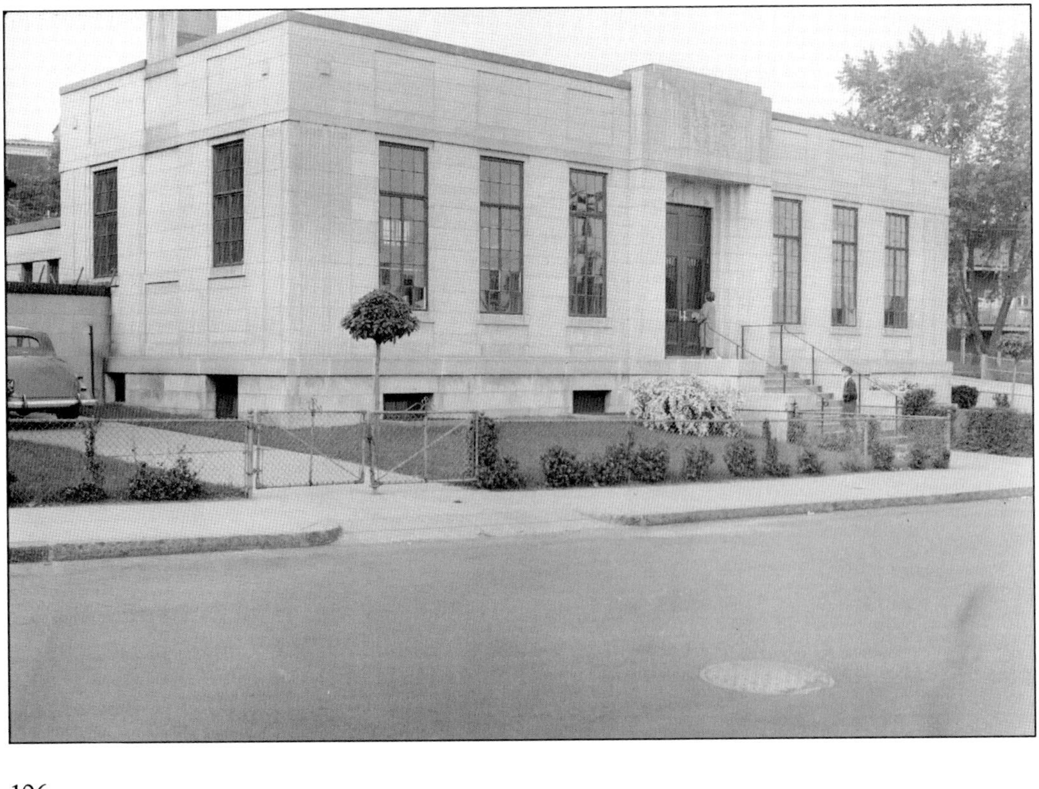

A seven-foot round granite marker was installed in the pavement between Quincy Market and Faneuil Hall in 1976. Inscribed by sculptor Frankie Bunyard, the stone honors the mayors who made the markets happen and reads simply, "Honorable Josiah Quincy, Mayor / 26 August 1826 / Faneuil Hall Marketplace / 26 August 1976 / Honorable Kevin H. White, Mayor." A detail of the marker is shown here, complete with the detritus of an active city marketplace. (Author's collection.)

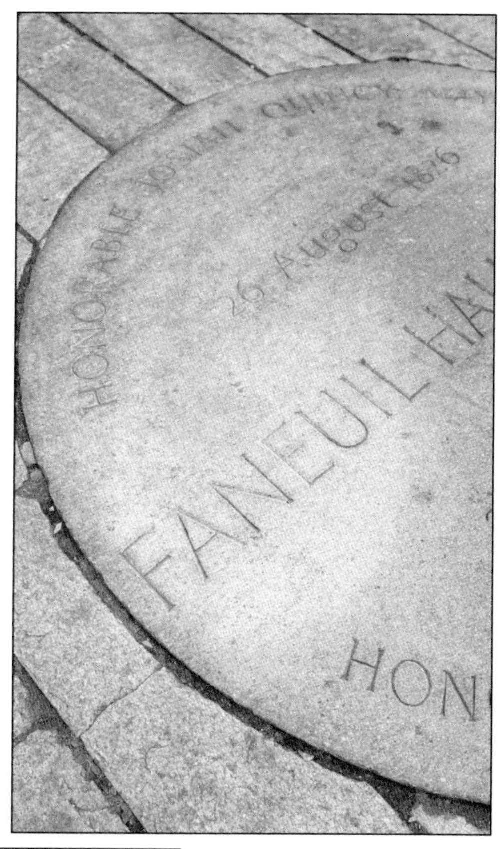

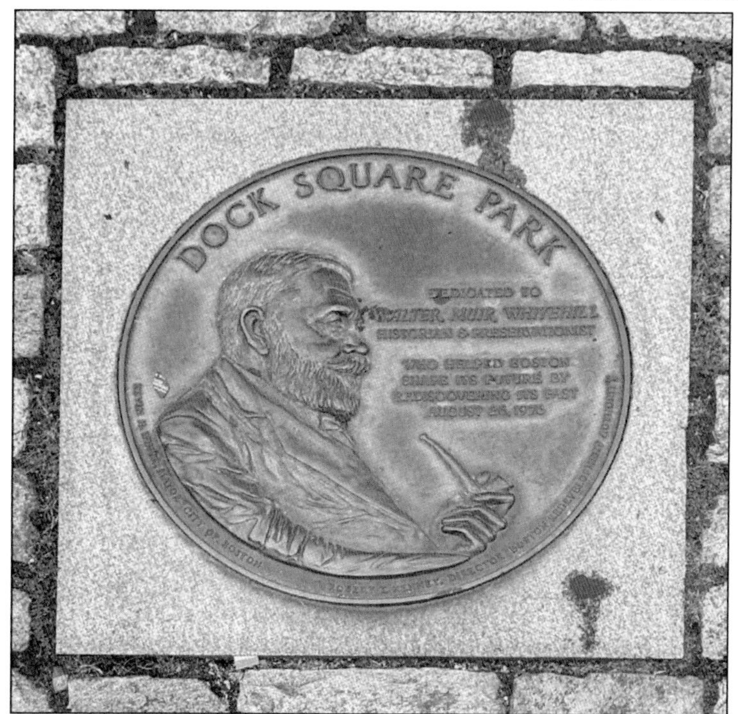

A plaque honoring Walter Muir Whitehill was unveiled as part of the opening ceremonies for the Faneuil Hall Marketplace in 1976. The marker reads, "Dedicated to Walter Muir Whitehill / Historian & Preservationist / Who helped Boston shape its future by rediscovering its past." The medallion is at the base of the Samuel Adams statue. (Author's collection.)

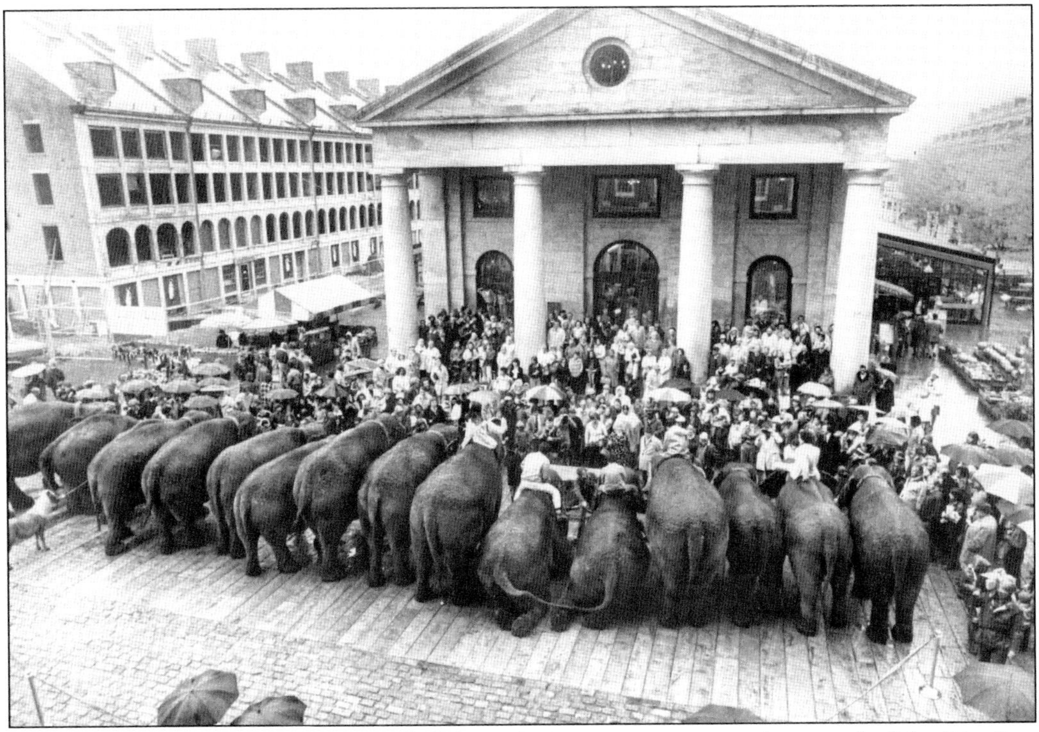

For years, circus elephants were paraded through Boston to promote the arrival of the Ringling Bros. and Barnum & Bailey Circus. Elephants would arrive by rail and march to the Boston Garden, where the circus was held. Here, the elephants seem to be making a pit stop by Quincy Market. The photograph is undated but is probably from the mid-1970s, when the North Market was still under renovation. (MHS.)

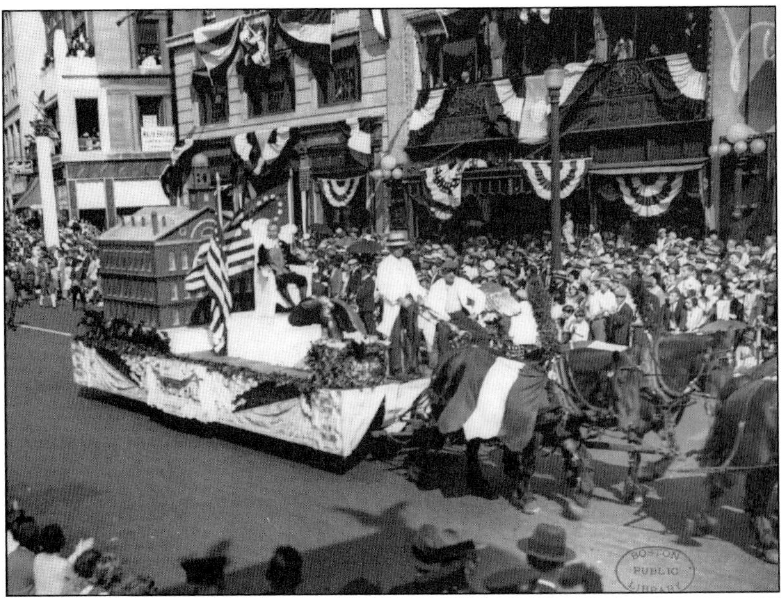

Chartered by Congress in 1919, the American Legion provides services to veterans. The nonprofit organization held its 12th annual convention in Boston in 1930, and crowds turned out on October 5 to watch the Legion's parade through the city, which included this float with a model of Faneuil Hall. (BPL.)

Five

Reinventing Quincy Market

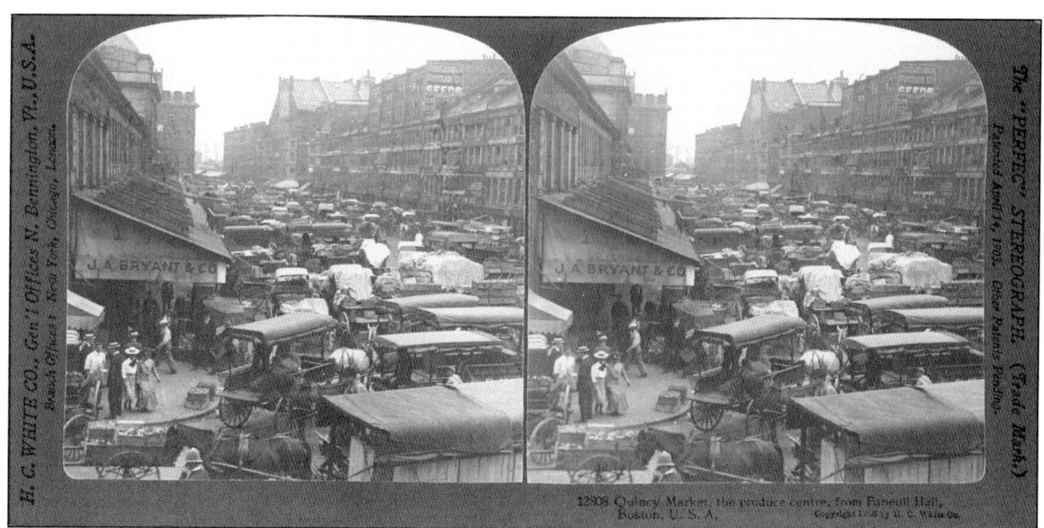

Quincy Market, North Market, and South Market had fallen into disrepair by the 1950s, and most of the tenants were gone. After almost tearing down the historic structures, the City of Boston reversed course and developed a plan to revitalize the buildings. Renovations began in 1973, and a new festival marketplace opened on August 26, 1976, exactly 150 years after the original Quincy Market opened. (LOC.)

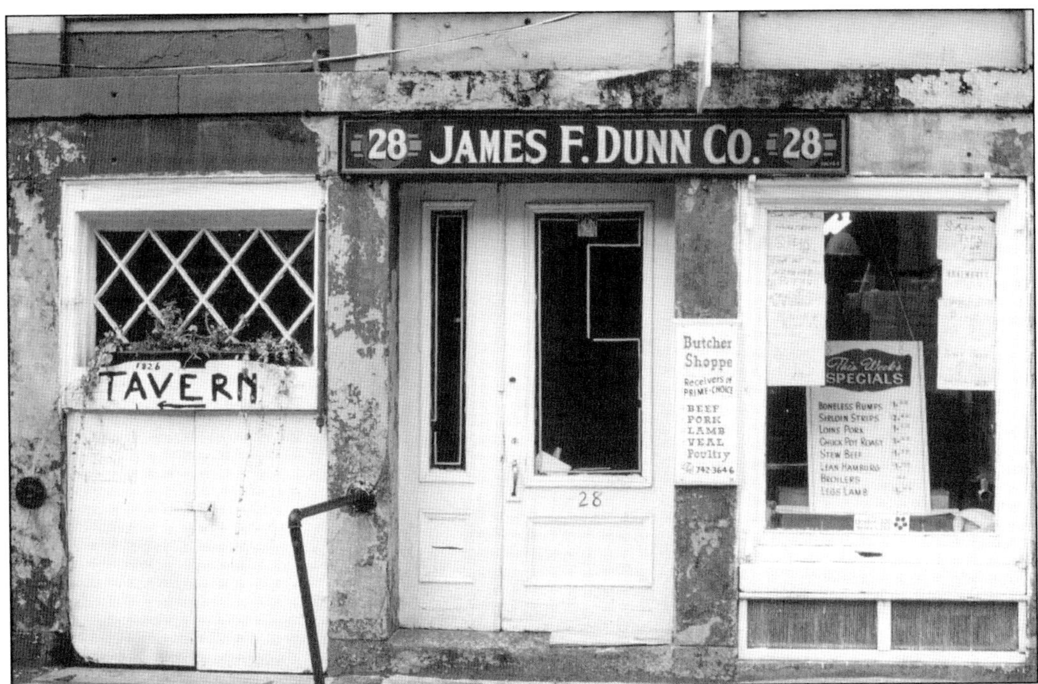

By the 1950s, Quincy Market was a mess. John Quincy Jr. described the sorry state of the once grand marketplace: "On any given day the remains of produce, meats, and other food stuffs lay strewn across the gummy asphalt that now partially covered the old brick and cobblestone streets," he wrote. The market detritus attracted rats "in droves." (Photograph by Edmund L. Mitchell, BPL.)

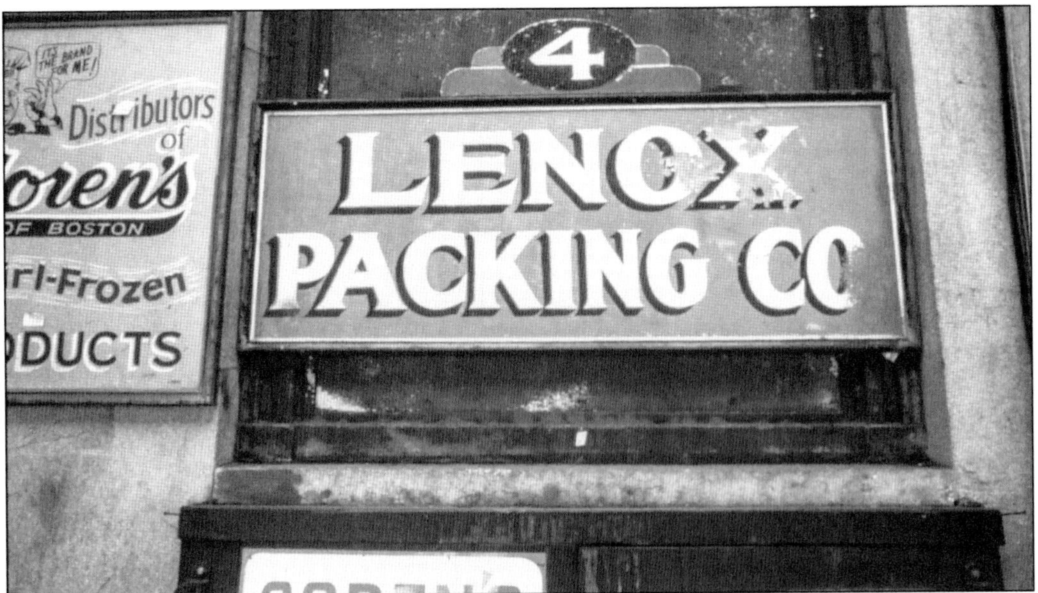

Moreover, the buildings were badly deteriorated. Basements were flooded, plumbing was antiquated, and columns were cracked. After the city eased design restrictions in 1855, subsequent updates were haphazard. "Much of the once-uniform granite façade was now covered over—or completely removed and replaced—with pressed metal, colored plastic, vinyl, aluminum, mismatched bricks, or other makeshift materials," Quincy wrote. (Photograph by Ernst Halberstadt, BPL.)

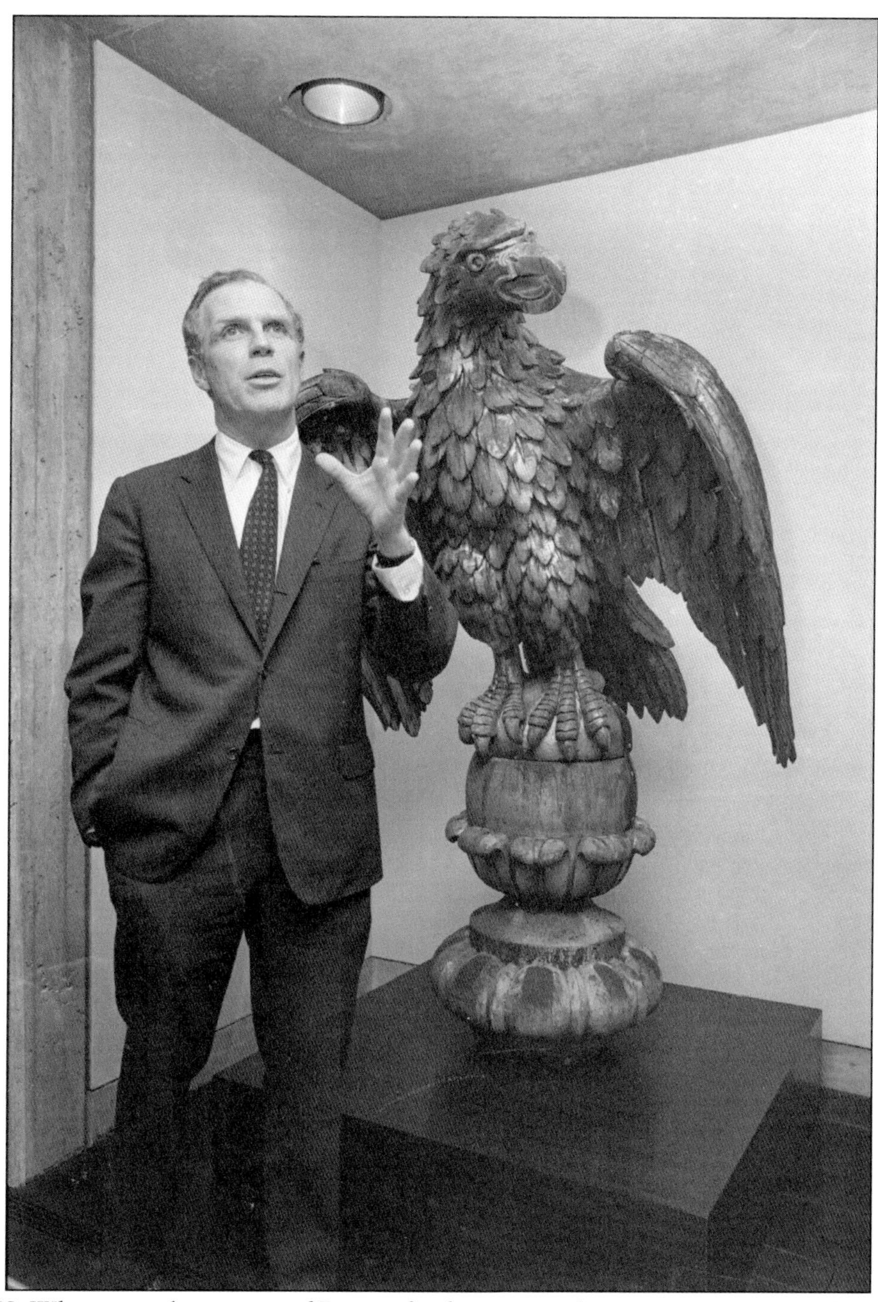

Kevin H. White served as mayor of Boston for four terms, from 1968 to 1984. He led the city during an era of racial unrest that culminated in court-ordered busing to desegregate the public schools, and the whiff of scandal followed some of his appointees. However, he was also credited with turning Boston into a world-class city, in part by transforming Quincy Market into something new: a festival marketplace. Just like former Mayor Josiah Quincy was said to be disgusted by the dilapidated wharves and the stench of the sewage near the Town Dock, White was disheartened by the sight of the deteriorated market buildings outside his city hall window. "It was an eyesore, right in front of me," White reportedly said. White is shown here in city hall's Eagle Room in 1969. (Photograph by Gene Dixon, BPL.)

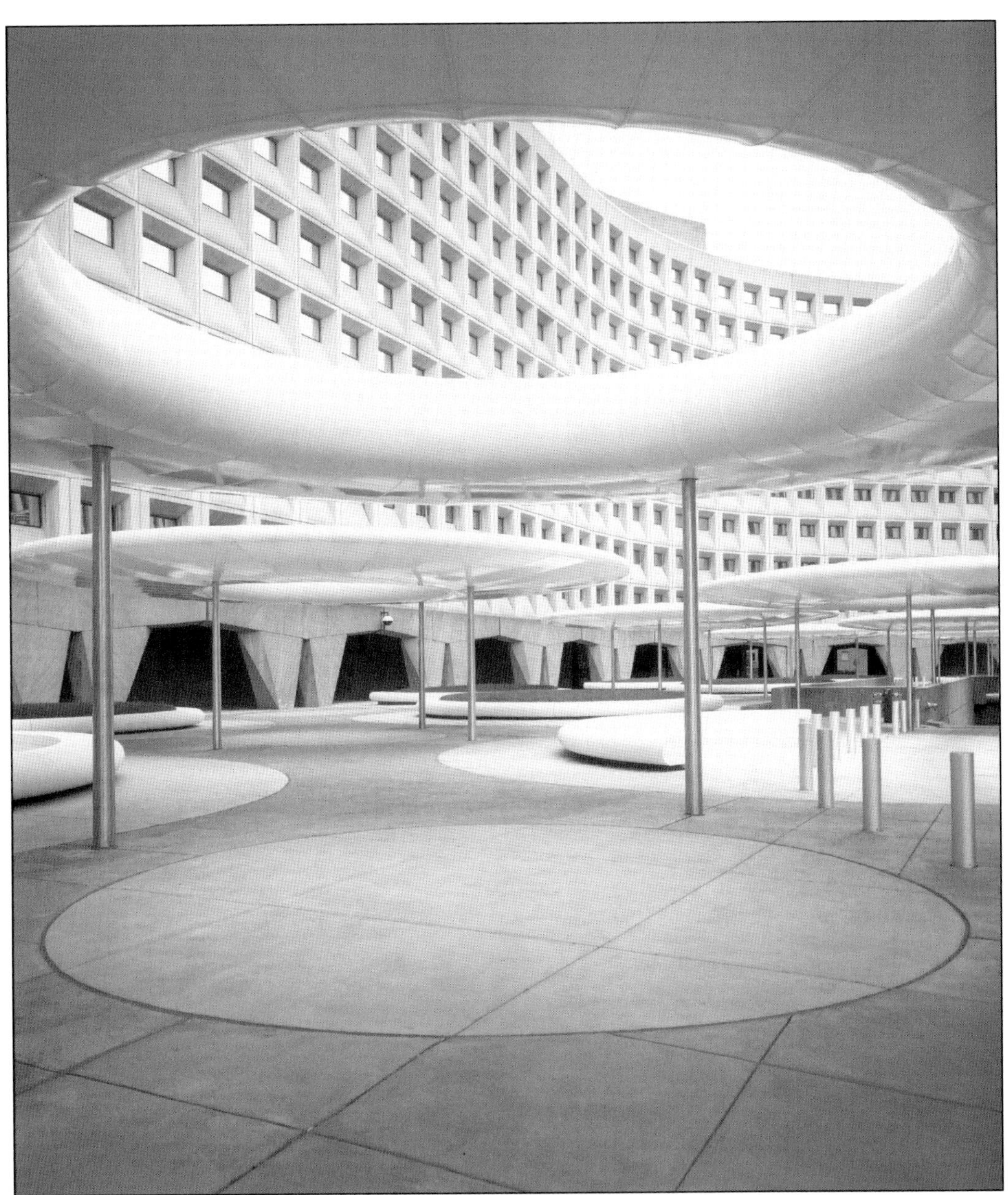

Quincy Market's long journey from eyesore to icon began when White's predecessor, Mayor John F. Collins, appointed Ed Logue as director of the Boston Redevelopment Authority (BRA) in 1961. Logue saw value in the historic structures, despite a staff recommendation to demolish them, and he pursued options for preservation. Lending his support, preservationist Walter Muir Whitehill influenced key city stakeholders to save the markets. In 1966, the BRA commissioned the Society for the Preservation of New England Antiquities and the Architectural Heritage Foundation to conduct a feasibility study for reusing the market buildings. Architect Frederick "Tad" Stahl and developer Roger S. Webb led the research and prepared a road map for restoration. Thanks, in part, to the Stahl-Webb report, the US Department of Housing and Urban Development (HUD) awarded the city $2.1 million in January 1969. Shown here is the HUD building in Washington, DC. (Photograph by Carol M. Highsmith, LOC.)

On July 1, 1971, the BRA selected a development team led by Philadelphia-based Van Arkel and Moss Associates to restore the market buildings. R.M. Bradley and Company was designated as the management company, with George B.H. Macomber Construction Company as the builder and Benjamin Thompson and Associates (BTA) as the project architect. The relationship was short lived, however, and the BRA ousted Van Arkel and Moss in 1972 for failure to perform. (Photograph by Edmund L. Mitchell, BPL.)

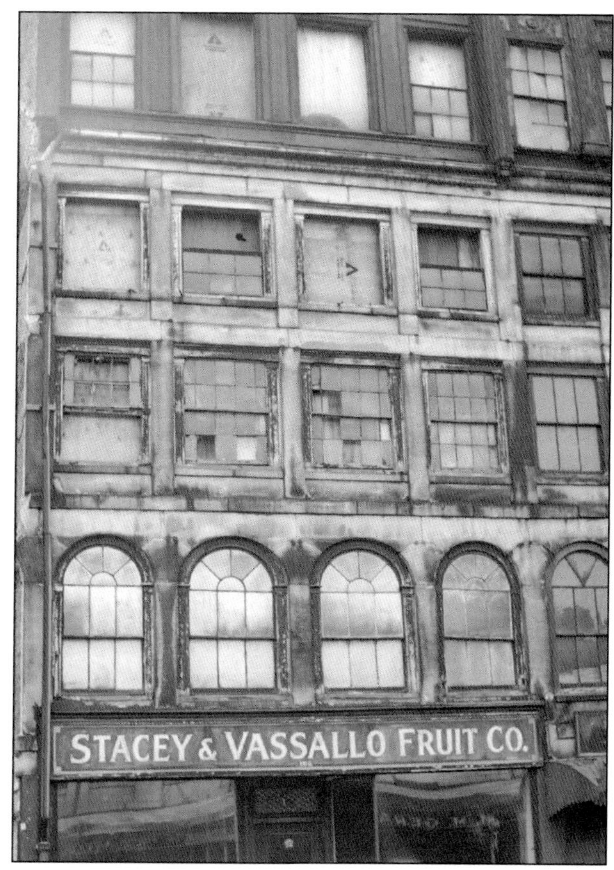

To avoid losing momentum, the BRA implemented the first phase of its market restoration plan in October 1972. The authority hired a team led by Tad Stahl to stabilize the North and South Markets and return the rooflines and facades to their 1826 appearance. (Photograph by Ernst Halberstadt, BPL.)

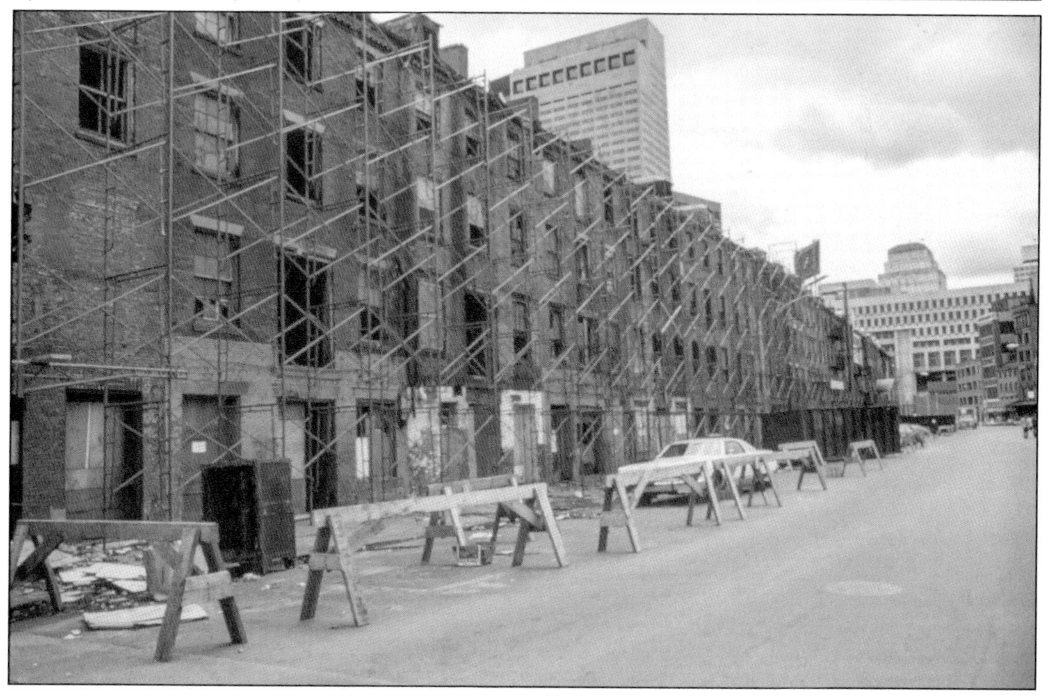

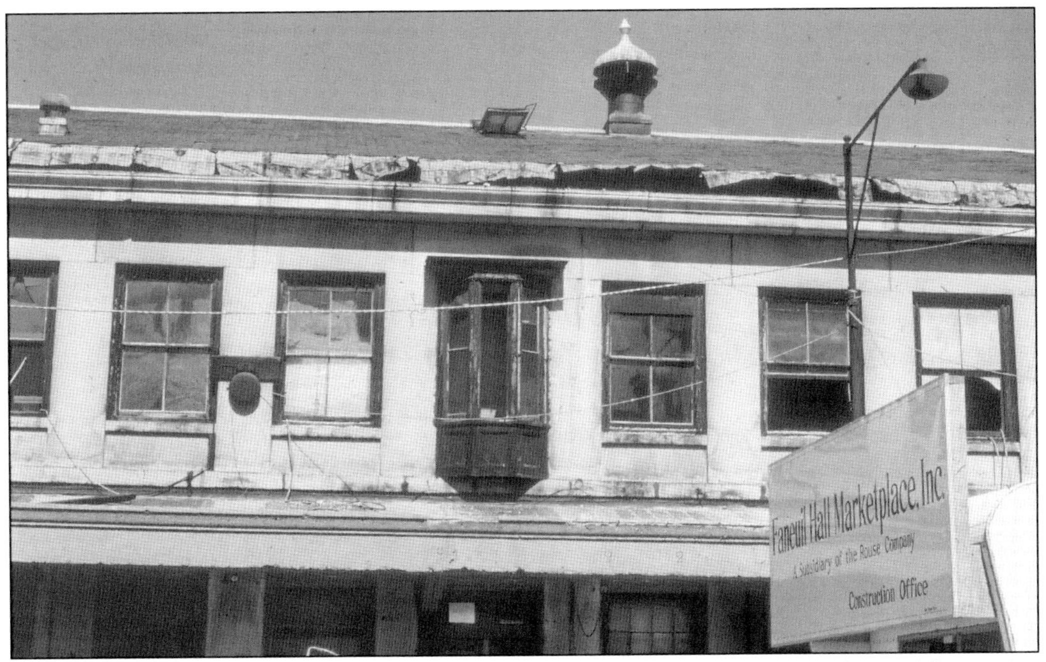

On March 22, 1973, the BRA designated a new team to complete the second phase of the market restoration. The Maryland-based Rouse Company served as the developer and management company; two firms from the Van Arkel and Moss team were retained, with BTA as project architect and planner and Macomber as builder. (BPL.)

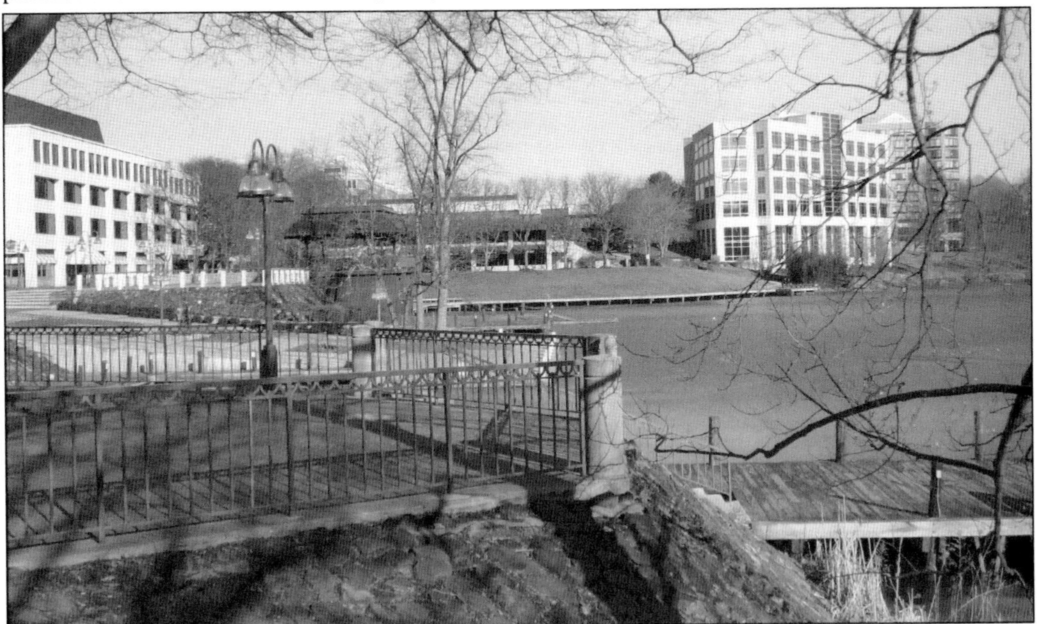

The Rouse Company was a real estate development firm founded by James W. Rouse and Hunter Moss in 1939. Before the BRA tapped Rouse for Quincy Market, the company had developed the planned community of Columbia, Maryland, in the late 1960s (shown here). With the Boston project as a model, Rouse went on to build festival marketplaces in other cities, including Harborplace in Baltimore and South Street Seaport in New York City. (Preservation Maryland.)

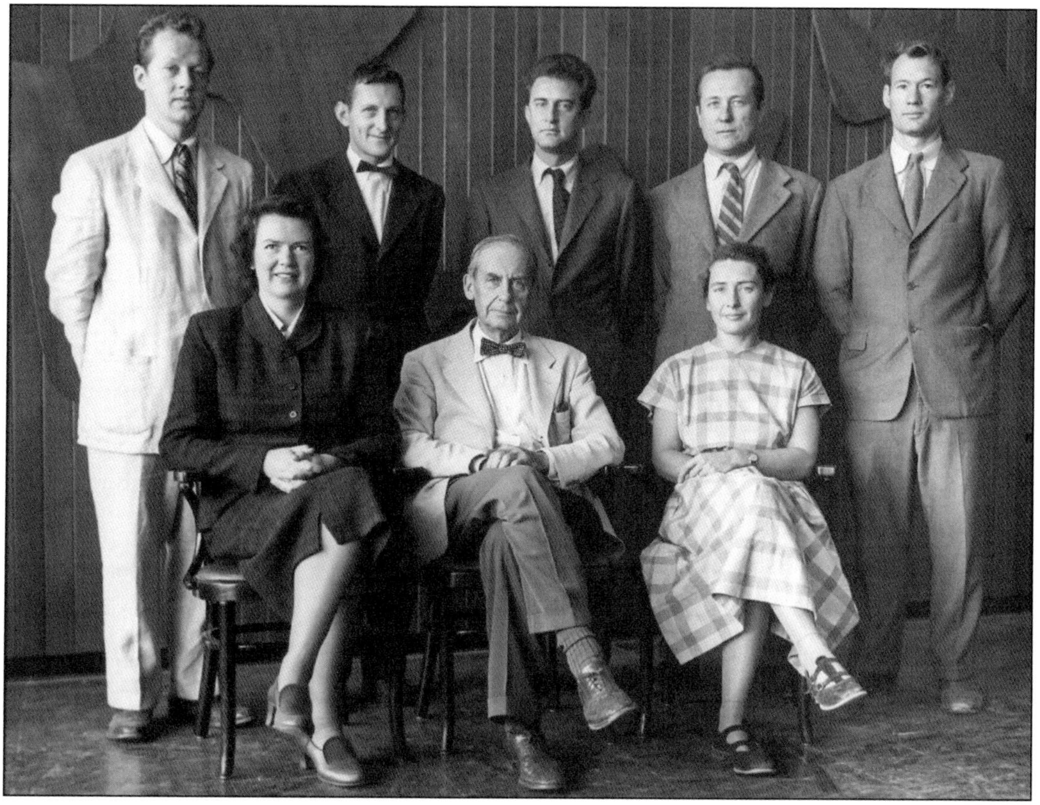

Benjamin C. Thompson was a founding member of the Architects Collaborative (TAC), established in Cambridge, Massachusetts, in 1945. TAC embraced a philosophy of collaboration over individualism. Shown here in 1950, from left to right, are (first row) Jean B. Fletcher, Walter Gropius, and Sarah P. Harkness; (second row) Thompson, Norman C. Fletcher, Robert S. McMillan, Louis A. McMillen, and John C. Harkness. (Photograph by Walter R. Fleischer, Harvard Law School Library.)

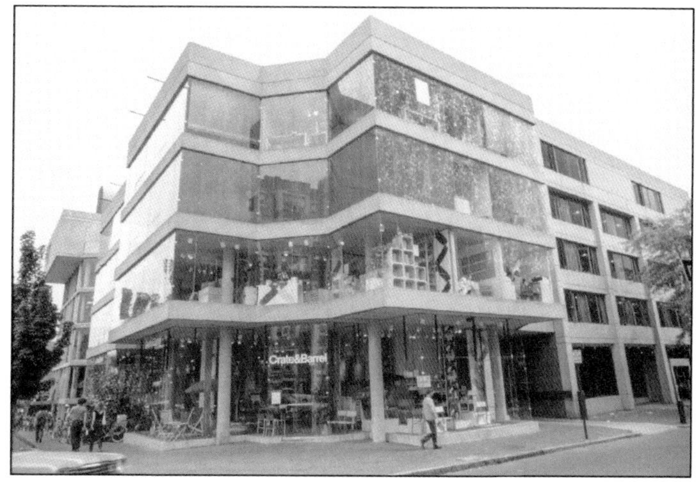

Thompson left TAC after 20 years and founded Benjamin Thompson and Associates in 1966; his wife, Jane McCullough Thompson, joined the firm in 1967. Thompson's 1969 design for the glass-walled Design Research headquarters received accolades (shown here after Crate and Barrel took over the space), but he may be best remembered for designing Faneuil Hall Marketplace. (Photograph by James F. Taulman, BPL.)

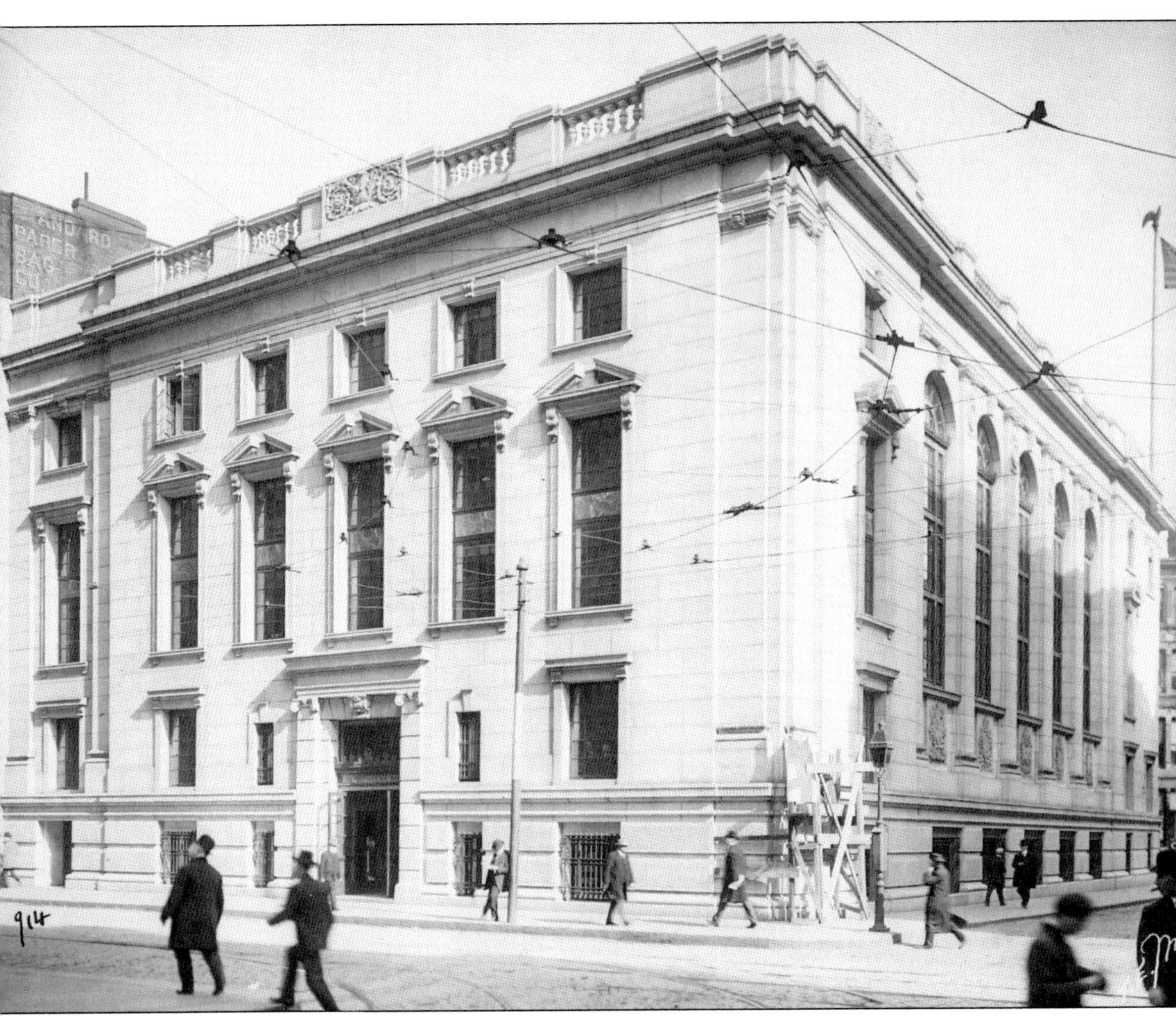

After selecting the Rouse team, officials worked out the legal and financial details. First, the city granted the BRA a 99-year master lease for Quincy Market and adjacent public streets for $1 per year. (The BRA already owned the North and South Markets.) This enabled the BRA to execute a 99-year sublease with Faneuil Hall Marketplace, a subsidiary of the Rouse Company, for all three buildings and the streets. Rouse would pay the city an annual base rent of $600,000 plus a percentage of the rental income. Next, Rouse had to find financing. By 1974, project costs were estimated at $33.5 million, and public contributions to date were nearly $12.5 million. The Teachers Insurance and Annuity Association provided permanent financing, and Chase Manhattan Bank of New York offered a construction loan. Chase insisted on a local match from Boston lenders, however, and the city's financiers were not sure the project would succeed. Eventually, after much lobbying, a consortium of financial institutions agreed to pool their funds and spread the risk. Faneuil Hall Marketplace could move forward. Shown here is the First National Bank in Boston around 1908. (BPL.)

Looking at the project from today's perspective—when every city seems to have a historic marketplace—it is easy to forget how revolutionary Faneuil Hall Marketplace once was. The new market was decidedly not a traditional shopping mall. There was no anchor store, no national chains, and (definitely) no free parking. The project was proposed as an assemblage of small, preferably locally owned businesses that would "mingle and compete," in the words of Benjamin and Jane Thompson. (Author's collection.)

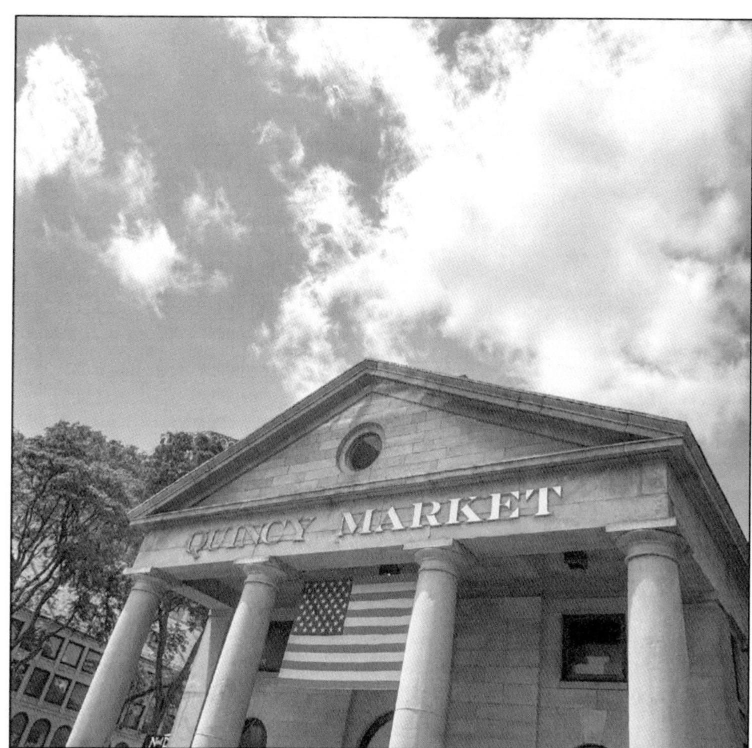

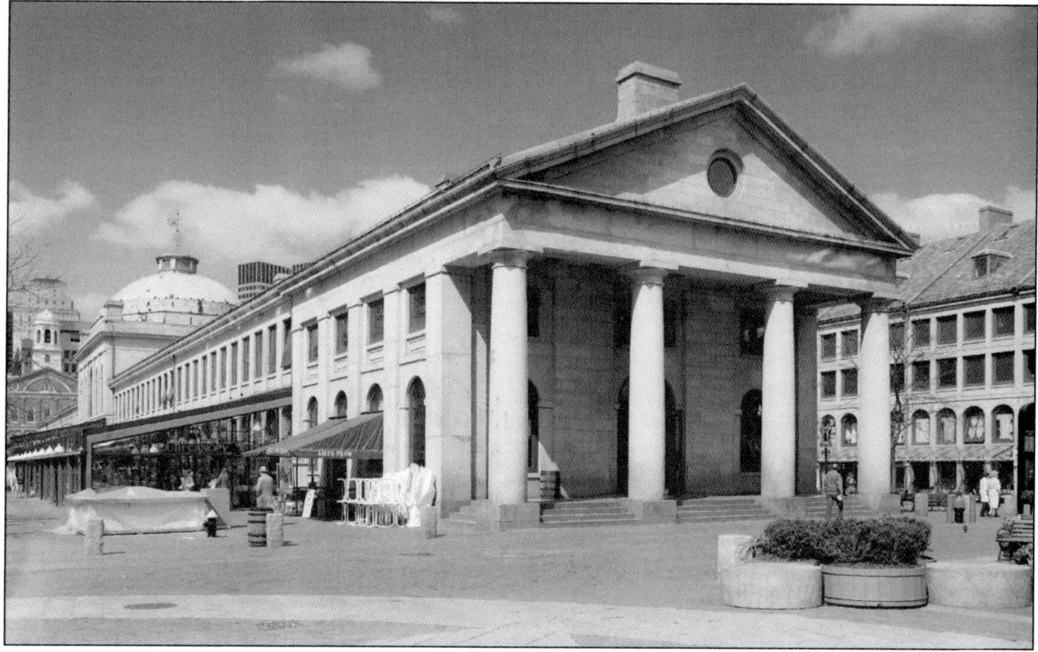

As BTA proceeded with the project design, Benjamin Thompson introduced changes that did not always conform to the building's original 1826 design. Although this dismayed preservationists, his stated goal was to respect the past while meeting the future. The Thompsons explained, "All that is usable and real will be kept and used, without denying the flow of the past into the present and the evolving future." (LOC.)

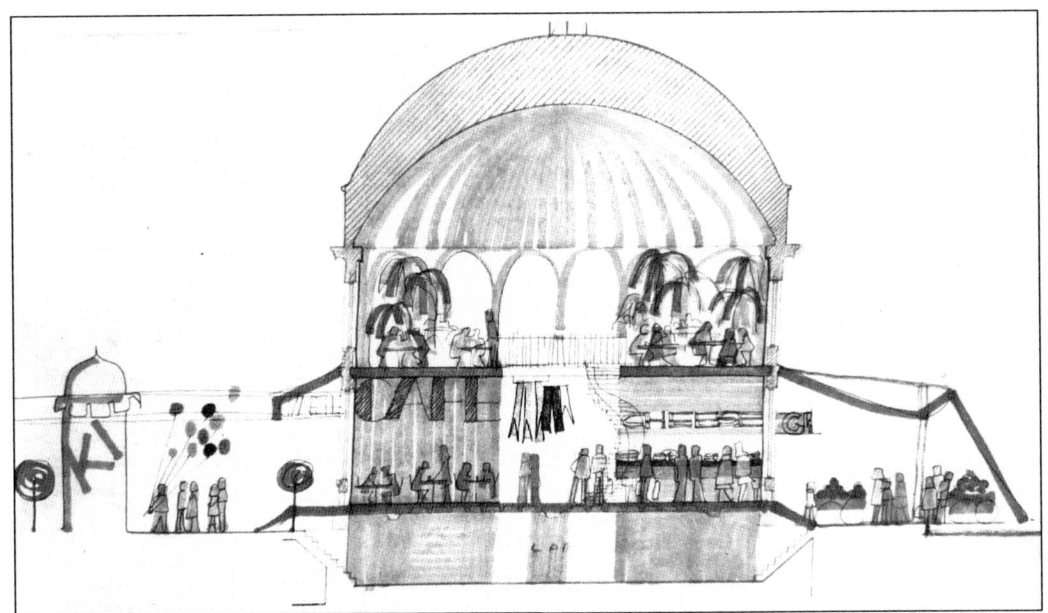

Just as the central dome was the defining feature of the 1826 Quincy Market, a reimagined rotunda took center stage in 1976. The new design removed part of the ceiling between the first and second floors to create a two-and-a-half-story atrium under the elliptical dome. Plaster was stripped from the rotunda's walls, and salvaged signs from the original market vendors were displayed on the exposed brick. A conceptual plan for the rotunda is shown here. (MHS.)

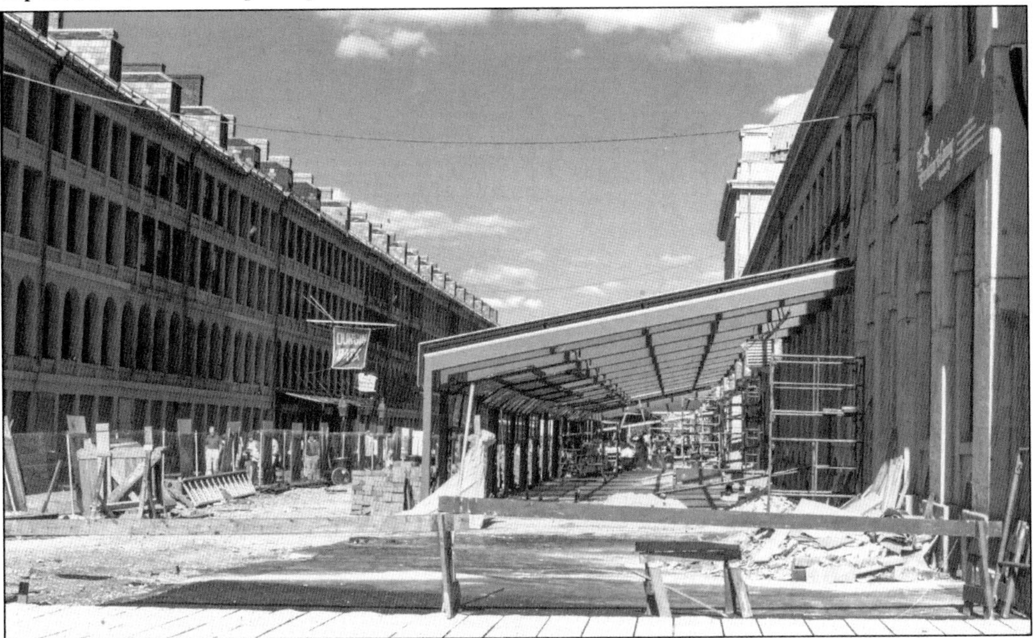

The renovation mimicked Quincy Market's awnings by adding a shed-roofed glass canopy along the building's north and south sides. North and South Market Streets were converted into pedestrian malls paved with brick and granite. Outdoor seating was introduced, trees were planted, and poles with globe clusters provided lighting. A new bull weather vane was installed. (Photograph by Edmund L. Mitchell, BPL.)

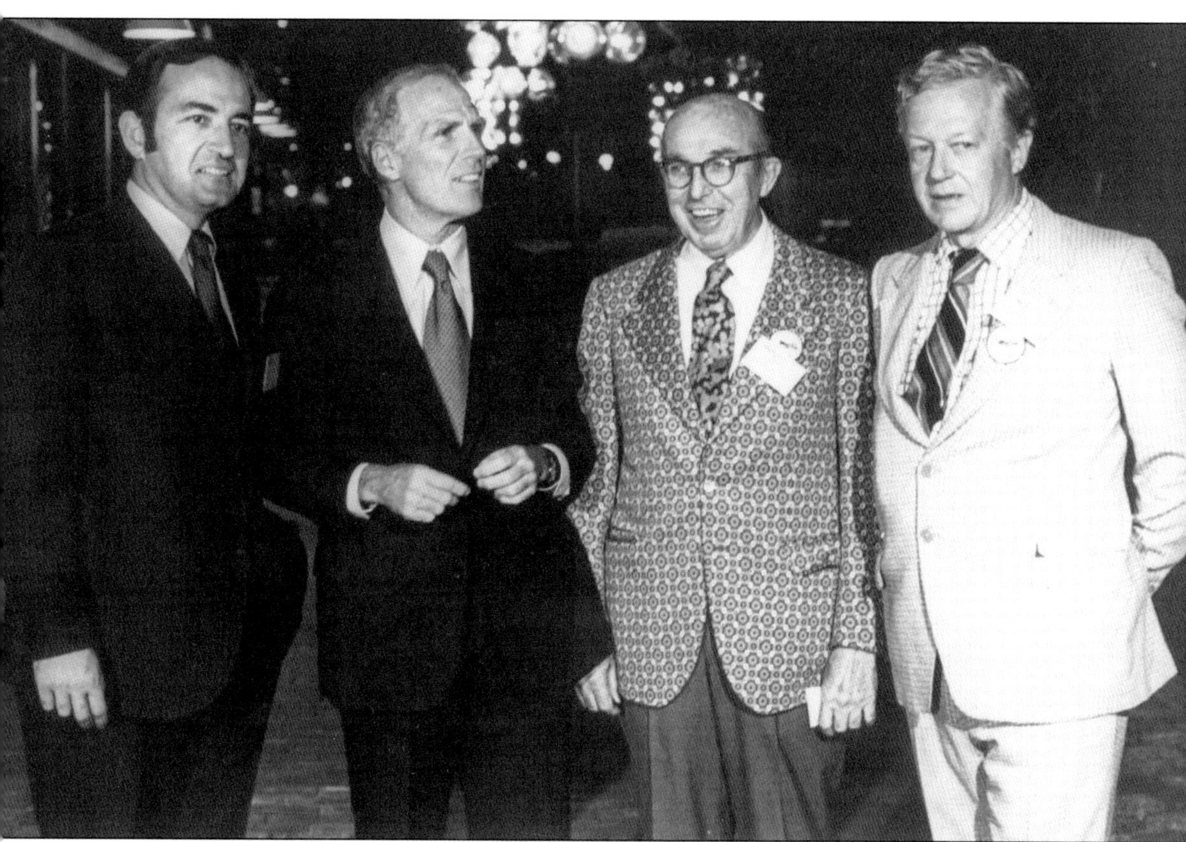

The revived Quincy Market building opened with great fanfare on August 26, 1976, exactly 150 years since the original Faneuil Hall Market welcomed its first customers. After Mayor Kevin H. White addressed the crowd, a man in colonial costume rang a bell and declared the market open. Attendees made their way to the rotunda, where they enjoyed free champagne and slices of a 2,000-pound cake in the shape of the market. Some 100,000 people turned out (an estimate the *New York Times* later called "excited but plausible") to explore the new marketplace. "This is truly an historical event, a rebirth, a happening," White declared. Shown here at a gala held the night before the market opened are, from left to right, BRA director Robert T. Kenney, White, Rouse Company chairman James W. Rouse, and project architect Benjamin Thompson. (MHS.)

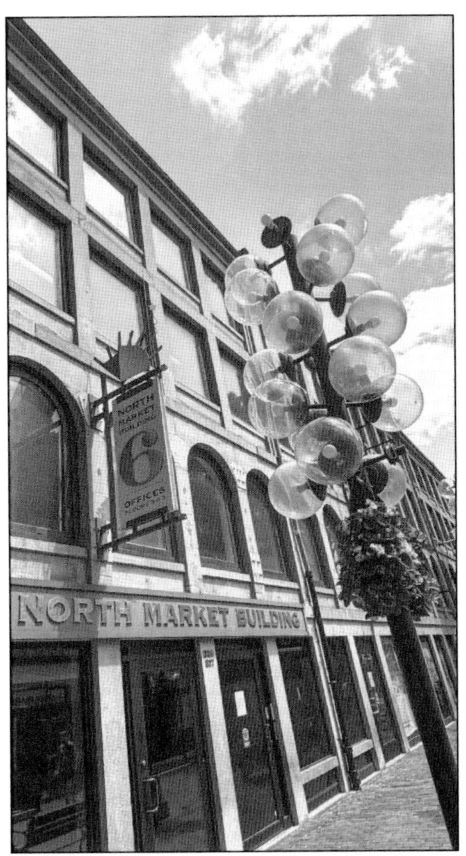

The South Market opened exactly a year later, on August 26, 1977, and the North Market followed on August 26, 1978. Again, festive celebrations marked the occasions, with champagne and massive cakes. Both markets had a mix of retail shops, restaurants, and offices; Durgin-Park continued to occupy its historic space in the North Market. (Author's collection.)

Quincy Market continued its 150-year focus on food. A press release issued around the time of the opening touted the offerings: "From fine Italian pastries and hearty New England soups to Cajun cooking and whole lobsters, there is something for everyone." The North Market and South Market retailers focused on fashion, accessories, home goods, and gifts. A greenhouse was constructed north of Faneuil Hall to accommodate the market's flower vendors. (Photograph by James F. Taulman, BPL.)

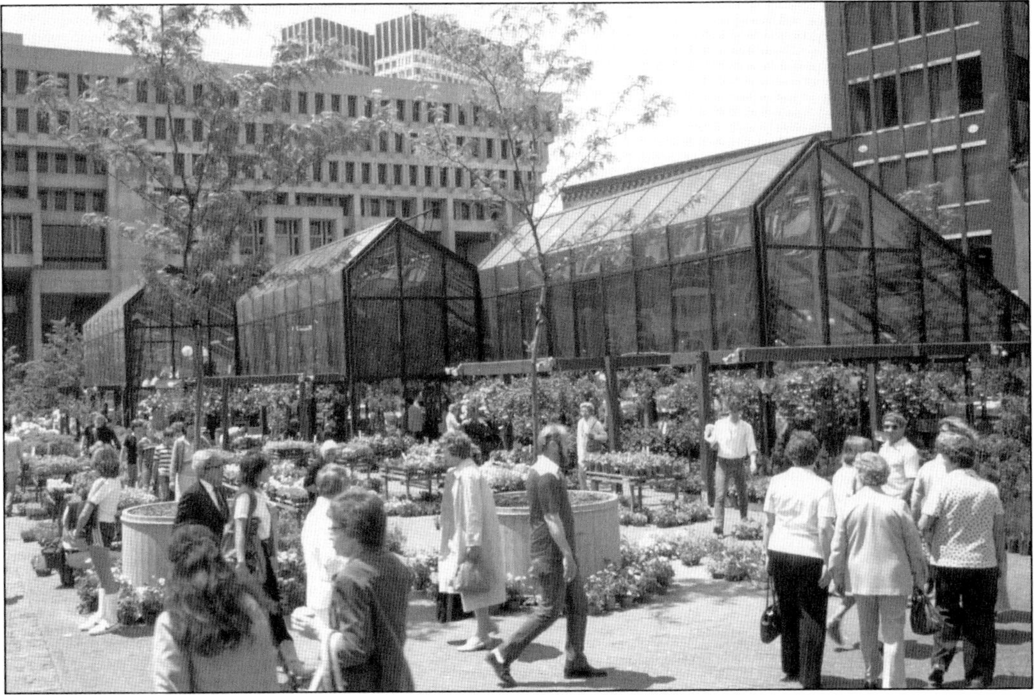

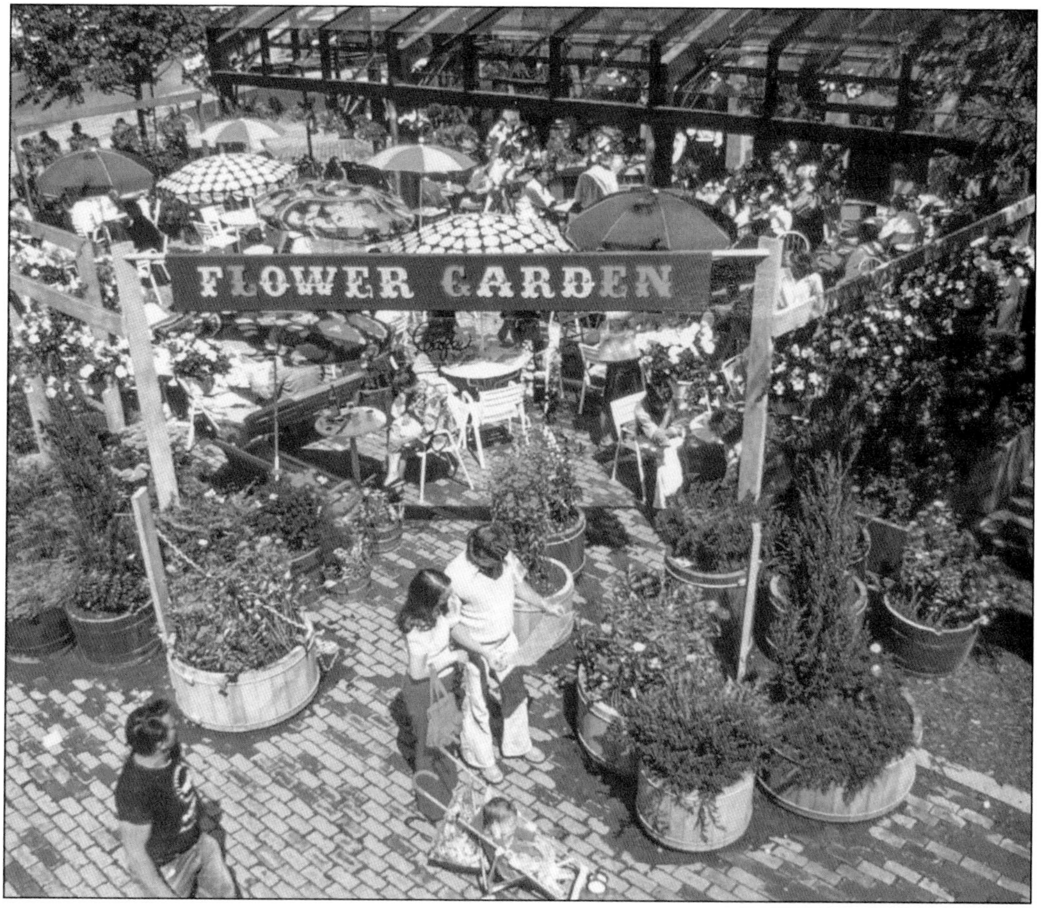

Faneuil Hall Marketplace had no shortage of restaurants and bars. Benjamin and Jane Thompson operated four, known collectively as Landmark Inn: Thompson's Chowder House, Flower Garden Café, Wild Goose Rotisserie, and Bunch of Grapes. Among the others were historic Durgin-Park, still serving authentic Yankee dishes, and Lord Bunbury, an English pub with an interior shipped from London. The Bull Market—presumably named after Quincy Market's weather vane—was created under the glass canopies for merchants to sell their wares from carts. And the entertainment pulled everything together. Street performers, singers, and musicians from around the world delighted audiences year-round. (Both, MHS.)

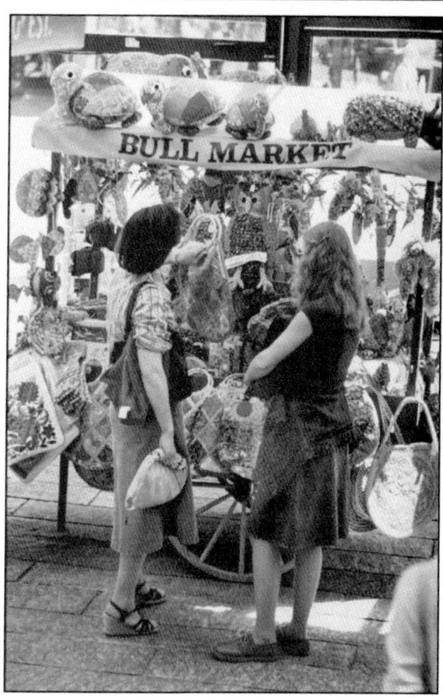

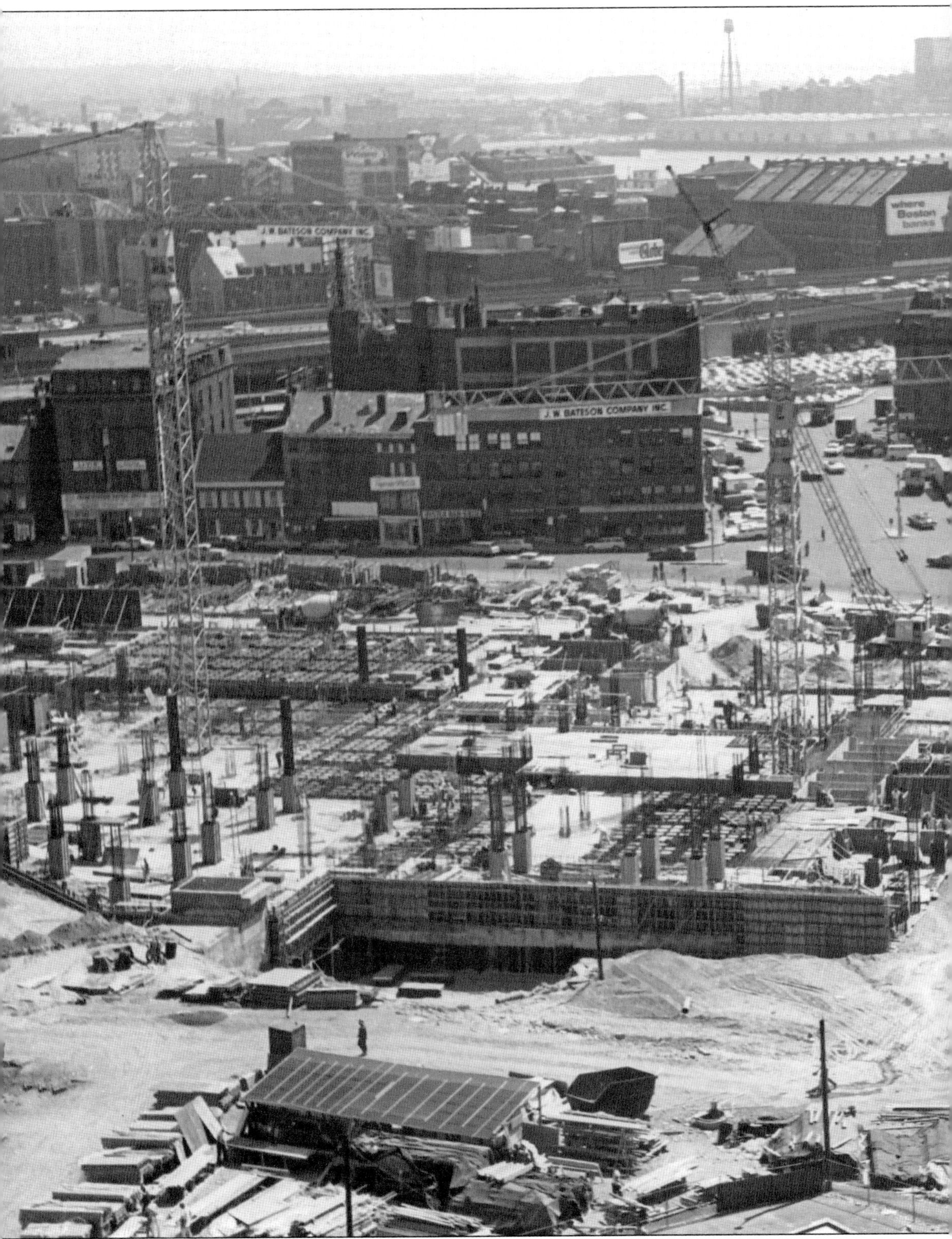
J. W. BATESON COMPANY INC
J. W. BATESON COMPANY INC
where Boston banks

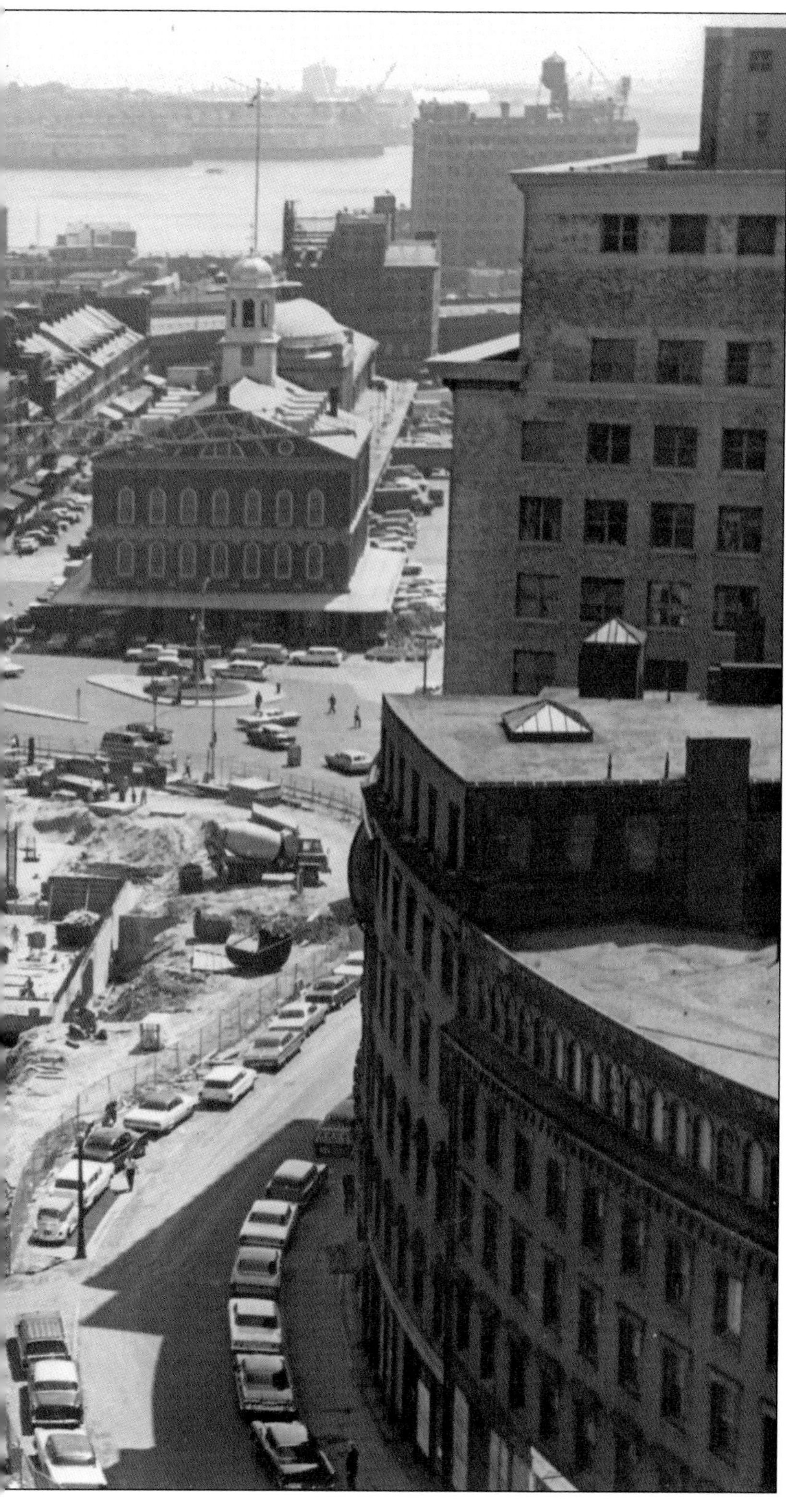

Former Boston City Councilor Lawrence S. DiCara drew a direct line from Boston's old Scollay Square to the city's redeveloped seaport, and that line traveled straight through Faneuil Hall Marketplace. If Mayor John Collins had not torn down all the burlesque houses in Scollay Square, he explained, Mayor Kevin White would not have looked out his window from the new city hall and thought about fixing up Quincy Market. And if the marketplace had not become a major tourist destination in the 1970s and 1980s, those visitors would not have seen the old Central Artery—"this horrible green, elevated rusting structure." Once the Artery was underground (thanks to a massive public works project known locally as "the Big Dig"), people could just walk over to the seaport. "So, it's all connected," he said. (BOS.)

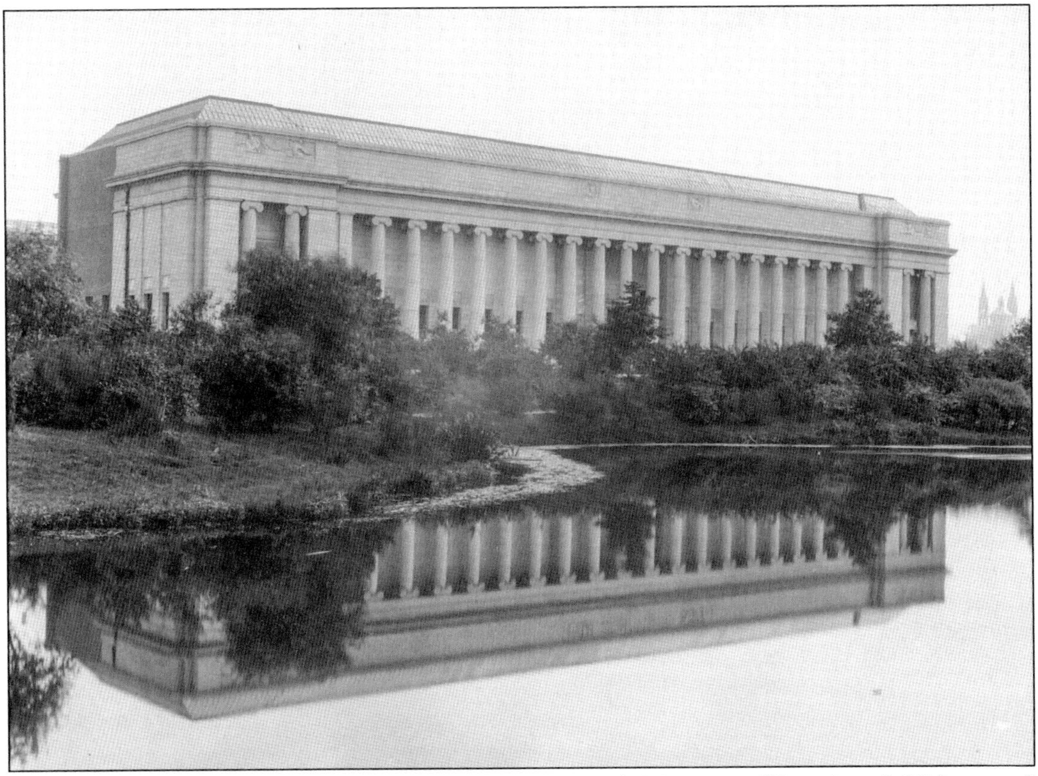

Boston's Museum of Fine Arts (MFA) opened a branch in the South Market in 1979, occupying 12,000 square feet donated by the Rouse Company. The satellite museum coincided with major renovations at the MFA, and museum director Jan Fontein told the *Boston Globe*, "The Faneuil Hall site will let us keep many great objects on public view during the renovation program, works which would otherwise have to be placed in storage." The MFA presented the Rouse Company with a reproduction of Gilbert Stuart's portrait of Josiah Quincy made with a large-format Polaroid camera. (BPL.)

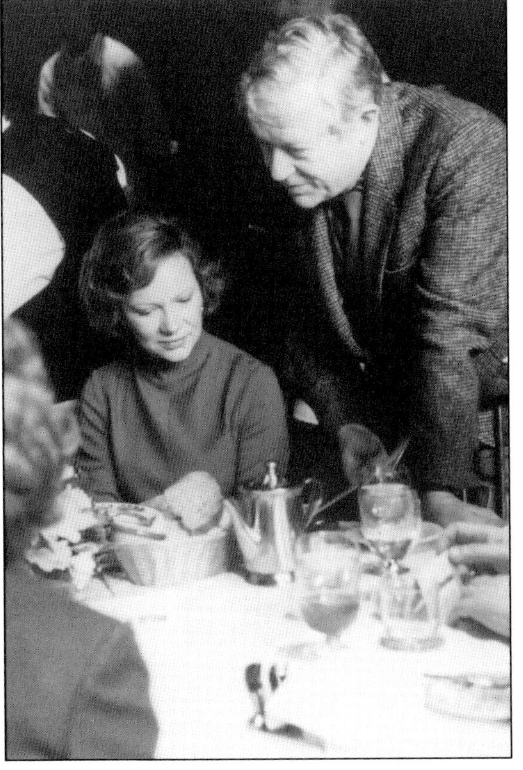

Former First Lady Rosalyn Carter made multiple visits to Boston in the 1980s. She is shown here with Benjamin Thompson at his Wild Goose Rotisserie restaurant in February 1980. (MHS.)

When Faneuil Hall Marketplace opened, many Bostonians ignored the official name and stuck with the familiar Quincy Market. Some even assumed Quincy Market included Faneuil Hall. The confusion was understandable. The new market's logo featured Faneuil Hall's grasshopper weather vane, which, intentionally or not, blurred the distinction between the three buildings that made up Faneuil Hall Marketplace and Faneuil Hall itself (which remains a separate entity). (MHS.)

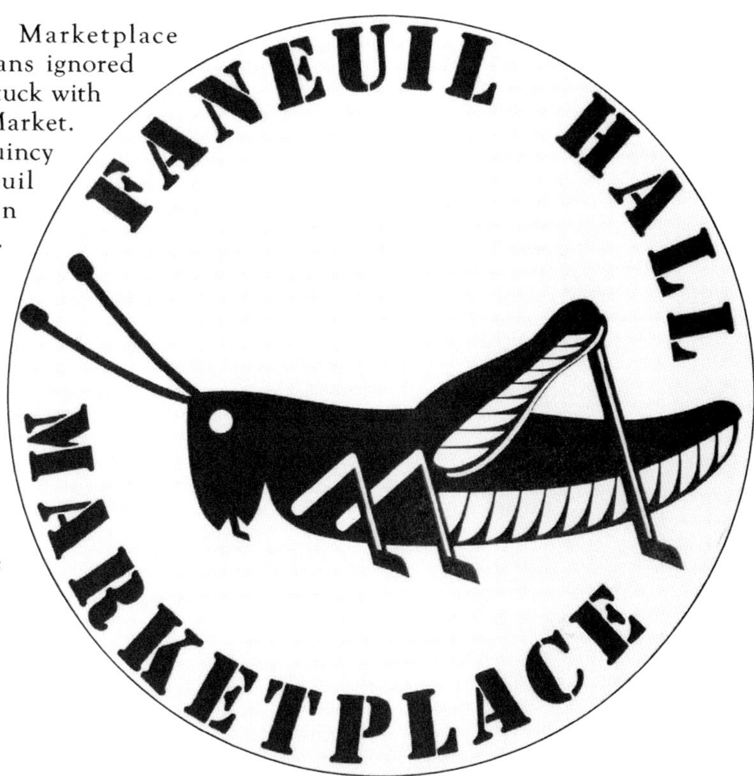

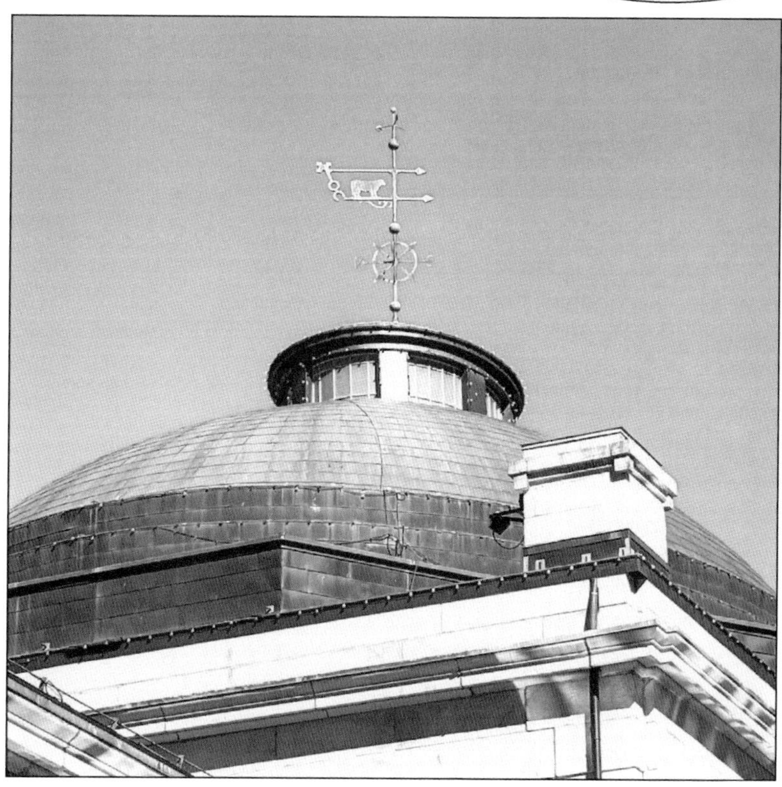

Quincy Market's weather vane never achieved the iconic status of Faneuil Hall's grasshopper. The choice of a bull was probably a nod to the market's meat vendors, but it is not clear when the weather vane was installed. Author John Quincy Jr. dug into the mystery and found only more questions. Early illustrations were ambiguous, with some showing a weather vane without details and others showing only flagpoles on the market roof. (Author's collection.)

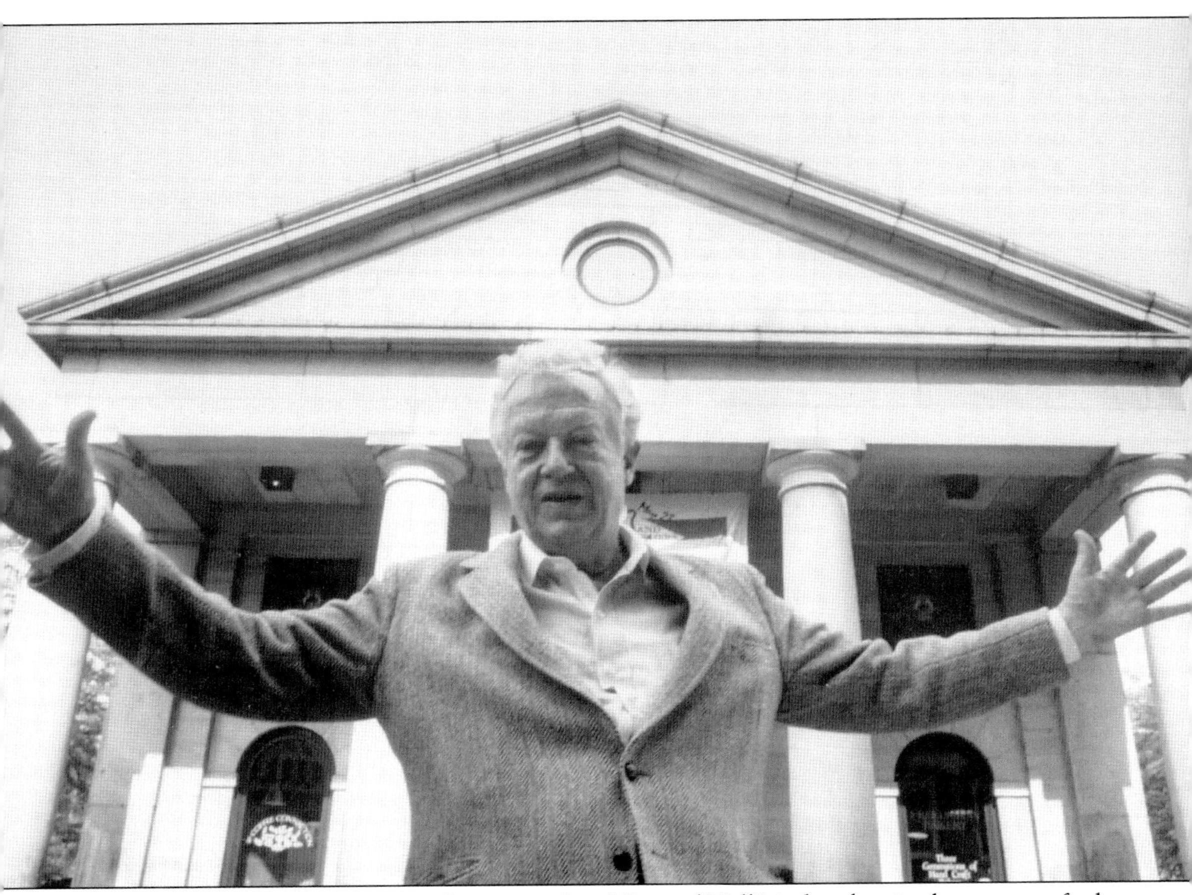

From the beginning, Benjamin Thompson placed Faneuil Hall Marketplace in the context of other great world markets. Jane Thompson described her late husband's deep understanding of marketplaces in a letter to John Quincy Jr., as quoted in his book *Quincy's Market*. "Historic marketplaces, sprung up at intersections of navigation and trade routes, were traditionally the seed and heart of great cities," she wrote. "Physically, people need the variety and abundance that markets bring. Socially, they need the communal security of mutual exchange and personal contact. Psychologically, they hunger for the festive activity that markets add to a central city." And since 1742—and no matter what people call them—Faneuil Hall, Faneuil Hall Market, Faneuil Hall Marketplace, and Quincy Market have survived fires, wars, earthquakes, protests, rallies, rodents, political whims, economic downturns, and evolving public tastes to form the heart of the Boston waterfront. Shown here is a celebratory Benjamin Thompson in front of the marketplace he revived (with a little help from a lot of friends). (MHS.)

Bibliography

Amadon, Elizabeth Reed, et al. "The Faneuil Hall Markets: An Historical Study." Part of "Faneuil Hall Markets Report," prepared for the Boston Redevelopment Authority by Boston Architectural Heritage and the Society for the Preservation of New England Antiquities, 1968.

Beagle, Jonathan McClellan. " 'The Cradle of Liberty': Faneuil Hall and the Political Culture of Eighteenth Century Boston." Doctoral diss., University of New Hampshire, 2003.

Boston Record Commissioners. *A Report of the Record Commissioners of the City of Boston Containing the Boston Records from 1729 to 1742*. Rockwell and Churchill, 1885.

Brown, Abram English. *Faneuil Hall and Faneuil Hall Market or Peter Faneuil and His Gift*. Lee and Shepard, 1901.

Frothingham, Richard. *History of the Siege of Boston, and of the Battles of Lexington, Concord, and Bunker Hill*. 4th ed. Little, Brown, 1873.

Kennedy, Lawrence W. *Planning the City upon a Hill: Boston Since 1630*. University of Massachusetts Press, 1992.

Quincy, John, Jr. *Quincy's Market: A Boston Landmark*. Northeastern University Press, 2003.

Quincy, Josiah. *A Municipal History of the Town and City of Boston*. Charles C. Little and James Brown, 1852.

Seasholes, Nancy S. *Gaining Ground: A History of Landmaking in Boston*. MIT Press, 2003.

Snow, Caleb H., MD. *A History of Boston*. Munroe and Francis, 1825.